FIRE AND IRON

RICHARD F. ALLEN

and FIRE IRON

Critical Approaches to *Njáls saga*

University of Pittsburgh Press

Library of Congress Catalog Card Number 71-134493
ISBN 0-8229-3219-9
Copyright © 1971, University of Pittsburgh Press
All rights reserved
Henry M. Snyder & Co., Inc., London
Manufactured in the United States of America

Grateful acknowledgment is made to the following for permission to quote
material which appears in this book:

The Belknap Press of Harvard University Press and Basil Blackwell
Ltd., for quotations from *Preface to Plato*, by Eric A. Havelock. Copy-
right 1963 by Harvard University Press. Reprinted by permission of
Harvard University Press and Basil Blackwell Ltd.

Oxford University Press, for quotations from *The Nature of Narrative*,
by Robert Scholes and Robert Kellogg. Copyright 1966 by Oxford University Press. Reprinted by permission of Oxford University Press.

Princeton University Press for selections from *Mimesis: The Representation of Reality in Western Literature*, by Erich Auerbach, translated by Willard R. Trask. Copyright 1953 by Princeton University
Press; Princeton Paperback, 1968. Reprinted by permission of Princeton University Press.

To the memory of ALAN M. MARKMAN

Simle þreora sum   þinga gehwylce
ær his tid aga,   to tweon weorþeð;
adl oþþe yldo   oþþe ecghete
fægum fromweardum   feorh oðþringeð.

Contents

Acknowledgments

I would like to thank the following persons and institutions for their assistance and support: Sharon Delano for overcoming the difficulties of the final typescript; the University of Pittsburgh for its grants of a Mellon Graduate Fellowship for the years 1965–67; the Viking Society for Northern Research for the use of its facilities but especially for the privilege of belonging to its membership; Michael Chestnutt and Professors Hans Bekker-Nielsen and Ole Widding for their hospitality and favors towards me during a far-too-brief visit to Copenhagen. I would especially like to acknowledge my gratitude to Professor Peter G. Foote of the Department of Scandinavian Studies, University College London, for his advice and help and many kindnesses during my researches in London in 1967/68 and to Richard M. Perkins of the same department for his assistance and for many useful conversations. I wish to thank my wife, Judy Allen, far less for the long hours of her time offered up to the drudgeries of typing and proofreading than for her sustained interest, useful suggestions, and keen criticisms.

Above all I would like to pay tribute to Alan M. Markman who, at the University of Pittsburgh, encouraged my first desire to study and to write on the Icelandic sagas at a time when my formal qualifications to do so would have struck many a man as nil.

He was a teacher who commanded the highest respect for the thoroughness of his scholarly discipline, for the breadth and detail of his knowledge, for his never-hidden deep love and engagement with all literature, and most of all for his ability to make his own convictions and his own biases perfectly clear while presenting with the same clarity other views. He urged his students into the pursuit of their own visions to whatever horizons they could reach. In short, his was a well-made and open mind. His friends, colleagues, and students will know what a loss it was that fatal illness overtook him at a time when he seemingly had many years left to lead and time to write his long-considered thoughts on the Old and Middle English literatures he so cherished and delighted in. As it befell, his students are his chief memorial; he left behind him more good men and women desirous to uphold his standards than ever he left behind articles in scholarly magazines; he did both, and from the latter he has his proper fame but from the former he has our love, for he did what a man in these times should do.

Introduction

I have undertaken in this book to construct a series of critical approaches to *Njáls saga* which try, in the light of recent discoveries about the nature of orally based narrative and in the light of other modern critical conceptions, to explain why this saga, the longest, the most popular, and the most complex of the Icelandic family sagas, conveys the sense of unity it does, why it strikes modern audiences as a powerful coherent work. That *Njáls saga* is the work of a single composer and that it does possess a coherent design are issues that have already been suasively argued and demonstrated in this century. To some extent these are the assumptions that provide the starting point for my own essays. But it is my hope that these essays in turn will present evidence that may reinforce and enhance the intuitive perception of almost all who read *Njáls saga* that here is a work with a grand design.

The family sagas comprise a great literature and interest in them is widening as they become increasingly available in satisfactory translations. With respect to *Njáls saga* it is indeed difficult for anyone to engage himself with this work for any length of time without becoming convinced that here is a composition that belongs in the very forefront of Western narrative art. And yet there is no critical book in English that is devoted to this saga; of other books only the translation of Sigurður Nordal's *Hrafnkatla* and Anne Holtsmark's *Studies in the Gísla Saga* confine themselves to single sagas and much of their concern is with matters outside the realm of strictly literary criticism. It is still true to say, in spite of recent and growing interest, that little consideration has been given to the sagas as *literature*, especially when one considers the amount, the unique qualities, and the sheer excellence of much of the Icelandic writings. These are reasons enough why such critical efforts as this book incorporates should be made. It is my hope that some of the approaches I have attempted here, although admittedly designed to suit *Njáls saga* in particular, will be applicable to other sagas as well, especially since, in order to come to *Njáls saga*, I have had to discuss matters that pertain to many other family sagas. Some of these matters will be all too familiar to scholars in the field; I have tried to write a book that will be pleasing and informative to a general audience as well as one that may provide some stimulus to specialists.

Some of the problems that confront anyone who wishes to read and experience the family sagas as an autonomous literature are introduced, the still-continuing controversy over the origins and hence the nature of the sagas is reviewed, and the discussion leads to the conclusion that these works must be viewed as imitations, composed by literate artists, of primary oral narrative. In exploring the consequences of this statement, one of the most distinctive features of the sagas (and of *Njáls saga*), the rapid, paratactic style that carries only those facts necessary to the advancement of the narrative and yet manages to put together what seems a realistic, thoroughly realized story, is examined in the light of Erich Auerbach's terminology in *Mimesis* and his discussion of the role the Christian vision had in shaping the very syntax of post-Roman historical and heroic narrative. This style is then seen as a function of the sagas' relationship to the structures and social role of primary epic. Here comparisons with the social functions of the Homeric poems and with the nature of the Greek society that produced them have seemed both unavoidable and illuminating.

As the units that form *Njáls saga* are analyzed, a scheme to comprehend these units is derived, based on the assertion that many statements pertaining to the aesthetics of orally composed literature will also be pertinent to *Njáls saga*. An analysis of how the beginning eight chapters of the saga foreshadow and sound the larger themes of the whole work provides some substance for this assertion.

Some of the methods Wayne Booth defines and applies in *The Rhetoric of Fiction* are employed to show how many of the conventions of the so-called "objective" saga style may be seen as the devices of a reliable narrator to determine the values of his story. The rhetoric available to the narrator extends to the very order in which he places his events, to the nature of those events, and to the point of view from which those events are told. It is possible then to step back still farther to see that the curve of *Njáls saga*, the broadest shape of the narrative, relates it both to other works of literature and to certain vital and universal experiences that the Icelanders, in building and maintaining their land, share with the rest of mankind. This approach uses a number of concepts and methods of archetypal criticism.

I have tried to avoid imposing a single theory of interpretation on *Njáls saga*, indicating instead what might be appropriate in a number of theories. I am aware that any such set of approaches will at given places seem to ignore crucial material, either from *Njáls saga* itself or from works of critical theory that might well augment or modify my statements. There is, for example, a need for a sustained close look at the very style of *Njáls saga* itself; this book does not attempt to provide that, although I have been privileged to read work in progress by Professor Whitney Bolton that represents a strong beginning towards such an approach. There is moreover much in the realms of archetypal and psychoanalytic criticism that I have not invoked in order not to write too sprawling a book. The Icelandic sagas ought to attract the attention of critics and historians who have a command of modern psychological constructs, for the sagas seem to be one part of the artistic expression of a severely self-repressed society. Surely what they do not say and what they avoid mentioning can be as significant and revealing as the events to which the sagas do devote their overt concern. One cannot help but wonder at times at a society which produced and admired extensive narratives in which so many people have so much trouble talking to one another.

One must, in speaking of such a work as *Njáls saga*, keep in mind the conditions under which this work was first composed, the mode in which it first existed, the audience to whom it was first addressed; these things I have tried to do. But there comes a time when one must also acknowledge that *Njáls saga* still exists *now*, that it is a powerful work that can strongly affect people, who, except for it, know nothing whatsoever about Iceland, that there are things in it that speak to us in a way they could not speak to its original audience simply because we have been born into a world at once pressed down, expanded, and altered by seven hundred more years of human thought and deed. What we see and bring out of *Njáls saga* also becomes part of *Njáls saga*. And that is cause both for pride and caution.

Some comments are perhaps necessary on the translations in this book. They are mine and any blunders in them are solely my responsibility. I have deliberately not tried to make the excerpts from *Njáls saga* consistent in style. Particularly in chapters 2 and 3, I have tried to follow the Icelandic word and phrase order as closely as possible without sounding hopelessly un-English since I am interested there in showing how given formal units are repeated, often in very similar language. Thus I have tried to keep the same English words for crucial words or phrases that do reoccur. Fights, for example, often sound much more flashy in the English translations where men cut, thrust, parry, slice, and stab, than they do in the Icelandic where men

must do much of their work with two verbs, *leggja* and *hǫggva*.
In other passages, however, that are dramatically or lyrically
powerful, I have tried to indicate or reproduce these effects as
best I could.   The best thing about such efforts is that they
never fail to enhance one's admiration for the surety and subtlety
of the original.   I have reproduced the alternation between past
and present tenses that is a striking feature of saga prose;
whether or not these alternations are functional or were even
perceived by the saga audience is a matter of debate.

There is, moreover, no compromise about the retention or
normalizing of Icelandic names that will satisfy everyone.   I
have kept personal names and many place names as well in their
Icelandic nominative forms.   Where it seemed more sensible to
adapt English forms of place names (e.g., the Althing, the
Rangriver Plains), I have followed the usage of the recent Penguin translation, *Njál's Saga*, by Magnus Magnusson and Hermann
Pálsson and I have also followed its usage with respect to nick-
names.   Translations from the sagas are based on the text in the
Íslenzk Fornrit series; thus for *Njáls saga* the translations correspond to the text in *Brennu-Njáls saga*, ed. Einar Ól. Sveinsson,
Íslenzk Fornrit, XII (Reykjavík, 1954).   Page references are to
this edition.   I have provided chapter references as well since
they correspond to the chapter divisions in the Penguin translation and may thus be useful.   Mainly for reasons of publishing
expense I have omitted the Icelandic text except where it is essential to a precise understanding and interpretation; those who
know Old Icelandic will know how to provide themselves with
this text; for those who are unfamiliar with this language lengthy
citations in it would be superfluous.   The same reasons apply to
the several long translated quotations from scholarship in Modern Icelandic.

One last word.   Critical essays are, perhaps more often than
they should be, sober and earnest affairs; *Njáls saga* itself is a
work that brings home the truth of Virgil's phrase, *sunt lacrimae
rerum*.   But *Njáls saga* is also full of humor, a high and broad

humor, daring and fine, which can manifest itself at one and the same time with moments of the utmost seriousness. Whoever composed *Njáls saga* was able to laugh at both the conventions of saga composition and at his fellow Icelanders. At the same time this man used, to great effect, those very conventions and used them to catch up and comprehend wisely and sorrowfully the men and the land about him. The vision of such a man is rare, as vital for us as for the men and women he wrote for; it is enduring. Those who encounter *Njáls saga* in their lives should seek to enhance its fame and that is my intent.

FIRE AND IRON

*Mun ek nú segja yðr alla mína ætlan, at þá er vér komum þar
saman, skulu vér ríða til Bergþórshváls með ǫllu liðinu ok
sœkja Njálssonu með eldi ok járni ok ganga eigi fyrr frá en þeir
eru allir dauðir.*

[I will now tell you my full purpose, that when we come together
there, we shall ride to Bergþórshváll with our entire company
and attack the Njálssons with fire and iron and not turn away
before they are all dead.]

1

Problems of Saga Criticism, Origins, and Genre

The Icelandic family sagas[1] are works easy to enjoy, powerful in their effect, but difficult to criticize. No label of epic, history, or historical novel—and all have been suggested if only as partial solutions—adequately describes their nature which is often called unique. It is hard for the literary critic to find an entry into the sagas which does not direct him to discussions of particular episodes and characters, or lead him straight away to large thoughts about heroic self-assertion, or beckon him down the road well travelled by philologists, collectors of folklore, and seekers after origins. The language of the sagas on the whole does not offer untoward difficulties and for this one thanks both the clarity of the saga-men themselves and the long efforts of scholars who have made the manuscripts available in finely edited texts. But to explain and analyze the effect of the compact narrative filled with facts and bare of ornament is another matter. The following pages touch upon some of the thoughts which occur to anyone hoping to comment on the literary art of the sagas.

First of all, the relationship of the sagas to historical events is a confusing one for historian and critic alike. The degree to which sagas seem to reflect historical truth varies from one work to another and it is, moreover, difficult to determine whether or not a given tradition is veracious. With some exceptions the only checks upon a saga's veracity are other sagas.[2] The *Landnámabók*, that remarkable collection of anecdotes and genealogies of Iceland's principal settlers, certainly goes back to material written in the twelfth century. It preserves traditions and information handed down from the ninth and tenth centuries. But extant manuscripts of it are from times contemporary with saga composition and at least one authoritative version was expanded with borrowings from the sagas.[3] Thus, if one is to be rigorous, the historicity of a given event cannot be settled by an appeal to *Landnáma*. Nevertheless, it is certainly not possible to regard the sagas as literary narratives only; nor is it possible to approach them without keeping in mind that they purport to tell what actually happened in the past. Certain turns in the plot or whole patterns of events have to be explained by the desire of the saga-man to preserve a fact or tradition. The sagas present a form which poses as history and which would have been accepted as such by their audience. Like other medieval histories they are filled with elements from folklore, but they make use of such elements and their other matter to fashion well-wrought episodes, to delineate character, and to achieve an integrity of form, all in a manner not to be found in other medieval historical writing and which altogether seems closer to art than history ought to be. And there is the further question: to what extent do the sagas reflect and comment upon the events of the Sturlung Age, during and just after which most of the major sagas are now thought to have been composed?[4] *Njáls saga* in particular seems to narrate events and raise issues relevant to happenings in that turbulent period.

In the past the problems of saga origins and of the relationship of the manuscripts to oral tradition have been bound up with the question of their historical reliability. These are problems to be examined later. Here one need only remark that comments on such matters as sentence structure, the use of conventional language and typical scenes, narrative technique, and form in its entirety, will be affected by what attitude is taken towards the manner in which oral tradition informed the manuscripts.

In spite of these vexed issues lying behind them, the sagas themselves remain very accessible to the reader who comes upon them. They demand less special knowledge and previous cultural information than any other medieval and heroic genre. More than most literature, ancient or modern, they establish their own conventions and make believable their codes. Indeed it is remarkable how firmly any one of the longer sagas creates by itself the picture of life and the habits of style and viewpoint that mark the family sagas as a whole. One does not need knowledge of medieval rhetorical conventions to respond correctly to the art of this prose, an art which remains apparent even through translations.[5] Nor is there any need to explicate in detail customs pertaining to courtly and chivalric matters before one can understand why men and women in the sagas say what they say and make the choices they make (which is not to say that the sagas were unaffected by such matters). These men and women have roots reaching back into the legendary past of Scandinavia's heroic age and in their deeds they may recall the heroes and heroines of that age, but they themselves are credible in present terms. The stories of their dealings with each other arise out of circumstances easy to reconstruct. In contrast with much of medieval literature the life the sagas depict revolves around the requirements of a comparatively simple society whose structure does not reveal a great disparity between social classes. This is not to deny that the sagas show a well-developed sense of aristocratic values; it is to assert that their setting enables one to respond to these values with ease.[6] The men and women of the sagas face death concerned not so much with why they die as how they die; they have an integrity of gesture and commitment to gesture attractive to this present age which has admired style when it has known nothing else to admire.

Although a given saga may provide much that is representative of them all, the sagas interact among themselves in a way, if not unique, at least unusual in literature. Any saga may be read by itself with pleasure, but a given saga often presumes knowledge of others. This knowledge, when acquired, opens a whole new range of effect. A brief remark in one saga can raise vistas of all the action of another. The first chapter of *Njáls saga* seemingly goes out of its way to tell us that "Hallgerðr's brothers were Þorleikr, the father of Bolli, and Óláfr, the father of Kjartan, and Bárðr."[7] Hallgerðr's brothers and their sons play virtually no part in *Njáls saga*, but the mention of them brings to mind the passion and tragedy of their story as *Laxdœla saga* tells it. The power of that story, even through this brief allusion, stirs the reader and intensifies his expectations of *Njáls saga* as it gets under way. And those persons who appear and reappear in several sagas call to mind all the stories in which they took part while at the same time they retain a certain consistency of character, much more than Sir Gawain, for example, possesses in his various roles throughout Arthurian literature, for the saga-men worked in the same country and at roughly the same time and drew not only upon each other's written work but upon memories of the deeds of their common ancestors in that same land.[8] Guðmundr the Powerful appears in *Njáls saga*, six other family sagas, and three other historical sources. Skapti Þóroddsson, who is shown in an unflattering light in *Njáls saga*, plays a more sympathetic role in *Grettis saga*.[9] But there is seldom gross conflict between representations of the same person. Because of these cross references, as one reads more and more, a whole saga-world emerges, the literary imitation of the world of Iceland's heroic age.[10] Even the genealogies begin to come alive. References to sagas no longer extant are reminders that for the medieval Icelanders this world was both wider and more complete than it can be now. Analogies exist, of course, to this linking of saga with saga. Homer's poems existed within the context of the lost Homeric cycle. The *chansons de geste* share characters and link plots. In the late Middle Ages the already vast worlds of Arthurian and Alexandrian romance show a tendency to merge. There are other examples from the corpus of Germanic heroic poetry to the cycles of the novel in the nineteenth and twentieth centuries. A certain parallel to this creation of a literary world dependent on a real terrain occurs in the works of William Faulkner who also depicted a culture at once villainous and heroic, growing out of the settlements of pioneering men.[11] The sagas are both bound to a single land which exists not in the imagination but in actuality and linked to ancestral memories in a tighter and more consistent way than is found in most of these other examples. Considering that active composition in the genre extended for well over a century, such an overall unity is remarkable.

In reading the sagas one encounters two features related in their effect: (1) the swiftly moving prose is halted by the passages of poetry which are present to a varying degree in almost all of the sagas, and (2) ordinary events and realistic depictions of Icelandic life exist side by side with the marvelous, the super-human. The verses are usually quoted when the speaker is under emotional stress; they serve to intensify, prolong, and memorial-ize an occasion of significance. They seldom advance the narrative except in cases where an insulting verse demands vengeance. The Icelanders, it seems, were capable of delivering without pause for reflection flawless verses in a variety of mea-sures among which are some of the most complicated forms ever devised by poets anywhere and this often between blows or at the height of a heated quarrel. The custom is too widely attested for it to be only a literary convention.[12] On the other hand the audience of the sagas seems to have had a certain craving for such verses, both for their own sake and perhaps as a relief from the terseness of the speech in prose. A number of manuscripts of *Njáls saga*, for example, expand the action of chapters 1 through 99 by the interpolation of many additional verses.[13] At any rate the effect is one not encountered elsewhere, not even in the Irish epic sometimes suggested as a source for this con-vention. It is somehow one of widening the range of genres which the sagas comprehend; it achieves a startling contrast between modes.[14] In *Njáls saga* the main exploitation of this effect is reserved until close to the end where the phrases of the *Darraðarljóð*, a poem in one of the old heroic measures, confirm the presence of superhuman powers behind the course of events.

The marvelous and the superhuman appear in almost all the sagas. At first it is difficult to reconcile the presence of such phenomena with the prevailing realistic mode of the sagas and with the powers of action the saga heroes possess, for although these men may be gifted with greater strength and wit than their comrades nothing in their nature surpasses mortal limitations. The saga hero is no figure of myth or romance about whom one expects miraculous happenings to occur; nor is there anything extraordinary about his environment, which still exists today in Iceland very much the same as it was. Nevertheless it is always difficult to make general remarks about the sagas. The fights of Grettir with the monstrous figure of Glámr and with the trolls behind the waterfall do evoke the same fear and wonder that we associate with the marvels of romance or with the great adventures of Beowulf whose epic story is indeed somehow linked with Grettir's.[15] Grettir with his enormous strength is preternaturally endowed and his encounter with Glámr lies at the heart of the saga, for it changes Grettir's fate. But in many other sagas the marvelous is, or seems to be, paradoxically mundane. It must be understood that prophetic dreams, shape-shifters, spirits all too substantially returned from the dead, and spectacular and ghastly apparitions were simply matter-of-fact possibilities of daily life in Iceland as for some they still are today.[16] *Egils saga* casually remarks about a neighbor of Egill's that "men were not agreed that he was not a shape-shifter,"[17] and *Njáls saga* introduces one of Hallgerðr's relatives, Svanr, by telling where he lived and adding that "Svanr was well skilled in wizardry; he was Hallgerðr's maternal uncle; he was an extremely difficult man to have any dealings with" (ch. 10, p. 32). Svanr's homestead, occupation, kin, and most prominent characteristic—the four major concerns of the saga-men when introducing anyone—are each given equal weight. There is no extra fuss about his wizardry. Such coolness of approach has lead one critic to remark how "this unreal world is described with the same detail and sobriety of style as is the 'real'."[18] This is true of the manner in which marvels are introduced and described, but I do not think it is true of the feelings with which they were apprehended.

In *Eyrbyggja saga* men are carting the corpse of a woman, Þórgunna, to burial. One night they seek shelter at a farmstead, but the farmer there refuses to offer them hospitality because he dreads their cargo. In the night he and his men are aroused by a great clatter in the kitchen; they discover Þórgunna there, as large as in life and stark naked, busy preparing a meal. She sets the table and serves the food. Everyone thinks it best to partake of it, whereupon she returns to her bier. In the morning the burial party sets out, but word has run before them, "and wherever the event became known, most men thought it good advice to grant them what hospitality they required. The rest of their trip was without incident."[19] It is clear from the story that the men have been greatly frightened, but the tale is told without comment. The marvelous was a part of the daily life of the Icelanders;[20] it was not at the edge of things but in and about the central events of men's lives; it was none the less real for being marvelous and none the less marvelous for being real. Beneath the matter-of-fact style is not simple acceptance, but awe and contained fear. Perhaps one element behind the terseness of saga expression is a fear of letting go, a fear that if one thing is admitted all might have to be. A certain survival value accrues to bare narration and cultivated understatement in such regions as Iceland.[21]

But, for one reading the sagas now, the effect brings about once again a widening of horizons. In much literature of recent centuries that deals with men and women in their daily world, the light of the artist falls on a narrow band of that spectrum along which the possibilities of literature extend. Events may have their roots in heaven or in hell, but they are only visible as they take place upon a small stage called the real world.

The vision of the saga-man was wider and he easily saw forces and shapes from heavenly or hellish realms and could place them in his tales with no sense of contrivance. For the Icelanders and, I think, for men in general throughout the Middle Ages subjective experience became objectively projected onto the outer world; fears and desires now considered to be part of the inner life took on a palpable existence before men's eyes. The wonders of nature—auroras and meteoric showers and volcanic eruptions among others—were easily seen as the portents and displays of powers from beyond the world of men. It is possible to view the whole vast medieval world structure from heaven to hell as an enormously elaborated projection of forces that are active within the psyche. The celebrated objectivity of the sagas—exercised as it is in a world where forces of the unconscious, the subjective interplay of human spirit, may become fully visible—formed a genre which most effectively and without religious explication could use marvelous events for symbols. To put it another way, when subjective experience becomes objectively visible, the observations of the saga-men become observations of psychic phenomena. Witch rides, dreams, and magic fogs become symbols of inward events, symbols of the spiritual condition of men and society.[22]

Wondrous events, particularly as they are placed and used in finely constructed works like *Gísla saga* and *Njáls saga*, give more than a glimpse of those shaping forces which the sagas incorporate and powerfully convey. In Gísli's dreams, alternate groups of good and evil women appear struggling for his soul. In *Njáls saga* the forces struggle not for the soul of one man but for dominion over a whole society. In this longest of the sagas a pattern emerges that may elsewhere appear only in part, a pattern of struggle between forces of order and chaos. The meaning of men's deeds is reflected and reinforced by a growing number of miraculous and terrible signs, the intensity and frequency of which culminate in the events surrounding the Battle of Clontarf. The pattern delineated by such signs and portents is not unrelated to the fundamental experience of the Icelanders, that of striving to establish and maintain their society which they had brought to this island at the northern edge of the world. In this sense one may then speak of the incorporation of myth in *Njáls saga* both because its basic curve, one of descent through disorder into terrible bloodshed followed by a slow reestablishing of order, is a curve whose shape relates the saga to other works of literature and because the successful incorporation into art of this curve is an achievement important to the sustaining and advancement of the human spirit.

Such speculations will be further developed, but for the moment they need only be touched upon insofar as they are thoughts that do occur upon a first reading of the sagas. But there is danger in reading these works as if they were the products of men working in the manner of modern novelists. Sagas occupied a far different role in their society from that which novels occupy in ours and they came into existence through far different routes about which a great deal of controversy still exists. Indeed, what Cedric Whitman has written of the Homeric poems is true also of the sagas: "Manifestly what is composed is the direct result of how and when it is composed."[23] For this reason it is necessary to turn back to the question of saga origins in hopes that a review of this problem will make it possible to place the family sagas within a wider social context where art and utility merge.

The composition of the family sagas extends over a century or more of saga writing, but the nature of their prose and of their narrative conventions is sufficiently alike to allow one to speak of a "saga style."[24] Because this style relies heavily on parataxis both in syntax and in its juxtaposition of events, because it employs familiar and traditional material for its scenes, and because it possesses a rhythm that seems naturally suited for speaking, it has suggested to every observer a close relationship to oral narrative. The problem lies in defining this relationship. The sagas at once possess some features not found in oral compositions and lack others that are. They have a rapidity of pace and density of fact not to be observed in literature known to be orally composed. They lack the insistent repetition of important facts and relationships and they lack the luxuriant elaboration of typical scenes, two features which often mark oral literature.[25] The epithets, similes, and metaphors which provide for so many critics useful entries into a work and which again mark much oral narrative are not found in the sagas. Figurative language is rare in saga prose, although all the more telling when it occurs. Sagas have a complexity of form not to be found in the repertoire of folktale tellers with whose skill and memory the art of the saga-men is sometimes compared.[26] They evince an ability to manipulate point of view in a way which seems to be a mark of written rather than of oral literature. Finally, however much the sagas use a common phraseology and vocabulary, this common fund of words and phrases is not generated by metrical demand and does not constitute a formulaic system that functions as a mnemonic device, as a word hoard for a teller of tales. The presence of this common fund of words and phrases ought not to be used to argue the direct oral composition of family sagas. There is no evidence that professional "makers" of family sagas ever existed or ever practiced such an art.[27] One is faced then with the paradox of a prose which strikes all at first sight as oral in nature, which constitutes a narrative filled with traditional material, but which possesses a density of fact and which is stamped with other marks that seem ascribable only to literate men composing for a literate audience.[28] This paradox, which is a fascinating one, has excited much controversy. As a fitting description of it the words of W. P. Ker still stand and can hardly be improved upon:

> Icelandic prose is very near to the spoken language; it is rich in idiom and in conversation, and the artistic form given to it by writing men seems to follow easily from the natural growth of the spoken traditional tale.[29]

Three centuries of divergent opinion, however, lurk behind Ker's "seems to follow easily." The past history and present status of the debate over saga origins have been recently set forth by Theodore M. Andersson (see n. 3), and there is need here only to touch upon the main outlines of this debate. The two great divisions of opinion may be identified by the terms *Freiprosa* and *Buchprosa*, suggested by Andreas Heusler.[30] Freeprosaists are those who argue that the sagas reflect pre-existing oral versions and incorporate the forms of oral tradition. In the past this view has often been associated with an early dating of the sagas and with a belief in their historical reliability, although Heusler stated and Andersson has emphasized that theories of oral origins for the sagas need not be bound to a belief in their truthfulness.[31] It must be pointed out that even the most ardent advocates of the freeprose hypothesis have not been dogmatic in their key statements. Finnur Jónsson, although giving primary emphasis to the importance of oral tradition, acknowledges that the writer following this tradition could shape and vary details of this material for his own purpose.

> When one thus grants to oral report a predominant importance both with respect to content and to stable form—as I have always done—the opinion can then, however, be held that the scribe can also have had influence, that he need not have been a purely mechanical copyist. He could have put a certain color on details and have formed words and sentences just as any oral tale teller could have done.[32]

Heusler's key statement, which is often quoted as representative of an extreme position, is perhaps even more indulgent to the freedom of the scribe than Jonsson's is.

> The language of our Icelandic sagas unites two qualities: it is unusually good (that is, here: clear, pithy, expressive in choice of words and in rhythm) and very natural and unlabored. Both taken together are to be explained only in this manner, that the writers discovered in their oral models a honed narrative style and followed it to the best of their abilities. In many

sagas one thinks first of a dictation: the parchment
picks up the heard speech of the narrator with the
fidelity of a phonograph.   But the abundant models
from free oral delivery enabled the writer to fashion
new examples with the same or similar freshness.[33]

From Heusler's remarks it can be seen that he admits the possibility of saga *writers* closely imitating an oral style and fashioning new episodes cast in the form of oral narrative. That these
oral narratives could exist seems clear from the work of Knut
Liestøl, a folklorist whose field work with Norwegian tale-tellers
enabled him to bring much common sense and experience to the
many references in the sagas themselves to the long tales told
by Icelanders (see n. 2).   There is no question that men in Iceland from the tenth through the thirteenth century (and on to
today) were capable of entertaining an audience with reports of
news and with tales of adventures, often of considerable length.[34]
The question remains to what extent could the family sagas have
taken their present shape within a tradition of oral narrative?
In past decades, when freeprose theories prevailed in histories
of Icelandic literature and in scholarly editions of the sagas, a
great deal of intellectual effort was expended in debate over the
content and shape of the "oral" sagas, by definition no longer
extant, which were thought to have preceded the existing ones.
In the manuscripts themselves scholars were inclined to detect
much meddling interpolative activity.   "Here is often seen to no
little extent the romantic tendency to admire those works which
we have not and to find much to blame in those which are preserved," complained Einar Ól. Sveinsson in his early work on
Njáls saga.[35]   In a later work, Sveinsson repeats this complaint,
which does need emphasis: "It may seem strange, but sometimes
it appears as though people overlook the fact that sagas, as we
designate them, the written works, really exist, while the oral
sources upon which they are supposed to be based, do not
exist."[36]

The bookprose theorists, led by such men as Sigurður Nordal

and Einar Ól. Sveinsson and represented in the introductions to
the saga editions of the influential *Fornrit* series published in
Reykjavík, also acknowledge the role of tradition in the formation of the sagas, but argue that the sagas should be regarded
primarily as fictional works composed by individual authors of
varying talent, working with a combination of oral tradition,
written references, and their own experience. Each saga must
be considered on its own merits. Some are manifestly close to
local traditions and preserve local tales, anecdotes, and genealogies; others owe much to the imagination of their shapers.
The style of the sagas is not a direct capturing of a preexisting
oral version but an imitation of an oral delivery. The sagas are
designed to be read aloud—but this is a somewhat different
statement from saying that they were recited by a storyteller
whose recitation was then set down more or less verbatim by a
scribe. Coincidentally with the advancing of these views has
come an intensive effort to date the sagas and to place them
along a curve of development. Behind the family sagas were
decades of extensive religious and historical prose writing in
the twelfth century as well as a flourishing oral tradition preserved in skaldic poetry and in the tales of legendary heroes.
Poetry and folk legend may have provided the tradition and even
some of the narrative molds in which saga narrative is cast, but
it is an essentially historical impulse which gives birth to the
genre. Family sagas take shape at the end of a sequence that
begins with saints' lives, moves to lives of those Norwegian
kings (Óláfr Tryggvason and Óláfr Haraldsson) who were ac-
claimed as saints, and from there comes to the lives of prominent
Icelanders about the Norwegian court, particularly the Icelandic
court poets, who counseled, fought for, and memorialized the
kings.[37] This trend joins with a desire to set down memorable
events in the various districts of Iceland itself. The development of the family sagas themselves leads from the first clumsy
efforts, around or even before 1200, of the *Heiðarvíga saga* and
from some extraordinary deviations from "saga style" in the
Fóstbrœðra saga into a period of initial flowering stimulated by

the composition of *Egils saga*, perhaps by Snorri Sturlusson, in the 1220s.[38] Saga writing then seems to have flourished in most of the major districts of Iceland throughout the rest of the turbulent thirteenth century which wracked Iceland with internal strife and brought it under the formal dominion of Norway in 1262. The last part of the century saw the composition of *Njáls saga* which is, in many ways, the culminating work in its length, mastery of style, and sweep of vision. The much-beloved *Grettis saga* comes still later. In it and in *Njáls saga* too some historians detect a proliferation of the marvelous and an increased interest in fantasy. Such signs point towards the shift of taste to European romance and heroic legend which inundated the older forms as the fourteenth century drew on.[39] It must be emphasized, however, that interest in the family sagas did not wane. It was in the fourteenth century that they were collected, revised, brought together in the great codices; certainly they were read.

This attempt by the Icelandic historians to review the sagas in the context of their age has exactly reversed some of the cherished datings of the older schools. It was formerly thought that the sagas took form in the twelfth century, but as that century wore on "a hundred or more vigorous tales of iron muscle and red blood, which were then in the making, had to give way to the anaemic saints' lives from the south."[40] Thus the short compact "classical" version of *Fóstbræðra saga* in *Hauksbók* was thought to be the original and the longer version in *Flateyjarbók* a "corrupted" one spoiled by monkish interpolators. But now the classical version is considered to be a fourteenth century restyling of a much earlier version to which the "interpolations" properly belong.[41] Nordal has demonstrated beyond doubt that *Hrafnkels saga*, once thought to be early (c. 1200), factual, and a prime example of a saga derived directly from oral composition, must in fact be late (c. 1300), fictitious, and written by a man who felt free to invent a story very much as he pleased.[42]

There are many variations in the positions either freeprosaists or bookprosaists may take. The chief difference between them

lies in their conception of the final shaper of the tale and in
the use which that shaper makes of the tradition which all agree
lies behind the sagas. Andersson has summarized the difference
between these two positions thus:

> Bookprosaists and freeprosaists can often be in sub-
> stantial agreement on what the sources of a saga were
> but rarely on the form of those sources or the way in
> which the saga author used them. In most cases the
> adherent of freeprose believes in a central core of
> formed tradition which could (but need not) be in-
> finitely varied by the writer, but which imparted to the
> saga its fundamental structure and narrative art. The
> believer in bookprose for the most part rejects this
> central core and sees the lines of a saga as the work
> of an author who imposed his artistic will on hetero-
> geneous materials. The gap between the theories is
> therefore real and fundamental though it has often
> been much exaggerated in the ardor of discussion.[43]

Recently the debate over saga origins has moved along two
sharply diverging paths, the one affirming the literary autonomy
and thirteenth century provenance of the sagas, the other re-
asserting the freeprose hypothesis in the light of an increasing
understanding of the ways and forms of oral composition. In
Über die Entstehung der Isländersagas, Walter Baetke doubts the
evidence advanced by freeprosaists for the existence of oral
sagas, criticizes the compromise of bookprosaists with their
opponents, and denies the view that sagas preserve any accurate
picture of tenth-century Iceland. For Baetke the opinions of the
bookprosaists lack sufficient rigor. "Almost all make, sometimes knowingly, sometimes unknowingly, concessions to the
theory of the oral saga."[44] The bookprosaists fail to see the
inconsistency of their stand; while they deny the existence of
whole oral sagas, they nevertheless will admit the existence of
shorter anecdotes from which a saga-man could have pieced to-

gether and worked up his tale. Where can the line be drawn between short pieces and longer self-sufficient narratives?[45]
Baetke considers the sagas of little historical worth and criticizes the assumptions of those who have had faith in the historical veracity of these narratives (see n. 2). Overall, the
family sagas must be considered as works of art, in a sense
more radical and closer to modern conceptions of artistic composition than that held by the bookprosaists. The sagas are
fictions that preeminently reflect the age in which they were
written, and hence they ought not to be regarded as the indige-
nous product of an isolated Teutonic bastion in the northern
seas but as works influenced by and related to the great cultural
and literary movements of high medieval Europe.[46]

Baetke's conception of the sagas does provide a basis from
which one may begin to criticize features of the sagas in terms
of the aesthetic function alone,[47] although the chief value of his
work is in its emphasis on the sagas as embodiments of thirteenth,
not tenth, century Icelandic spirit. But any attempts to criticize
the sagas as if they were works of fiction following modern no-
tions of form and composition must take into account the rehabilitation of freeprose theories undertaken by Theodore M.
Andersson in his book on saga origins and in other works.[48]
Like Baetke, but for opposite purposes, Andersson criticizes the
use which the bookprosaists make of oral tradition. Whenever
possible they ascribe the sources of saga genealogies and of
various narrative episodes to previous sagas or to well-known
documents of Icelandic history such as the *Landnámabók* or
Ari's *Íslendingabók*. When this attempt fails the bookprosaists
appeal to local oral tradition as a source for minor characters
and events which are otherwise unrecorded. Andersson senses
the inconsistency in this procedure. Referring to *Reykdæla saga*
he notes that

> chapters 2 to 17 contain the names of forty-two per-
> sons, of whom less than half were socially qualified
> to be listed in *Landnáma*, and who must therefore

have dragged out their existence in oral tradition. This brings us to the inevitable question: if oral tradition could harbor the memory of so many *viri obscuri*, why could it not remember the elite? Wherever the theory of contaminated oral and written sources is pursued to its logical conclusion, it leads to this fundamental contradiction.   We must either assume that oral tradition provided all or most of the names or take refuge in Baetke's logic and assume that all the names not explained by written sources were invented.[49]

Andersson feels obliged to appeal to oral saga.   His contention as I understand it is that narrative methods observable in the written sagas were first fashioned by and are reflections of techniques of oral narrative.   Andersson is influenced by Liestøl who, he says,

insisted that traditional material could not exist apart from some kind of form.   Conversely form could not exist without content. ... To concede a pre-saga narrative style is as good as conceding an oral saga. This does not of course mean that our written sagas are transcriptions of oral sagas. ... The writer undoubtedly could and did use written sources, supplementary oral sources, his own imagination, and above all his own words, but his art and presumably the framework of his story were given him by tradition. The inspiration of the sagas is ultimately oral.[50]

This final statement would seem to leave Andersson at no extreme remove from the views of Nordal and Sveinsson insofar as extant sagas are the issue.   But his words evidently have been read to mean that the family sagas, as we have them, lie very close to oral saga, just the point he seems cautious to avoid. This reading is unfortunately promulgated in comments about the sagas in a recent and widely read book on Western narrative in general.[51] And it has led another recent critic to predict with respect to the Icelandic saga that "it is only a matter of time before the resurging freeprose theory will seek additional confirmation in modern theories of oral-formulaic usage."[52]

However skeptical one must be of an extreme statement of the freeprose position, it is nevertheless becoming apparent that the structures of the family saga, the ways in which they assemble themselves event after event, seem to follow the examples and seem to recreate the patterns of extended oral composition. Whatever light has been generated by this review of theories of saga origins shows that sagas may best be seen as analogues of oral narrative. They are works which provide a literary imitation of epic narrative composed before an audience by a teller of tales. The word epic must immediately be qualified, of course. If primary epic itself may be seen as a union of history and heroic legend, folktale and sacred myth, saga must be placed beyond the breakdown of this primary union, a breakdown first brought about by the advent of literacy—and in Western Europe, by the advent of literacy and Christian culture. The family saga is a form evolved out of the mingling of literate values with the impetus and tradition of heroic legends. Hence the family saga appears in a form that represents itself as history and yet contains within it a complex amalgam of cultural information inextricably fused with the stuff of narrative; saga is at once highly entertaining and selectively instructive.[53]

Two forces are here at work to determine those qualities of the sagas which seem to relate them to primary oral narration. The first concerns the basic stuff of the sagas, the form and and manner of which was shaped by oral tradition. What Andersson and Liestøl say is true: such material cannot "exist apart from some kind of form." Such material is found in the typical events and groups of events out of which the sagas are composed: the individual quarrels, the course of feuds, the legal debates, the single duels and group battles, the assemblies, the bartering for brides, the love affairs, the trips abroad, the rides to the Althing, the hospitable receptions at the farm or in the assembly booth. The earliest legendary sagas we have word of must also have been composed out of such typical material if they obeyed any known pattern of folk narrative. The fact that tradition conveys patterned material is strengthened by this further observation: precisely those events which are retained by tradition are events which already fall into a kind of pattern, events which are, as it were, already memorable, events which make up a story already *sögulegt* ("worth telling," "significant"). Such events are likely to touch upon the vital interests of society.[54] It is also worth noting that both the relative simplicity of Icelandic life, linked as it was to the revolvings of the seasons, and the degree to which men seem (in the sagas at least) bound by legal considerations in their smallest actions imposed forms upon the daily and yearly actions of the Icelanders, or at least provided forms for transmuting those actions into art.[55] As the events of life became preserved in tradition, they became further subjected to the polishing and shaping of narrative impulse. The sagas, then, are made up of typical scenes and such scenes in turn are recalled and composed by a fitting together of smaller motifs, small events and gestures which are also stylized, also familiar and traditional. These motifs belong to given scenes, but they may vary enough to make each occurrence of the scene a new creation.[56] The saga-men compose by this technique, the origin of which is ultimately oral. Although a given saga-man may have behind him several generations of writing men and written works on which to model his own craft, his art—which re-creates a tradition— may be judged by criteria applicable to orally composed works.

The second force affecting the prose qualities of the sagas is the manner of their presentation. They were designed to be read aloud and were read aloud as entertainment for the inhabitants of the Icelandic farmsteads. Given the architecture and conditions of the time, such a reading would be public and would reach most levels of Icelandic society.[57] That such readings took place can scarcely be doubted, although the contemporary evidence is scanty. Probably the custom was simply taken for granted, as it seems to be in the one clear thirteenth-century reference there is, and even this does not mention a family saga. In the year 1258 a certain Þorgils Skarði

> rode to Hrafngil. He was well received there. He arranged for his men's quartering. He was asked to choose what there should be for entertainment that evening, sagas or dancing. He asked what sagas were available. They told him that there was the saga of Archbishop Thomas [à Becket] and Þorgils chose that because he honored the Archbishop more than other holy men. The saga was then read up to the point where the Archbishop was set upon in church and the mitre hewn away from him. Men say that that Þorgils paused there and said, "That must have been a fair death indeed." A little later he fell asleep. They left off the saga and prepared the table for dinner.[58]

While it is regrettable that Þorgils's taste did not lead him to request a family saga, it is pleasing to think that he spent what proved to be his last night in this world with the edifying example of the holy blissful martyr freshly set before him.[59]

Although there are no references to the reading aloud of family sagas, the introductions to other works, including both legendary sagas and saints' lives, make it clear that no distinction can be made between reading and hearing these sagas; the two terms are virtually synonomous, as they were for medieval culture in general.[60] There is no reason to suspect that the case would be any different with family sagas, especially since medieval Icelanders did not make the generic distinctions scholars now make.[61] In later centuries there is excellent documentation of this practice of saga entertainment, *sagnaskemtan* (M. Icel. *sagnaskemmtun*), "storytelling," which was often a reading aloud of sagas for the night's entertainment of the farmstead community, and much evidence exists that manuscripts of the family sagas were widely circulated for this purpose. Indeed, to judge from the nature of the surviving thirteenth- and fourteenth-century manuscripts, it is difficult to imagine how else the sagas could have been enjoyed unless they were re-created from the parchment by a skilled reader familiar with his story.

Re-creation is a reasonably precise word in this context, for of course there is none of the paragraphing, indenting, and very little of the punctuation marks which ease the task for the readers of modern editions. The recognition of direct speech and of the speakers, and matters of intonation, dramatic pauses, and emphasis, were left to the choice, skill and interpretation of the man reading the saga aloud to others. Sagas passed through the medium of the human voice and elements must have been added there that cannot be retrieved today. The only clearly marked large unit is the chapter, distinguished in the case of the two principal manuscripts of *Njáls saga* by large colored capitals and by colored chapter headings. Although these divisions, in *Njáls saga*, often occur at logical breaks in the narrative, their primary purpose appears to be that of enabling the reader, at a glance, to tell just where he is in the story. It might also be noted that the texts of the Icelandic manuscripts use abbreviations for many frequently occurring words and letter groups (wherein verb tense is at times left to the choice of the reader); such abbreviation is used to an even greater degree than is found in other medieval vernacular texts.[62] Of course, any person trained to read in Iceland would be trained to interpret the conventions of this script. One cannot from their appearance alone argue that the manuscripts must have been employed in reading aloud. But the age of the solitary reader, off in his corner with a book, was centuries away.[63] Everything we know about secular literature in the rest of medieval Europe indicates that it reached its audience through public readings.[64] Contemporary references to such readings as well as the established practice in later centuries of *sagnaskemtan* suggest that the point need not be belabored that the reading of the family sagas was a public occasion and that their major mode of existence thus was embodied in the relationship between lecturer and listener.

Such being the case, there would have been a constant pressure upon and incentive for writers of saga prose to shape their style for easy delivery both for their own convenience in reading aloud and for quick comprehension on the part of their audience. The modern analogy to this occurs (or should occur) whenever one adapts a paper written for publication into a talk delivered to a group of listeners. One senses a pressure to break up complex sentences into shorter units, to decrease the amount of syntactical subordination, and perhaps to curtail striking flourishes of style. These pressures are especially effective when the main interest in what one is narrating is the story itself. The Icelanders of course were accustomed to or at least exposed to a spoken prose of a different order from that of the sagas. In sermons, homilies, and accounts of the lives of holy men they would often meet the alliterative phrases, the extended and balanced clauses, the drawn-out similes, and the religious metaphors which characterize the *sermo simplex* style as it was adapted from Latin models. In fact the extant versions of the *Tómass saga Erkibyskups* which so pleased Þorgils Skarði afford good examples of this clerical style, although it is not certain if the version Þorgils heard was similar.[65] But in such writings the main interest lies not so much in the story as in what the story means. The rhetorical figures of the clerical style are designed to elicit this significance by means of devices which arouse the emotions and intrigue the intellect. There is no need for such devices in the family sagas. Their subject matter, the putative deeds of ancestors, deeds set in a framework of contemporary values and ethics,[66] guaranteed the interest of the audience which wanted to know what happened and how. The thrust then of saga style was towards the dramatic. One can see this in the increasing use of dialogue and long set speeches in the later sagas. The saga reader must have done his best to dramatize what he was reading, to bring

out the characters of the speakers, to act out the scene. This
little vignette from *Ljósvetninga saga* must have been perfectly
suited to such a purpose. Guðmundr the Mighty is an overbearing man, here assigned the seat of honor that Ófeigr feels is
properly his own.

> And when the tables were brought in, then Ófeigr
> placed his fist on the table and said, "How large do
> you think this fist is, Guðmundr?" Guðmundr said,
> "Large indeed." Ófeigr said, "Do you think that
> there might be strength in it?" Guðmundr said, "I
> certainly think so." Ófeigr says, "Would you think a
> blow from it a strong blow?" Guðmundr says, "Very
> strong." Ófeigr says, "Do you think that any harm
> might follow?" Guðmundr said, "Broken bones or
> death." Ófeigr answers, "How would such a death
> seem to you?" Guðmundr said, "Very bad, and I
> would not wish to have such a death." Ófeigr said,
> "Then don't sit in my place." Guðmundr says, "As
> you wish," and he sat down on the other side.[67]

In a declamation of this passage the phrases "Ófeigr said" and
"Guðmundr said" could be safely omitted (although they add a
certain ritualistic intensity to its effect); it is possible, however, to view them only as "quotation marks" that would guide
a reader.[68]

Thus a situation exists where a written genre set down and
perfected by literate and well-educated men moves towards the
mimesis of an oral style.[69] This is not a new idea, but in view
of some trends in saga criticism, it needs to be emphasized
again and again. Sigurður Nordal has described this process:

> It is reasonably clear and would be still clearer, if
> more of the older sagas were extant in their original
> form and not shortened and polished by later copyists
> (e.g., the texts of *Egils saga* and *Glúms saga* in the
> *Möðruvallabók* and of *Fóstbrœðra saga* in *Hauksbók*),

that the development of the saga style in the thirteenth
century and on into the fourteenth went in the direction of giving the story a more "oral" quality. This
has led men's sight astray in later times. It is correct
to say that sagas developed in such a manner that
they might be recited. And it may well be that in a
similar fashion the best educated authors trained
themselves to tell stories, as, for example, Sturla
Þórðarson was able to tell the *Huldar Saga*,[70] and
likewise the authors of some sagas may have practiced reciting sagas or parts from sagas as they were
composing them. But even so the saga style is
equally far from what the primeval oral style must
have been before the Writing Age as it is from the
daily speech of the thirteenth century which sometimes peeps through in *Sturlunga saga*. It is precisely
the highest achievement of the craft of writing—an
achievement which few attain—to make books "talk."
As absurd as it may seem, it is none the less true
that in the flourishing period of saga composition, the
more sagas resembled oral narration—which is what
men today think they should do—the more they became created and fictional compositions [*skáldskapur*],
that is to say, at once more independent of oral tradition and of the crutches of foreign stylistic models.[71]

Finally, where do all these considerations bring the reader
who approaches *Njáls saga*? Here is a work that even the pro-
ponents of the Higher Criticism could agree had been assembled
with a master hand, although they viewed it as an amalgamation
of any number of preexisting shorter sagas, reports, anecdotes,
and verses, as an amalgamation which failed to fuse into a
unity.[72] And yet, when one returns to this saga after reading
others, one is struck by the internal evidence and pervaded by a
conviction difficult to explain that whoever wrote this saga knew
exactly what he was doing from beginning to end.[73] And after

the work of Einar Ól. Sveinsson it is difficult not to see this saga as the composition of a master craftsman who came late in the thirteenth century after other men had already brought the genre to a high degree of perfection. This man fashioned much of *Njáls saga* in his own imagination, relying for inspiration and material on the art and stuff of other sagas, on a miscellany of written genealogical lore, local oral tradition, and brief allusions in historical sources to the deeds of Gunnarr and Njáll some three centuries before.[74] He wrote for an audience a generation removed from the culminating broils and intrigues of the Sturlung Age, for an audience that perhaps wanted to reflect on the significance of such national turmoil, on the nature of the kind of events which had led Iceland to come under Norwegian rule and law. *Njáls saga* presents, in a three-hundred-year perspective, similar issues: the conflicts between strong men of free will, the workings of malice through the actions of little men, the long struggle of a society to control the passions of its chief men and to reconcile its codes. For these reasons the use, abuse, and conflict of law, in all its roles, pagan, secular, and Christian, figure so largely in the saga.[75]

In a way the author of *Njáls saga* enjoyed the best of both worlds. He could write and re-create traditional forms and material for an audience trained to hear and appreciate fine craftsmanship and conditioned to follow the development of themes in a mode that imitates the patterns of oral composition. But because he was writing, and because his work was to be preserved in manuscripts, he could also allow himself some of the fine touches, the minute but telling details discernible in this work, details which strike one as the touches of a man consciously reflecting about, perhaps even revising his work.[76] This saga, the longest of the sagas and one that seems in art and form culminative and inclusive of much that has gone before it, seems also to have been the most popular, to judge by the number of surviving manuscripts.[77] It existed for an audience, a national audience, and its form and content cannot be separated from the expectations and demands of that audience, cannot be analyzed without

appeal to its "radical of presentation."[78]   This relationship between work and audience is an oral one in the twofold sense I
have discussed: in the nature of the traditional material out of
which the work is fashioned and in the re-creation of that work
through public readings to an audience which was trained to respond to this mode of composition and which was reared as well
in the Christian culture of thirteenth-century Iceland.   The following two chapters develop some of the implications this statement has for the style, patterns, and unity of *Njáls saga*.

2

Saga Style: Christian Context and Epic Background

I wish to suggest two forces that are responsible for shaping certain features of saga style. They are (1) an interaction between the saga-man's evaluation of what events in Icelandic history were worth telling and his Christian awareness of the potential immense significance of each man and each man's deeds and (2) the shift of saga away from the epic synthesis so that the epic burden of explicit cultural information is curtailed in favor of a compelling narrative swiftness. The "density of fact" in saga narrative, of which I have previously spoken, provides a useful starting point for such a consideration.

The sagas move from one important point to another. In works like *Hrafnkels saga* and *Gísla saga*, all is excluded that does not directly contribute to the advancement of the plot or the delineation of major characters. *Njáls saga* moves with a more deliberate stride, but in it, too, matters which may have appeared as digressions or wanderings of the main path turn out to be thematically related to major concerns of the saga. In typical sagas, moreover, the passage of time is abruptly handled; between one conversation and the next, days and months may intervene. Years may pass by in a remark like "And now things are quiet for a while." These intervals are seldom defined precisely by historical dates, a matter that can bring woe to those who try to reconcile saga time with real time.[1]   But the inner chronology of the saga is carefully set forth.   The audience is always told in what relation events are to one another, whether one event occurred before, during, or after another.[2]   Altogether, a large amount of time is covered in a short space.   *Hrafnkels saga Freysgoða* is not a long saga (it has less than ten thousand words), but it covers the full course of a man's career and touches upon the generation preceding him as well.   *Egils saga Skalla-Grímssonar*, in perhaps seven hours of reading time, covers 165 years in its main action, 310 altogether if the epilogue is included.[3]   The main action in *Njáls saga* covers about sixty-five years, but the work in its entirety spreads over a century.   It seems difficult to reconcile these statistics with the undeniable statement that sagas convey an impression of close imitation to reality.   But if one examines more closely the elements of this imitation, one begins to see how the sagas comprehend a wide expanse of time that nevertheless contains many effectively detailed dramatic scenes.

In almost any chapter several kinds of narrative may be discerned.   The first might be called distant narration, a rapid chronicling of events, of the mechanics, for example, of who rode to visit whom.   The second is close imitation, giving details of an action in the saga man's own words and from his point of view:

> Gunnarr sees that a red tunic passes before the window and he lunges out with his halberd into the man's body.   Þorgrímr's shield came loose from his grasp and his feet slipped from under him.   He tumbled off the roof and then makes his way to where Gizurr and the other men were sitting about on the ground.   (ch. 77, p. 187)

The third is also close imitation in direct speech, interchanges between the characters, sometimes in extended dialogue, sometimes in just a brief glimpse of a conversation's high point:[4]

> Gizurr looked up at him and said, "Is Gunnarr at home?" Þorgrímr answers, "That's for you to find out, but I do know this, that his halberd was at home." Then he falls down dead. (p. 187)

Often such moments of close imitation provide an occasion for the utterance not of individual thought but of traditional lore:

> Þjóstólfr told Glúmr that he didn't have the strength for anything except for tumbling about on Hallgerðr's belly. Glúmr said, "'The worst companions come from home.'⁵ Here I am taking insults from a thrall like you!" (ch. 17, p. 49)

Margaret Jeffrey notes that such "single speeches give the impression of being true reproductions of actual talk." But overall a great deal is clearly omitted. "The narrator gives us the kernel of a dialogue. ... That is to say, that which he gives us is real; but it is, at the same time, to a high degree an abstraction from the real."⁶

The best way to show the admixture in saga narrative of distant and close imitation, of time rapidly passed over and moments carefully depicted, and to show how the narrative moves into speech at the moments of greatest emotional stress is to let a segment of this narrative speak for itself:

> When spring came, Hrútr had to travel to the Westfjords to take in money for his goods, but before he left home, his wife speaks with him. "Do you intend to come back before men ride to the Althing?" "Why do you want to know?" says Hrútr. "I want to ride to the Althing," she says, "to see my father." "And so you shall," he said, "and I shall ride with you." "Good," she says.
>
> Then he rode away west to the fjords and put all his money out at interest and rode back home.
>
> And when he returned, then he gets ready for the Althing and summoned all his neighbors to ride with

him. Hoskuldr came too, his brother. Hrútr said to his wife, "If you still have it in mind to go to the Althing as you said, then get yourself ready and come with me." She quickly got ready, and then they ride until they reached the Althing.

Unnr went to her father's booth; he was glad to see her, but she was somewhat depressed. And when he noticed that, he said to her, "I've seen you in better moods; do you have something on your mind?" She burst into tears and made no answer. Then he said to her, "What did you ride to the Althing for, if you won't tell me your secret? Or don't you like it out there in the west?" She answered, "I would give all I had never to have come there." Mǫrðr said, "I'll soon find out about this."

Then he sent a man to fetch Hǫskuldr and Hrútr; they came at once. And when they met Mǫrðr, he stood up and gave them a good greeting and asked them to sit down. They talked for a long time and their conversation went well. Then Mǫrðr said to Hrútr, "Why does my daughter think things are so bad out west?" Hrútr said, "Ask her, if she has any charges against me." But nothing was brought up against Hrútr. Then Hrútr had his neighbors and his household men questioned about how he treated her. They gave him good witness and said she was allowed to manage all her affairs as she wished. Morðr said, "You must go back home and be content with your lot because all the testimony favors Hrútr more than you."

Then Hrútr rode home from the Althing and his wife with him, and things were well with them during the summer. But when winter drew on, then trouble arose between them and it was worse the closer it got to spring. Hrútr had another trip to make west to the fjords and he announced that he would not ride to the

Althing. Unnr, his wife, said little about that. Hrútr
went off, when he was ready to go. (ch. 6, pp. 22–23)

The reader senses that he has been present at an important
scene (and so he has, see chapter 3 below) and that he has been
informed of all he needs to know—yet this short passage covers
a year of time.

There is one remaining narrative element found in the sagas.
This consists of passages of sheer fact, information about
character and genealogies which will be essential for an understanding of later action. Such passages, static in themselves,
nevertheless provide the fuel for the narrative to consume.

There was a man named Njáll. He was the son of
Þorgeir Gollnir, the son of Þórólfr. Njáll's mother
was called Ásgerðr and she was the daughter of the
chieftain Áskell the Silent. She had come out to Iceland and taken land to the east of the Markar river,
between Qldusteinn and Seljalandsmúli. A son of
hers was Holta-Þórir, the father of Þorleifr Crow (from
whom the men of Skogar come) and of Þorgrímr the
Mighty and Þorgeirr Skorar-Geirr.

Njáll lived at Bergþórshváll in the Land-Isles; he
had another farm at Þórólfsfell. He was wealthy and
handsome, but this feature was to be noted, that no
beard grew upon him. He was so great a lawyer that
no one was his equal; he was wise and prophetic, of
sound and benevolent counsel, and all advice which
he gave men turned out well. He was gentle and
noble-minded, farsighted and long-remembering. He
solved the troubles of each man who came to him for
help.

His wife was named Bergþóra; she was Skarp-
Heðinn's daughter. She was a high-minded woman
who bore herself well, but she was somewhat harsh-
tempered. They had six children, three daughters and

three sons, and they all come into this saga later.
(ch. 20, pp. 55–57)

Almost all this information, which is allotted a chapter by itself,
is necessary to later developments—Njáll's kinship with Þorgrímr
the Mighty, for example, comes into the saga ninety-eight chapters further on.   Shorter sagas often group most of such information at their beginning, but in *Njáls saga* these passages of
sheer fact are distributed throughout the saga.   As one encounters
them it seems as if the input of facts, describing the characters
and their relationships, stirs the saga to action and determines
the result.   Even the genealogies, for which apologies are often
made, have important functions.   To the Icelandic audience they
were a convenient shorthand which indicated the rank and blood
of a man, and they possessed a natural interest for an audience
descended from the people mentioned in them.   For the saga-man
they compactly indicated ties of kin between his characters, and
hence, the extent to which one person might feel obliged to come
to the aid of another.   They can be put to other rhetorical uses
as will later be shown.   In general, information of this nature is
given once and not repeated; one is expected to keep it in mind.

As a work like *Njáls saga* progresses, with each scene and
each set of facts linked and contributing to the following, either
directly through cause and effect or indirectly through parallels
of act and theme, a given passage of narration comes to bear a
heavy charge, a cumulative intensity of dramatic interest and
associations.   The unadorned style and the paratactic mode of
expression contribute to this effect.   The reader's, or listener's,
attention is kept strictly to the fact, to what is happening.   No
interesting figures of speech, no heroic epithets or oft-repeated
formulas, occur to ease, if only for a minute, the demand that the
reader or listener devote his utmost attention to the story before
him.   It is the reality of the event that the reader cannot escape
as he contemplates what is set before him.   It is impossible,
even today, to stand at Bergþórshváll without being overcome,

terrified even, by the knowledge of what happened there a thousand years ago. The land has not changed; the saga, with its
insistence upon the event, is present in one's mind; it is not
difficult at all to see the assault upon and burning of Njáll's
house and family. What is difficult is to accept that event. For
in the sagas there is no protecting cushion of ostensible rhetoric, lyric, or striking rhythm to smooth over the harshness of
events. Only at the most terrible moments may the saga-men
relent—indeed the burning of Njáll would be intolerable were it
not for the comforting words it is granted him to say; Gunnarr's
death is offset, if only slightly, by a commemorative verse and
the words of Gizurr, the man who led the attack: "A mighty hero
have we now laid even with the earth and difficult that was for
us. His defense will endure in memory, so long as the land is
lived in" (ch. 77, p. 191). Nor is there any description of landscape in the sagas, except for those details which will influence
the action later on.[7] As many writers point out, the saga-men
did not need to provide description of a terrain presumably well
known to their audience. If sagas were told on the route marches
to the Althing or in the armed camps which were a feature of the
Sturlung age, the whole panorama of a saga's setting might have
been visible as the saga was told, for Iceland is a land of clear
air and long views.[8] It must be assumed that the sagas had a
scenic dimension for their audience which they do not have today
outside of Iceland.

The paratactic mode of saga expression, where fact after fact
follows without an overt intrusion of the saga-man, where little
is explained but much is shown, brings the reader into the story.
A highly subordinated style presumes a director or manipulator
of the narrative, who stands as an interpreter between the reader
and events.[9] But the reader of sagas must involve himself in
the sagas to explain and understand them; he must try to adjust
his inner life and emotions to the saga world he is shown so
that he may re-create emotions and motivations of the actors in
that world. Of course he is given more help than is first ap-

parent. In the very choice of events and facts which are selected for him to see and hear there is a great deal of ethical guidance. But it is up to him to make the most of what he is given. Curiously enough, the sagas, for all their economy of statement and swiftness of pace, are fatiguing to read. They demand a great deal from their audience, a good memory and a constant alertness. If one does not read them in haste chiefly for the sake of their great moments, one finds that they impose their own deliberate pace, that they need to be read, and perhaps told, in relatively small units.[10]

In the great sagas there is a sense that a firm hand is in control, that each portion contributes to the overall unity of theme and action. In fact, the type of narrative found in the sagas could not have come into existence unless a high degree of selectivity and control had been possible for the saga-men and, it might be added, for the historians who preceded them or were contemporaneous (perhaps, on occasion, identical) with them. I can only remark that this selectivity, which leads to the swift pace and narrative density of the sagas, was possible because the Icelanders were confident of their importance in the scheme of things. What happened to them on their island was what held the chief interest for them. Their vision was focused on Iceland and it saw there a society that functioned within a well-established framework of law and ethics. They were not dependent on events in far-off lands and cities to impart direction to their lives. Given that situation it was possible for the saga-men to know for sure what was *sögulegt* and what was not.

With this in mind, it is instructive to compare the sure touch of the saga-men with the passage in Gregory of Tours's *History of the Franks* which Erich Auerbach discusses in *Mimesis* (pp. 77–95)—the story of Sicharius and Chramnesindus. There is much in this story that reminds one of the stuff of the sagas. There is a quarrel between two Germanic warriors, petty Frankish aristocrats, and a settlement that leads to an exaggerated friendship between them (compare the relation of Hǫskuldr

Hvítaness-Priest with the Njálssons). Then, later, rash words are spoken in drunkenness, the old enmity is rekindled at once, and sudden assault and murder follow. Other touches remind one of the techniques of the saga-men.[11] And yet Auerbach's opening comment justly is: "I imagine that the first impression this passage makes on a reader is that here an occurrence sufficiently confused in itself is very obscurely narrated" (p. 81). And part of the difficulty, as Auerbach shows, is that Gregory was in no position to decide which details were essential and which were not for his story. He could not decide because he had no framework in which to set the activities of his many characters.

> For if we ask ourselves how Caesar or Livy or Tacitus or even Ammianus would have told this story, it immediately becomes obvious that they never would have told it. For them and their public, such a story would not have had the slightest interest. Who are Austrighiselus, Sicharius, and Cramnesindus? Not even tribal princes, and during the heyday of the Empire their bloody brawls would probably not even have elicited a special report to Rome from the provincial governor. This observation shows how narrow Gregory's horizon really is, how little perspective he has with which to view a large, coherent whole, how little he is in a position to organize his subject matter in accordance with the points of view which had once obtained. (p. 84)

It is of incalculable significance to the development of saga narrative that the Icelanders did have a perspective in which to view their deeds and did have confidence, based on their heroic legends and Viking past and strengthened by two centuries of fashioning their own society, a confidence that enabled them to commemorate the deeds of Icelanders in that society.

Auerbach's work, concerned as it is with the ways in which

Western literature has represented reality, opens the way for
further definition of and speculation about saga style, although
Auerbach himself never discussed the sagas. I have mentioned
the paradox with which the sagas confront the reader—the unique
combination of structural features apparently derived from oral
narrative with a compactness of story and corresponding lack of
redundancy that belong to works produced in a literate society.
Auerbach's celebrated distinction in *Mimesis* between two basic
modes of imitation, which he called foreground and background
styles, throws into relief the paradoxical nature of saga style.
Auerbach contrasted two passages, one from the *Odyssey* where
Odysseus's old housekeeper, Euryclea, recognizes him by the
scar on his thigh, the other from Genesis, where Abraham proves
willing to sacrifice his son Isaac. Here we have, according to
Auerbach, two ways of representing reality that differ from each
other in the extreme:[12]

> On the one hand [*Odyssey*, foreground] externalized,
> uniformly illuminated phenomena, at a definite time
> and in a definite place, connected together without
> lacunae in a perpetual foreground; thoughts and feel-
> ing completely expressed; events taking place in
> leisurely fashion and with very little of suspense. On
> the other hand, the externalization of only so much of
> the phenomena as is necessary for the purpose of the
> narrative, all else left in obscurity; the decisive
> points of the narrative alone are emphasized, what
> lies between is nonexistent; time and place are unde-
> fined and call for interpretation; thoughts and feeling
> remain unexpressed, are only suggested by the silence
> and the fragmentary speeches; the whole, permeated
> with the most unrelieved suspense and directed toward
> a single goal (and to that extent far more of a unity),
> remains mysterious and "fraught with background."
> (pp. 11–12)

The only critic I know of to apply Auerbach's remarks to the sagas, and to *Njáls saga* in particular, is Denton Fox in an article, "*Njáls Saga* and the Western Literary Tradition."[13] Noting the lack of suspense,[14] the self-effacement of the narrator, the "exclusive concentration on objective phenomena," and the "traditional and unidiosyncratic style of all these works," Fox concludes that the sagas are works of foreground style. And yet, when one reads Auerbach's definition in its entirety, one wonders if such a classification can so confidently be made. The mode of saga narrative seems markedly different from that passage of the *Odyssey* which Auerbach singled out. One cannot say that phenomena in the sagas are "connected together without lacunae." They are set side by side, but great gaps of time may exist between one event and the next in contrast to the leisurely and linked progress of Homeric narration. Thoughts and feelings are not completely expressed in the sagas; rather, they give glimpses and snatches of conversation, crucial glimpses, of course, from which one must labor to reconstruct the feelings and motives of saga characters. In fact, a number of Auerbach's comments on background style are appropriate to saga narrative. We do have "externalization of only so much of the phenomena as is necessary for the purpose of the narrative," "the decisive points of the narrative alone are emphasized," a great deal of "thought and feeling remain unexpressed," and in works like *Njáls saga* or *Gísla saga*, we do feel that "the whole ... is directed toward a single goal" (why a man and his family were burned to death within their house, why Gísli had to die). The play, moreover, of supernatural powers—the striking portents and celestial displays in *Njáls saga*, the dream women who appear to Gísli—surrounds these sagas with an aura of mystery because, in contrast to the Homeric poems, the activities of these powers are never explained. In short, the sagas exhibit features of both styles.

Now Auerbach goes on to discuss the development of Western literature in terms of the evolution and intermingling of these two modes of representation. Coupled with this discussion are Auerbach's reflections on the decisive effect the story of Christ's Passion had for all postclassical conceptions and representations of the tragic and sublime, and the radical change which biblical exegesis worked upon the very syntax of literary language. When Auerbach's commentary is read with Icelandic literature in mind, it suggests that saga narrative, whatever its debt to oral tradition and heroic legend, could only have taken its final shape within a Christian culture. Auerbach observes that the matter of the New Testament conferred upon every man an immense dignity, a potentiality of moving within the realms of the tragic and sublime. Commenting on the story of Peter's denial of Christ, he observes that Peter "is the image of man in the highest and deepest and most tragic sense" (p. 41). Yet his story (as given in Mark) is told in the simplest of fashions. Such a mingling of styles, of material of high significance, told, by classical standards, in bare, even uncouth terms

> was graphically and harshly dramatized through God's incarnation in a human being of the humblest social station, through his existence on earth amid humble everyday people and conditions, and through his Passion which, judged by earthly standards, was ignominious; and it naturally came to have—in view of the wide diffusion and strong effect of that literature in later ages—a most decisive bearing upon man's conception of the tragic and the sublime. (p. 41)

And later Auerbach speaks of "the true and distinctive greatness of Holy Scripture—namely, that it had created an entirely new kind of sublimity, in which the everyday and the low were included, not excluded, so that, in style as in content, it directly connected the lowest with the highest" (p. 154). The Christian vision of events and interpretation of history introduced "an entirely new and alien element into the antique conception of history" (p. 73), that of figuration. Here one event prefigures another, for example, the near-sacrifice of Isaac is the pre-figuration which the sacrifice of Christ fulfills. Such a connection

> can be established only if both occurrences are vertically linked to Divine Providence, which alone is able to devise such a plan of history and supply the key to its understanding. ... This conception of history is magnificent in its homogeneity, but it was completely alien to the mentality of classical antiquity, it annihilated that mentality down to the very structure of its language, at least of its literary language, which—with all its ingenious and nicely shaded conjunctions, its wealth of devices for syntactic arrangement, its carefully elaborated system of tenses—became wholly superfluous as soon as earthly relations of place, time, and cause had ceased to matter, as soon as a vertical connection, ascending from all that happens, converging in God, alone became significant. (p. 74)

What is important here is not the concept of figural interpretation—it would be almost without exception perverse, I think, to apply it to Icelandic family sagas. What is important is the effect this concept had on syntactical modes of expression so that the most simply related event could nevertheless assume a great charge of meaning.

With this quotation and the preceding one in mind, consider the death of Grettir Ásmundarson. Here the wretchedness of Grettir's death mingles with the heroic sublimity of his long ordeal and resistance to produce an effect which, I submit, would not have been possible in pagan heroic literature. Perhaps for similar reasons it can be stated that Milton's *Samson Agonistes* is superior to its source. Milton, with his knowledge of the classical and Christian connotations of a hero's death, knew what that death meant. In it is the same mingling of wretchedness and heroic triumph; it is an effect which men in a Christian culture especially can achieve. It is certainly not found in what remains of pagan Germanic heroic tale.

> They pressed the attack, but Illugi [Grettir's younger brother] defended them both valiantly. But Grettir was unable to fight, both because of his wounds and his sickness. Then Qngull [their foe] ordered that they should press Illugi under their shields—"Because I have met no one his equal, even any older man."

Illugi is taken prisoner.

> After that they went at Grettir; he had fallen forward on his face. There was no opposition from him because he had already died from his wounded leg; his thigh was festered up to his anus. Then they inflicted many wounds upon him until little or no blood flowed. And when they thought that he was quite dead, Qngull took hold of Grettir's sword and said that he had borne it long enough. But Grettir had seized the haft fast in his grip and it would not be loosened.

They try to free the sword and fail. Qngull cuts off Grettir's hand. Then he does a botched job of hacking off Grettir's head. His miserable aping of heroic manners casts only shame upon him; at the same time the parody of such manners in no way diminishes Grettir's achievements and fame. Qngull's boast is a disgraceful (and perhaps intentional) echo of Gizurr's after the death of Gunnarr of Hlíðarendi:

> "Now I know for certain Grettir is dead and a mighty warrior have we laid even with the earth," said Qngull. "We shall now take the head with us to the mainland because I do not want to lose out on the reward that has been laid upon his head; they will not be able to ignore the fact that I have slain

Grettir." His men told him to do as he pleased, but nevertheless they found little to like in the deed and all thought it unmanfully done.[15]

Possibly the audience would make a reference here to the desire of Judas, who was willing to betray Christ for a handful of silver; such a motif is even clearer in *Gísla saga*. But Grettir's end is grim enough that he ought not to suffer what has befallen his brother-in-arms, Beowulf, at the hands of some critics. At least the Old English *Beowulf* has passages that seem to be specifically Christian in content, and these passages have supported some of the more remarkable exegetical constructions that have been built upon that poem. There are not many overt Christian references in the family sagas to justify scholarly detours into patristic writings.[16] What I am suggesting here is that the particular combination of heroic spirit and bodily mortification, the exaltation of a man who was not a leader of his tribe or nation but an outlaw, and the simple yet effectively detailed narration of *Grettis saga* are all the result of a mingling of native tradition with Christian sensibility.

One further comment by Auerbach on Gregory's *History* is appropriate, for he remarks that such a work, with its wealth of homely anecdote and detail would not have been conceivable in classical times. Gregory, he says, lays

> hold of what is alive. Not every priest could have done that; yet at that period no one could have done it who was not a priest. Here lies the difference between the Christian and the original Roman conquest: the agents of Christianity do not simply organize an administration from above, leaving everything else to its natural development; they are duty bound to take an interest in the specific detail of everyday incidents; Christianization is directly concerned with and concerns the individual person and the individual event. (p. 92)

It is in the sagas' power to make their audience think that it has been brought face to face with the great moments, the critical events in the lives of individual persons, for all that their audience views these lives and deeds from outside.   Men like Gunnarr, Gísli, and Grettir are more than stock figures set within the frame of heroic narrative—they are separate individuals and their deeds are done in conformity with their characters.   Later I will pay attention to the traditional and standardized formulas and patterns of saga narrative.   But within these forms the saga-men have set vividly realized men and women.   They conform and respond to tradition, and yet they stand out from it.   The concern of Gregory of Tours for the people of his history and the concern of the saga-men for the people of their stories are akin.

As is apparent, the initial effect of Auerbach's remarks was to suggest that many features of the sagas, which have been explained as the final polishing and shaping of Germanic heroic narrative,[17] have to be reconsidered in the light of the Christian culture in which the sagas were set down, a culture where any deed of any person could become significant.   It is a long way from Homer, and the *Beowulf*-poet, and certainly Virgil, and nearer to the worlds of Gregory of Tours, Giraldus Cambrensis, and William of Malmsbury when it is possible to have a "hero" who puts his enemy out of action by half-drowning him in puke and who diverts his old age with a childish scheme to fling his treasure about the national assembly so that he might have the pleasure of watching men scrabble for it and come to blows.[18] And the aristocratic chieftains of the Sturlung Age were not above shutting an enemy up within his house so that he would be forced to befoul the premises with his excrement—the insult was as mortal as it was undignified and the Icelanders resorted to it frequently enough to have a word for it, *dreita inni*.[19]   There is a mingling, which Auerbach speaks of, of the trivial and the undignified with the tragic and sublime.   The one frequently leads to the other—in *Njáls saga* men die because two women squabble over who should sit where; Gunnarr slaps Hallgerðr for stealing some cheese and is betrayed by her for that when his life is at stake.

More to the point, one wonders if the Vulgate Bible itself, either read in Latin or retold in the vernacular by local priests, could have had some effect on saga prose,[20] although it is misleading to suggest as Lars Lönnroth does that the clerical *sermo simplex* style is reflected in the style of the sagas.[21] The two are quite different. But many features of twelfth- and thirteenth-century medieval European culture appear in Iceland with little cultural lag. It is evident from the *Biskupa sögur* (lives of the bishops) that many from Iceland's leading families travelled abroad and received a good education. It is on the face of it hard to believe that sagas took shape unaffected by mainland currents which obviously influenced many other branches of Icelandic literature.[22] Lönnroth argues that the family sagas were influenced by continental historical writing and rather sarcastically refers to those present historians who now lay stress on a growing division between layman and cleric in thirteenth-century Iceland and who believe that as the clergy were "freed from secular influence ... the literate laymen are thought to have then taken over the writing of sagas and started a heathen renaissance in secular literature. This renaissance is regarded as the swan-song of the Icelandic people prior to their being finally overridden by the Norwegian King and Catholic Church."[23] And yet, in the end, it is impossible to demonstrate any extensive direct linkage between family sagas and medieval European literature. The older writers are surely correct on this point; the most distinctive features of the sagas and of histories like *Heimskringla* and *Sturlunga saga* are unique. From the beginning, even in the work of Ari Þorgilsson, who wrote in Latin and was unmistakably indebted to Continental models, Icelandic historical writing shows a clarity and pithiness of expression, a lack of didactic and emotional statement, and an incisiveness of choice that invites not comparison with but contrast to the European works that certainly provided the impetus for the first growth of Icelandic literature. Auerbach's remarks remain suggestive, but they have a general, not a specific, relevance to saga narrative. It is tempting to suggest a parallel evolution of Judeo-Christian creation and hero myth with Germanic creation and Germanic heroic myths in order to explain why many of Auerbach's remarks on Christian literature seem applicable to sagas, but any such suggestion must be so tentative and abstract that it must shelter in a scheme appended to this chapter (see appendix on p. 56). Perhaps in the sagas we have a genre based on the stuff of Germanic legend and tradition, observed and set down by men possessed of a Christian sensibility but free from religious tendentiousness.[24] And from here one is led back to the earlier considerations above which viewed sagas as a mimesis of oral narration and to an agreement with Fox that they are "foreground" narratives, but foreground narratives that have been changed by the circumstances in which they existed and the function they served. The route to a critical theory of the sagas takes us to the practice of *sagnaskemtan*, about which more must be said.

The practice of *sagnaskemtan* has certain cultural and social functions, and these functions in turn are reflected in the very style and shape of the sagas themselves. Sagas were read out for entertainment at public and social gatherings; the implication is that they reached a fairly broad audience. There is an analogy between the saga speaker and the epic poet who sang his songs before an audience which included the ruling classes of society. One may assume that the Icelandic audience was at once entertained and instructed by the material of the sagas. Looked at in one way, a work like *Njáls saga* provides a course in how to behave. The points covered touch upon the most important actions of Icelandic life—matters of law and hospitality, when to settle a quarrel and when to seek vengeance, how to gain honor and glory, and conversely, how to behave like an utter rascal; in general, how to conduct one's life in the most fitting manner possible, and last and most importantly, how to die well. Sagas

presented their audience with a series of events which made
apprehensible moral precepts necessary to Icelandic culture.
Njáls saga illustrates this point—over and over scenes culminate in proverbial phrases of wisdom. Njáll himself, the wise
and farseeing man, is given the main burden of utterance.[25]

Pálsson in his book, *Sagnaskemmtun,* has recognized the
didactic nature of the sagas and agrees that some of them at
least may be considered as a "mirror for chieftains" (p. 102) in
which exemplary behavior is reflected. In *The Icelandic Family
Saga,* Theodore M. Andersson demonstrates (although it is not
his specific intention) how an instructive series of events can
become part of a literary structure. Andersson describes one
of the components of saga rhetoric, a device which he calls
"staging." This device is observed just before the climax when
"a saga frequently lapses into a fuller and denser narrative.
There is a deceleration of pace, a magnifying of detail, and a
dwelling on incidentals in order to focus the central event one
last time and enhance its importance in relation to the rest of
the story" (p. 54). After analyzing a number of such episodes
Andersson is able "to abstract the following constituent elements of staging," which are

> the planning of a strategy, topographic details (es-
> pecially the route to be followed), the relaying of
> intelligence, inciting, assembling of men, reconnois-
> sance, dreams and omens, warnings and the rejection
> of warnings, a description of the enemy or ambush by
> a companion while still at a distance, belittling of
> danger by the hero and refusal to withdraw, dismissal
> of companions, heroic dialogue, and courageous re-
> sistance at a great disadvantage. In constructing his
> climax the saga author makes a selection from these
> possible motifs, the story is therefore variable,
> but it is always recognizable as a variation on a
> standard pattern. (p. 57)

Andersson notes how this format has the dramatic effect of delaying the climax and enhancing and framing the significance of the central event; it also increases suspense over just how the action will resolve itself. But certainly the sagas here lapse "into a fuller and denser narrative" because such matters were also of vital interest to the audience. The description showed this audience in detail how to make and meet an attack, how to act in a situation in which members of that audience might very well find themselves.

This concern with cultural behavior extends to the portrayal of character in the sagas—they are not unique personalities in any modern sense, but individual characters who fit themselves somewhere along the possible spectrum of social types. In *The Nature of Narrative*, Scholes and Kellogg observe that the

> especially distinguishing characteristic of the family sagas, which sets them apart from all other literatures of the Middle Ages, is their interest in what we could call manners. The individual attributes, which function as atoms in the molecular construction of saga characters, are very frequently social attributes. They are not merely physical characteristics or attributes referrable to ethical absolutes, but are expressed in terms of observable and agreed-upon standards of social judgment. (pp. 173–174)

If we may view the events and characters of the sagas as lessons and illustrations, we can say that the repetition of these lessons and illustrations, presented many times in typical scenes and types from saga to saga, would have two effects. The first would have been a stabilizing one, exerting a conservative influence on Icelandic cultural patterns. Composed as it is, out of traditional material, the fabric of the sagas would resist alteration, would only slowly adapt itself to innovation. Insofar as sagas determined social behavior, the effect would have been to retain a continuity of social behavior over generations. Some such mechanism was perhaps necessary for the proper functioning of the Icelandic nation, which may roughly be described as a republic. Here responsibility for maintaining order and stability was vested not in an overlord with military retainers, but was distributed among a large group of chieftains and landed farmers who were entitled to have a voice in national affairs. It was necessary that members of this society should share a reasonably uniform set of ethical values and material expectations to keep under control the inevitable acrimony that arises between rival factions. That there was no effective executive branch to enforce the decisions of the local and national assemblies was all the more reason for other controls on social behavior to develop. To put it succinctly, medieval Iceland possessed two unique things—its constitution and its prose family sagas. It seems likely that the two are related, that the first is a precondition of the second, that the second helped preserve the first. Indeed, the flowering of saga literature in the thirteenth century has been seen as a response to the foreign secular and churchly pressures that were working to tear apart the structure of Icelandic society. The sagas are a defense called forth to reaffirm the old values, perhaps not the old pagan values of the saga-age they tell of, but the ones the Icelanders had worked out in the two centuries after their conversion.[26]

As a second effect, the sagas, if they were stabilizing and conserving forces in Icelandic culture, may have gained some of their strength and relevance through a process of feedback. Is it not possible that men familiar with the sagas, impressed by the deeds and imbued with the spirit they depict, could themselves go out and act in a manner worthy of the sagas, perform memorable deeds themselves, and thus earn a place in the story? Something of that emerges in the pages of *Sturlunga saga*, dreary and bloody reading as much of it is. The intertwining between life and art, between events and the vision which chose what events to relate, was a complex one in thirteenth-century Iceland.

This question of the social function of the sagas needs to be raised because the precise conditions in which they did flourish may help explain important saga features, among which are certain means by which they achieve effective narration, their event-by-event chronological ordering, the nature of their characterization, and what I have called their narrative density, their swiftness, compactness, and lack of redundancy. I have suggested that sagas may be regarded as a mimesis of oral narration and that they imitate primary oral narration because they are in debt to it, because their authors strove to perfect this resemblance, and because they were audience-controlled, existing in a mode between speaker and listener.[27]   A fourth reason may here be added: saga structures retain the features of oral narrative because such structures are the most effective ones for impressing upon an aural public the memory of instructive deeds, of engraining social patterns into such an audience.   Eric Havelock, using the term *saga* to refer to oral report in general, observes in *Preface to Plato*:

> The saga in its purest oral form spoke far oftener of doings than of happenings.   But it can fairly be generalised that the saga considered from the standpoint of a later and more sophisticated critique is essentially the record of an event-series, of things-happening, never of a system of relations or of causes or of categories and topics. ... The fundamental units ... are sets of doings and of happenings. Information or prescription, which in a later stage of literate culture would be arranged typically and topically, is in the oral tradition preserved only as it is transmuted into an event. (pp. 173–74)

Oral narrative then will structure itself by placing events one after another without explicit classification, binding together, and subordination of such events to each other. The order need not be chronological, as the *Odyssey* and *Beowulf* both demonstrate, but chronological ordering is certainly an obvious and effective way to position events in a memorable pattern.

Since what is done must be done by somebody or some active
agent, it follows that such narrative will deal with characters in
action and these characters will be of a certain set.

> The psychology of oral memorisation and oral record
> required the content of what is memorised to be a set
> of doings. This in turn presupposes actors or agents.
> (p. 171)

> What kind of people can these be? Not anybody and
> everybody. If the saga is functional, if its purpose is
> to conserve the group mores, then the men who act in
> it must be the kind of men whose actions would in-
> volve the public law and the family law of the group.
> They must therefore be "political" men in the most
> general sense of the term, men whose acts, passions,
> and thoughts will affect the behaviour and the fate of
> the society in which they live so that the things they
> do will send out vibrations into the farthest confines
> of this society, and the whole apparatus becomes
> alive and performs motions which are paradigmatic. ...
> In sum, the saga, in order to do its job for the com-
> munity and offer an effective paradigm of social law
> and custom, must deal with those acts which are con-
> spicuous and political. And the actors who alone can
> furnish these paradigms in this kind of society we
> designate as "heroes." The reason for the heroic
> paradigm is in the last resort not romantic but func-
> tional and technical.[28] (pp. 167–68)

This quotation reads as virtually a brief for *Njáls saga*. Gunnarr,
Njáll, and his turbulent sons are certainly "political" men in
Havelock's sense of the term; their deeds involve the public and
family law; their fate affects and draws into the story men and
chieftains from virtually every district and every rank in Iceland.

What I have said presumes the existence of oral family saga
before the composition of such sagas as we now possess, or, at

least, the existence of an extensive and formal oral tradition about the deeds of Icelanders in the saga age. Such a presumption is by its nature undemonstrable, except insofar as the structure of the written sagas does suggest that they modelled themselves upon the forms of oral narrative. This modelling was maintained and further shaped by the circumstances of *sagnaskemtan*, by the requirement that, when read aloud, sentences could be easily enunciated and easily comprehended. The refinement of an oral tradition into written composition and the preservation by a literate culture of such compositions in fixed forms throws light on the origin of the narrative density of sagas. I would suggest that this is a feature that could occur when a quasi-epic literature takes form within a literate culture. In a wholly oral culture such as that in which the Homeric epics were formed, such as Iceland apparently was until the end of the eleventh century, spoken narrative, whether cast in deliberate verse or in what we would now perceive as prose, must bear a vast burden of cultural and didactic information.[29] It is only by the tradition maintained through the unceasing efforts of each generation of story tellers that the information necessary for the functioning of a complex but unlettered society may be preserved.[30] The structures of Homeric epic were evolved not so much for the sake of their art but for their ability to carry information, or, rather, art and function are inseparable. The associative formulas and structures of oral epic enable the poet to move in the broad filled-in foreground style which Auerbach, when he took Homer as his exemplar, was bound to describe. There are few abrupt leaps in time; everyone and everything is accounted for. Each event carries within it a hoard of cultural information, from guidance on ethical matters to a wealth of practical details. Altogether the Homeric epics are encylopedic works, covering all things necessary to a society, telling us in great detail of religion and religious ritual, law, education, warfare, seafaring, hunting, agricultural practices, clothing and armor, and whatever else was necessary for Homeric culture to preserve.

The sagas in their entirety also possess some of this encyclopedic function. *Njáls saga* in particular strikes one as the kind of cumulative work that will appear as a consummation of a body of heroic literature.[31] But in the sagas the weight of the cultural information is shifted to the realm of manners and ethics because they no longer function as repositories of practical knowledge. That is taken care of by other kinds of writing. The sagas, as we have them, came into existence at a time when letters and books were already established in Iceland; indeed, when the general literacy of the populace may have been considerably higher than that of other medieval cultures.[32] Thus the burden of information that in the past had to be carried orally and often rhythmically could now be transferred to books and shifted into prose. Certain matters no longer needed to be preserved in oral forms—we know that the law and various religious regulations and calculations were among the first things to be written down in Iceland. The decline of skaldic poetry in the thirteenth century also attests that events no longer needed to rely on and fit themselves to its complex mnemonic forms in order to be preserved.[33] Eric Havelock describes what happened in fifth-century Greece when an analogous shift occurred in the modes and technology of preserving information.

> But the alphabetic technology had in theory made it possible for preserved knowledge to discard both the rhythm on the one hand and the syntax of the image-series on the other. These had been companion but separate devices for framing words in memorisable form. How interesting therefore it becomes to notice that to carry out this double task at a single blow seems to have been too much for the energy even of the Greek mind. Of these two verbal modes, each at first might be discarded, separately from the other, but not the two together. Thus when the more obvious choice was made, and meter was dropped, the result was not a prose of ideas (whether or not we would

style this as "philosophic") but a prose of narrative, which retained the paratactic genius of epic, reporting experience still in the guise of events happening and of actions performed. Thus "history" is born on the coasts of Ionia, and also a descriptive geography presented as history. (p. 294)

The analogy that is urged here cannot be pressed all the way. Havelock suggests that the narrative mode of Greek historical writing reveals a direct debt to the narrative mode of preceding poetry in whose structure history was inextricable from the epic synthesis. The family sagas also employ this "syntax of the image-series"; from this, however, one should not infer that behind the prose sagas were extended oral poems.

But the habits and models of oral narration, practiced and perfected as they seem to have been in preliterate Iceland, influenced the shape and style of historical writings composed in Iceland, no matter what foreign and Christian models were introduced to the knowledge of educated Icelanders. Certainly it is true that in Iceland the first strong manifestation of literary activities is found in the historical writing that comes hard upon the setting down of vital legal and religious matters. One of the directions this activity eventually took is towards history as entertainment, towards the perfection of long narrative prose fictions. Cultural information, facts pertaining to religious and legal activities sort themselves out, become confined in codices of their own. Thus narrative genres were freed from having to carry along a burden of cultural information.[34] Narrative, oral or written,[35] could move closer to entertainment, could concentrate on perfecting narrative form as such. The sagas, in one sense, may be looked upon as prose epics relieved of their didactic burden so that the bones and structure of narrative, of *mythos*, show through. And it is in this sense that the sagas may be classified as foreground works. The features of foreground style in Auerbach's description are preeminently the features of oral narration. They are a consequence of the associative spinning-out of events through the oral-formulaic techniques and through associative clusters of larger patterns. The encyclopedic content of epic is largely fulfilled by such linkages, such associations that may appear digressive, which may be elaborated into extensive simile (Homer provides the most sophisticated example). It is precisely such obvious associations and linkages that are absent from the sagas, that have been knocked out because they no longer serve a functional purpose. Hence these works come to lack certain features of a fully foregrounded style. What remains is the structural framework and episodic arrangements of paratactic narrative, in which only events contributing directly to the plot appear, juxtaposed to one another without subordination. It is because the saga form developed towards a clear and perfect articulation of significant events that critical approaches to the sagas must concentrate on the patterns by which these events are represented and on the large overall structures in which these patterns are contained.

SCHEME: PARALLEL EVOLUTION OF MYTHS

"It is tempting to suggest a parallel evolution of Judeo-Christian creation and hero myth with Germanic creation and Germanic heroic myths in order to explain why many of Auerbach's remarks on Christian literature seem applicable to the sagas ... " (p. 46 above).   Such a parallel evolution might tentatively be diagrammed thus:

	Judeo-Christian Tradition	*Germanic Tradition*
Model	Bible	Mythical and Heroic Poetry
Chief mythical events	Creation	Cycle of Creation-Dissolution (*Vǫluspá*)
	Christ's Passion	Passions of Gods and Heroes (Baldr's death, Sigurðr's death)
	Last Judgment	Ragnarǫk (*Vǫluspá*)
Displacement into events of this world	Deeds and sufferings of the chosen people and early Christians which prefigure and fulfill God's scheme	Establishment of Icelandic society Sufferings and heroic deeds of Icelanders
These events are preserved and reflected in literature	The wide range of European history, romance, drama, allegory and other genres shaped by Christian concerns	Family sagas (*Laxdœla saga*, a clear case of saga following outlines of earlier heroic legend; reference in *Gísla saga* to similar situation in Eddic poetry)

NOTE: Interaction and cross references may take place vertically and horizontally among the elements of this scheme. *Vǫluspá* as it now exists seems obviously influenced by Christian concepts; Njáll's body after death is unharmed and shines with a holy luster; Hǫskuldr Hvítaness-Priest, betrayed and struck down by his foster-brothers, dies with words of Christ-like forgiveness on his lips. I hope I need not emphasize that the worth of such a scheme is in its suggestiveness rather than in any rigorous working out of it and that the relationships it diagrams are first of all literary ones and only secondarily historical ones.

3

Elements in *Njáls saga*: Description, Theory, Application

The various typical elements of which *Njáls saga* is composed form a critical scheme which will be used here to discuss the first episode of the saga (ch. 1–8). Chapter five of *Njáls saga* presents a scene (counterparts of which are found throughout saga literature) which must have been close to the hearts of a Norse audience—a shipboard fight with pirates. Hrútr Herjólfsson, in typical fashion, has sailed to the court of the Norwegian king, has been received there as a king's man, and has been outfitted with ships and a crew. Sailing for Oresund, Hrútr sights the lurking ships of Atli Arnviðarson, a notorious outlaw. Hrútr confers about tactical dispositions with his mate, Úlfr the Unwashed (1—the hero sights the enemy and takes measures). The scene shifts to Atli who also consults with his men about his dispositions (2—the enemy sights the hero). The fleets converge and the two sides identify themselves and exchange boasts (3—meeting, identification, boasting). Battle ensues; it follows a standardized pattern. After an initial stand-off (4—stand off), Atli succeeds in boarding Hrútr's ship and hacks his way towards Hrútr and Úlfr (5—one side boards the other):

> Hrútr turned now to face Atli; he hacked at once at
> Hrútr's shield and cleaved it through from top to bot-

tom [6—the main opponents face each other].   Then
Atli was hit on the hand by a stone and his sword fell
to the deck.   Hrútr seized the sword and sliced off
Atli's leg; then Hrútr gave him his deathblow [7—death
of foe].   (p. 18)

Hrútr and his men are victorious and seize much booty (8—spoils
of victory).

In chapter eighty-two Þráinn Sigfússon, who has been wel-
comed and fitted out by the Norwegian king as Hrútr was, comes
into collision with another piratical outlaw, one Kolr (1):

The weather was good.   Then Kolr sighted the ships,
which were approaching, and said that he had dreamt
about Earl Hákon [the Norwegian ruler] and said these
must be his men and ordered his own men to take up
their weapons [2].

The saga-man, according to his option, omits (3) the exchange of
identity and boasts.   They fight for a long time with no decisive results (4):

Then Kolr leapt aboard Þráinn's ship [5] and cleared
his way and kills many men; he had a gold helmet on.
Now Þráinn sees that his side is not prevailing; he
urges on the men around him, and he himself goes
first to meet up with Kolr.   Kolr hacked at Þráinn and
the blow struck Þráinn's shield and cleaved it through
to the bottom [6].   Then Kolr was hit on the hand by a
stone; his sword fell to the deck.   Þráinn struck at
Kolr; the blow struck his leg so that it came off;
after that they killed Kolr [7].   Þráinn cut off his
head but threw the body overboard and kept the head.
They seized a lot of booty [8]. . . . (pp. 199–200)

Other viking fights in *Njáls saga* (there are five altogether) follow this pattern.   The next two examples are details from one of
Gunnarr's fights and one of Kári Sǫlmundarson's:

> Hallgrímr thrust at Gunnarr with his halberd. There
> was a beam across the ship and Gunnarr leapt back-
> wards over it; Gunnarr's shield was in front of the
> beam, and Hallgrímr thrust into it and thus into the
> beam. Gunnarr hacked at Hallgrímr's arm and shat-
> tered the bones, but the sword did not bite; then the
> halberd fell to the deck. Gunnarr seized the halberd
> and ran Hallgrímr through. Gunnarr carried the hal-
> berd ever afterwards. (ch. 30, p. 81)

Kári's style is the same:

> Snækólfr turns to meet Kári and immediately hacks at
> him. Kári leaps backwards over a beam which lay
> across the ship. Snækólfr hews at the beam so that
> both edges of the sword are buried in it. Kári hacks
> at him and the sword struck upon the shoulder and the
> blow was so great it sliced off the arm and Snækólfr
> was dead on the spot. (ch. 84, p. 204)

It is no coincidence that Kári fights with much the same dex-
terity and nimbleness as Gunnarr—both leap backwards over the
beam and then strike at their opponents' arms as their weapons
embed themselves in the wood. The similarity of other feats of
arms performed by the two reinforce this parallel. It is a deliberate parallel, for Kári is Gunnarr's replacement; he is the hero
who brings *Njáls saga* to its conclusion; his manner and appearance are similar to Gunnarr's and he is explicitly compared to
him on several occasions.[1] Preparations for this comparison begin, without explicit comment, at Kári's first appearance, for,
like Gunnarr, Kári possesses resplendent clothing and armor,[2]
and he conducts himself in battle as Gunnarr did.

It is evident that viking fights in *Njáls saga* follow a stereotyped pattern and are made up of combinations of smaller motifs,
here the specific details of close combat, and I will not belabor
the point. This is a stock situation, one in which the same
phrases often (but not always) occur for the same motifs. The

objection might be made that such scenes are perforce structured and stereotyped. Given the nature of Norse weapons and the limited choice of tactics in shipboard fighting, there is a limited choice of ways men can meet in battle and die beneath weapons. If two men are having at one another with heavy swords, it is likely that one will thrust and the other parry until someone's guard fails and opens the way to the decisive blow. But as Peter Hallberg forcefully points out, these scenes from the classical sagas are certainly refined from reality. They are idealized battle scenes where blows are delivered once and for all and men bite the dust cleanly, often with an appropriate quip.[3]

The battle scenes in *Njáls saga*, particularly when compared with the contemporary descriptions of battles in *Sturlunga saga*, strongly suggest that in this area of representation *Njáls saga* is working with artistically wrought narrative forms. But this statement is true in other areas of life which the saga represents. I take the space to give more examples because the extent to which *Njáls saga* is made up of stock motifs and scenes, which combine into oft-repeated patterns, needs emphasis.

No one can fail to note how events in *Njáls saga* are grouped around law suits. An insult is incurred, which may lead directly to a summons and suit, or lead there indirectly through a pattern of revenge and settlement. This pattern, of course, is one that underlies a majority of the family sagas, and more shall be said about it later. But no other saga is quite so concerned with the attempts to contain the violence of blood feuds within a lawful settlement. The rhythm of the saga pulses with the yearly assembling of Iceland's chieftains and their followers at the Althing.

The first law suit comes early in the saga, in chapter eight. Hrútr's wife, Unnr, has declared herself divorced from him on grounds of incompatibility and gone back to live with her father, Morðr Fiddle. The next year Hrútr and his brother Hoskuldr assemble their forces and ride to the Althing. There Morðr sues Hrútr for the return of Unnr's dowry. Hrútr, who feels injured because of the divorce and who thinks Morðr is pressing his claim too aggressively and greedily, demands that the matter be settled in single combat between him and Mǫrðr. (Before the conversion of Iceland, such an appeal to force was a lawful substitute for court action.) Mǫrðr, an older man, is no match for the warrior Hrútr; he sensibly declines to fight, whereupon "there was a great shouting and outcry at the Law Rock, and Mǫrðr had from this the greatest shame" (ch. 8, p. 28). The chapter does not end here but includes an aftermath whose importance shall be taken up later.

The pattern seen in chapter eight is next repeated in chapters twenty-one through twenty-four. The outline is the same, but the framework is considerably expanded. Mǫrðr has died and Unnr has run through all her resources. This event is part of the thematic pattern of wastage and imprudence, of excess, which occasions so much mortal woe in *Njáls saga*.[4] She asks her kinsman Gunnarr to revive her suit against Hrútr for the recovery of her dowry. The business of the summonings, which, in chapter eight, takes place at the Althing and occupies one sentence,[5] is here greatly filled with two stock events that can appear in other contexts, a secret counselling and the successful trickery of a host by a disguised guest. Gunnarr goes to Njáll for advice, the first occasion of many such requests. Njáll tells him in detail how the case may be reopened. Gunnarr will have to trick Hrútr into revealing the proper formula for a new summons. Njáll predicts at length just what Gunnarr will do and what will happen. The scene has its parallel in chapter seven where Mǫrðr secretly counsels Unnr about what form her divorce procedure must take. The scene between Gunnarr and Njáll may seem awkward and not credible. But this is the first time the audience sees Gunnarr and Njáll in action; they have just been introduced. The long-winded prediction establishes Njáll's credentials as a man skilled in law and able to see into the future. His accurate description of Gunnarr's conduct and the audience's subsequent beholding of it establishes Gunnarr as a bold and intelligent man, possessed of a wit and humor that enhance attractive qualities already established through his warriorlike prowess. Gunnarr disguises himself as a peddler and finds himself invited to Hrútr's table unrecognized. By pretending interest in Hrútr's former suit with Mǫrðr, he tricks Hrútr into telling him how Hrútr may be summoned; whereupon Gunnarr does just that. The whole business provides an extreme example of how a motif (here that of summonings) may be condensed into a few words or expanded into pages and combined with other narrative formulas.

Chapter twenty-four is concerned with the law suit. Both sides ride in with supporters, prepared to resort to violence if need be. This motif echoes and swells in *Njáls saga* until it culminates in the great battle at the Althing between the Burners and their prosecutors. Gunnarr initiates his suit, but Hrútr over-turns it by pointing out technical errors in Gunnarr's approach. Njáll offers to save the case with his legal wisdom. Here too in embryo are motifs that are developed at great length in later episodes—technical errors place the prosecution on the defensive and wise men behind the scenes engage in a seesaw duel of wits. The motif is just sounded here, however, and not de-veloped. Instead the saga-man forcefully relates this episode with the preceding one in chapter eight. Gunnarr cuts through the proceedings to challenge Hrútr to single combat. Hrútr at first is inclined to accept the challenge but Hǫskuldr warns him that " 'you will have no more success against Gunnarr than Mǫrðr would have had against you, and instead we shall both together pay out the money to Gunnarr' " (ch. 24, p. 67). And so the case is settled. The chapter ends with two scenes of aftermath as Hrútr and Hǫskuldr, Gunnarr and Njáll discuss the outcome of events with each other. The parallel has been neatly drawn. Gunnarr has done to Hrútr what Hrútr did to Mǫrðr Fiddle and in both cases the issue was the recovery of Unnr's dowry. On a deeper level, in both cases, the victor has won by an appeal to violence. But settlement by such means only leads—if by devi-ous ways—to more trouble. Hrútr runs up against Gunnarr; Gunnarr gives his winnings to Unnr who uses them to catch her-self a husband no one approves of and who will subsequently give birth to the man who will contrive Gunnarr's death, plot the destruction of the Njálssons, and make the blunder that leads to the great battle at the Althing.

Successive readings of *Njáls saga* make apparent the similarly structured frames into which the author fits the events of his story. As a final example, a comparison of chapters eleven and twelve with chapters sixteen and seventeen shows that the events therein conform to a high degree. In the first set the main motifs are: (1) the *insult* to Hallgerðr (a face slap); (2) Þjóstólfr, Hallgerðr's foster-father, contrives to *get alone* with Hallgerðr's abuser (her husband) and *take vengeance*; (3) *announcement* of the slaying to Hallgerðr; (4) *flight* of Þjóstólfr and *boasting* of the slaying to the person who receives him; (5) *pursuit* of Þjóstólfr by the kinsmen of the murdered man; (6) *bafflement* of the pursuers; and (7) a *recompense*, willingly given by Hǫskuldr, Hallgerðr's father, to the next-of-kin of the slain man. Chapters sixteen and seventeen adhere to almost the same structure, although the details of each motif are different. Again there is: (1) the *insult*, again a face slap; (2) *vengeance* taken in an *isolated* spot by Þjóstólfr; (3) *announcement* to Hallgerðr; (4) *flight*, this time to Hǫskuldr, who kills Þjóstólfr as soon as the latter *announces* the killing; (5) *pursuit* of Þjóstólfr; (6) *bafflement* in that the intended victim is already dead; and (7) another generous *compensation* from Hǫskuldr to the kinsmen of Hallgerðr's second unfortunate husband. Reading the saga a first time, one may sense the broad similarity of the two episodes; closer examination reveals that their structure is virtually identical. Having on hand an effective way to represent a situation, the saga-man simply repeats it at need. This procedure, of course, is similar to that of oral composition. Cedric H. Whitman remarks of Homer's art that the "formula, not the word, was the epic unit. And the same is true of the longer repeated scenes. They might be lengthened or shortened, but they were units, to be used as such" (*Homer*, p. 110). The remark applies to the art of the sagas as well, if one substitutes for the poetic formula the concept of the small event, the minimal fact.

Indeed, one may begin to define the levels of narrative units

in saga composition at the syntactical level, where one deals
with the phrase that bears a single fact. The first sentence of
chapter two in *Njáls saga* contains four such units.

> It was a certain time, that the brothers rode to the
> Althing, Hǫskuldr and Hrútr; there was a great gather-
> ing of men there (*Þat var einu hverju sinni, at þeir
> bræðr riðu til alþingis, Hǫskuldr ok Hrútr; þar var
> fjǫlmenni mikit*). (p. 7)

Each of these units adds to our knowledge. The first by saga
convention sets the events to follow in chronological relationship to what has gone before; the second tells that two brothers
rode to the Althing, the third states who these brothers were, the
fourth states that the assembly was crowded. The first and
fourth are certainly stock phrases which are found many times in
saga literature; the second and third also have their twins and
their analogues. This level is one step up, it will be noted, from
a strictly grammatical level. A phrase here may include an entire sentence—"they rode to the Althing." On this level one
observes two kinds of units. The first are such as have just
been described above. The second kind is structurally the same
but functionally much different. It includes images such as:
(1) similes, rare, but all the more striking when they do occur—
"He travelled across the ice as swift as a bird might fly" (ch. 92,
p. 233); (2) descriptive sentences that have strong symbolic
referents—"There the fire at times flared up and at times died
down" (ch. 130, p. 336); and (3) proverbial statements, gnomic
utterances—"the hand rejoices in the blow but for a little
while."[6] These units raise different critical problems from the
first type, a matter to which I shall return.

The next level up is the level of gesture, of the small deed, of
stylized movements, events, and speeches that go together to
make larger scenes. I call these units *motifs*. After Hrútr and
Hǫskuldr arrive at the Althing, they catch sight of Mǫrðr Fiddle
and follow him back to his booth and enter:

> Mǫrðr was seated in the back part of the booth; they
> greeted him. He stood up to meet them and took
> Hǫskuldr by the hand and sat him down beside him,
> and Hrútr sat down next to Hǫskuldr. (ch. 2, p. 8)

The motif here is the act of greeting and welcoming. It too is a
highly standardized procedure and a seemingly indispensable
one, for this little rigamarole is reenacted on nearly every occasion when one person in *Njáls saga* comes to talk to another
person. The degree of the welcome's warmth and the positioning
of the guest are, of course, formal indications of the mood in
which the visit is received. Scenes of welcoming also impart to
the audience a lesson in manners. By the end of *Njáls saga*, if
a person knows nothing else, at least he will know how to say
how do you do. To actions on this level the word *theme* is often
applied, especially in discussions of oral poetry. But that word
has been used in so many other contexts that it seems best to
choose a different one.[7]

Such motifs, little blocks of formalized action, are joined together to make scenes. The scene may be defined as the level
of sustained individual or social action, as a compact unit of
significant action which has a beginning, middle, and end.
Mǫrðr's welcome of Hrútr and Hǫskuldr is the beginning of a
scene whose topic is bride-bartering. The dialogue between the
parties is made up of the following motifs: general small talk
not relevant to the purpose of the visit (a formality observed in
most such conversations); a direct statement of the proposal;
questioning of Hrútr's qualifications by Mǫrðr; offer of terms by
Hǫskuldr; further stipulation of terms by Mǫrðr; acceptance by
Hrútr; formal hand-shaking and betrothal, which concludes the
scene. This is a simple deal. Other scenes of bride-bartering in
Njáls saga usually include these motifs and in addition give the
woman a chance to state her own choice in the matter.

This scene in chapter two appears to be the center piece of a
narrative unit, which is here marked out by chapter divisions.
The chapter has told of the ride of Hrútr and Hǫskuldr to the

Althing and of the agreement with Mǫrðr for the marriage of his daughter Unnr that summer. It continues with Hrútr's ride back. On the way he is met by a kinsman newly arrived from Norway, who tells Hrútr of an inheritance that has been left to him there. It is a considerable amount of money. Hrútr rides over to see Mǫrðr and they agree to postpone the marriage for three years while Hrútr sets out to claim his inheritance. Hrútr sets sail and arrives in Oslo Fjord, which event concludes the chapter. Now this is a familiar pattern in Icelandic sagas. A marriage is postponed while the hero goes adventuring overseas.[8] On a more general level, it is a component theme of bride-wooing. The hero must prove himself worthy of the bride by seeking adventure and by overcoming obstacles. There is thus a strong tendency for a challenge to follow, for an adventure to intrude upon a betrothal scene. From a strictly logical point of view the news of Hrútr's inheritance seems to be a bit contrived; a person accustomed to later fictional forms senses a slight clanking of machinery and feels that the whole business of Hrútr's trip to Norway is a digression from the main direction of the saga. But the logic here is not the logic of modern fiction; it belongs to the logic of the oral tale. The latter event, the call to adventure, "belongs" to the first, the betrothal of the bride, and the whole series of events that follow belong overall to the theme of bride-wooing, a theme which, surprisingly enough, emerges (in my opinion) as the dominant one of the first thirty-four chapters of the saga. Having once started on this route, the saga-man feels compelled to show the whole working out. This is a process that Ian R. Maxwell describes as the principle of the integrity of the episode.[9] This principle takes one rather beyond the limits of the chapter unit, and indeed most critics would say that chapter divisions in saga literature are not important, that they are "notoriously inconsequential."[10] This may be the general case but it does not pertain to the two principal manuscripts of *Njáls saga*. There most chapters are aesthetically satisfying collections of scenes that do fall into a convenient narrative unit. Often, in this saga, the unit is the passage of time between one

Althing and the next. Chapters may also be clusters of scenes drawn together by "patterned sequences," a process by which one traditional scene calls forth others that exist in association with it, a process by which even groups of such patterns may call forth other groups. [11]

At this point one reaches the level of that unit which I will call the *episode*. This is the level where *mythos*, the shaping power of plot, takes hold of events. The first such episode in *Njáls saga* is the story of the dealings between Hrútr and Mǫrðr Fiddle and occupies chapters one through eight. It can be sub-divided. Chapters one through two set forth the sides and the marriage proposal. Chapters two through six tell of Hrútr's ad-ventures overseas. Here a curse is put upon him by the jealous Queen Gunnhildr and this curse leads (in chapters seven through eight) to the failure of Hrútr's marriage, his divorce, and Mǫrðr's suit against him. But the saga-man feels that all this material belongs to one clearly defined unit ("strand" or "part," *þáttr*, is the word he uses for it), for he ends chapter eight by saying, "and now is finished the episode of Hrútr and Mǫrðr" (p. 29).

Episodes may then be gathered up to form still larger *episode clusters*. Chapters one through eight and chapters nine through eighteen, which tell of the misfortunes of Hallgerðr's first two husbands, clearly form a large division. Together they establish the roots of evil that will join, decades later, in catastrophe. [12] In *Njáls saga*, episodes and episode clusters are often marked off by sections which I call *interludes*. These are the sections described above that pause to introduce new persons and to pre-sent their genealogies, chief characteristics, and such vital statistics as are necessary to the plot. Thus chapters nineteen and twenty introduce Gunnarr of Hlíðarendi and Njáll and his family; the next episode begins with chapter twenty-one. The first episode cluster has brought the plot so far; certain situa-tions have been developed and character traits established. To this body of facts the saga-man then feeds a whole new set of information; the plot absorbs it, and works upon it, advancing to a new and seemingly inevitable conclusion that is a new point of balance, a completed narrative, which demands more facts before it too can develop.[13]

Episode clusters merge into still grander patterns that form the large divisions of the saga. With the completed work one reaches the level of the entire plot, the entire structure of the story, which here has either been preserved by tradition or is represented as having been so preserved by the man who re-creates it. Finally one may speak of an *archetypal level*, a level of still further abstraction where the typical curve of the plot becomes apparent as one takes a stand back away from it. The word *archetype* may here be used in the following senses: (1) to refer to a pattern common to a number of works—one may at this level compare works whether or not they belong to the same genre or have originated in the same culture; (2) to refer to archetype as myth, as evidence that the repetition of the same basic story exists in order to satisfy certain cultural and psychological needs of a society (the remark also applies to stock patterns on lower levels of narrative); (3) to refer to the structure of the myth as this structure is related to patterns of the human psyche—the pattern itself, as an abstract symbol or form, has function and therefore acquires meaning.

The more one reads among the genres of saga literature, the more it becomes clear that this literature is composed out of a large but nevertheless finite choice of discrete events.[14] Almost any event, from the level of the phrase upwards, can be shown to occur more than once in saga literature. A sufficient number of such events are repeated often enough to give the sagas an overall similarity. Indeed, *Njáls saga* by itself is long enough to provide a considerable catalogue of such recurrences. The literature that is formed from selection of such events will be a traditional literature—it will not create something uniquely new that has not existed before; it will re-create, restate, what has existed before. There is no adverse criticism implied in this observation. Much of the power and effect of this literature comes from its ability to stir in the memory thoughts of actions similar to the story being heard. Saga literature, like oral literature, has a built-in allusiveness. By proper mastery of its forms the saga-man can compose[15] a work that is remarkably coherent and filled with symbolic suggestiveness. But this mastery displays itself in ways different from later literary techniques which have provided the basis for many of our critical concepts.

Recently Robert Scholes and Robert Kellogg in their book, *The Nature of Narrative*, have suggested a terminology and method of approach to the typical units of oral poetry, which I would like to modify and extend to *Njáls saga*. Such a procedure seems justified because, on levels of composition higher than the poetic formula, the structuring of saga narrative and oral poetic narrative are similar. Scholes and Kellogg propose that the word *topos* be used in place of the term *theme*, which has hitherto stood not only for motifs and scenes and even large patterns, but which has also covered the conceptual referents of such units. They prefer *topos* because

> from a structural point of view the somewhat stereotyped rhetorical elements [used by classical writers] . . . are similar enough to the stereotyped groups of ideas in orally composed narrative poetry to warrant the same descriptive terms.
>
> A *topos*, whether it occurs in an oral narrative or a written one, is a traditional image. It is not identifiable or even analyzable on the basis of either the formulas or the uniquely arranged words a poet might use to construct it, but rather on the basis of the image to which the words refer. . . . Briefly, it may be said here that insofar as a *topos* refers to the external world its meaning is a *motif*; insofar as it refers to the world of disembodied ideas and concepts its meaning is a *theme*. Traditional *topoi* consist, then, of two elements: a traditional motif, such as the hero's descent into the underworld, which may be extremely durable historically; and a traditional theme, such as the search for wisdom or the harrowing of hell, which

> may be much more subject to gradual change or re-
> placement in the course of time. The *topoi* of oral
> narratives are identifiable on the basis of their con-
> sistent association of a given motif with a given
> theme.... The thematic content of the *topoi* of ancient
> narrative is, of course, extremely difficult to analyze.
> The Homeric *topoi*, like those of the Germanic oral
> poetic tradition, were at one time closely associated
> with religious ritual, and their thematic content may
> therefore still be vaguely sacred, even though the nar-
> rative is remarkably free of direct references to cult.
> (pp. 26–27)

Since Scholes and Kellogg use the term *motif* to denote a traditional action, objectively observable, I will substitute for it the
term *object* in order to avoid confusion with *motif* as I use it to
designate a small stereotyped gesture or act.

Their terminology developed here applies to the narrative
levels of scene and episode. I would like to use it in a somewhat more flexible manner to examine the entire scale of traditional images out of which sagas are composed. The analysis
of the *topos* can be presented thus:

External World—————*Topos*—————————Theme
(Motif or *Object*)   (Traditional Image)   (Ideas and Concepts)

Such a division, of course, may be made of any image in literature. What we need to keep in mind is that "the *topoi* of oral
narrative are identifiable on the basis of their consistent association of a given motif with a given theme." Lord Warburton
kissing Isabel Archer and Will Ladislaw kissing Dorothea Brooke
may be "traditional images" of Victorian literature that look the
same. But their themes are quite different because the characters are unique individuals who bring to these scenes their own
special, unduplicated experience. When Gunnarr of Hlíðarendi,
Gísli Sursson, and Grettir Ásmundarson die as outlaws, fighting

to the end, surrounded by their enemies, the thematic reference
to those three images is very much the same.

On the first level of saga narrative, that which included the
minimal fact, images, symbolic descriptions, and gnomic statements, the *topos* presents itself in this fashion:

I.A. MINIMAL FACT

Object	Topos	Theme
1. The ride	1. "They rode to the Althing."	1. Assemblage

I.B. FIGURATIVE AND GNOMIC STATEMENTS

Object	Topos	Theme
2. Hildigunnr	2. "You are the greatest monster" (ch. 116, p. 291).	2. Woman as de-stroyer, in-citer
3. The destroyed house at Berg-Þórshváll	3. "There the fire at times blazed up, at times died down."	3. Course of blood feuds
4. The occasions which prompt this saying	4. "Cold are the counsels of women" (ch. 116, p. 292).	4. Woman as destroyer

The figurative statements and the proverbs are small concrete
phrases that immediately refer one to the large themes and the
whole structure of the work. Here there is room for personal
touches of the saga-man. Example three is not a traditional
image or formula—it is an individual and telling stroke by the
composer of *Njáls saga.* It strikes one as an image symbolizing
not only the fluctuations of passions in *Njáls saga* but the course
in general of the blood feuds which are the heart of saga literature. It does stand out, and because it does the reader will reflect upon its significance.

In the schemes for the next levels of motif, scene, episode
and episode cluster, the thematic component of the *topoi* remains
constant; the referent is to matters of social manners and cultural significance.

II. MOTIF (small units of typical acts)

Object	Topos	Theme
1. Elements of hand-to-hand combat	1. Gunnarr catches a spear in mid-flight and hurls it back.	1. Heroic agility
2. Details of a proper welcome	2. A man welcomes a visitor to his booth.	2. Hospitality

III. SCENE (level of sustained personal or social action)

Object	Topos	Theme
A set series of motifs depicting frequently encountered situations	1. A shipboard fight	1. Warfare
	2. A trial	2. Nature of legality, justice
	3. A feast	3. Lordliness
	4. Bartering for a bride	4. Bride-wooing
	5. Inciting	5. Duty of revenge

Level IV may be called the level of the chapter unit, if it is understood that this phrase need not refer to the physical chapter divisions in the manuscripts but to the patterned sequences of events which are components of a large theme. We are here moving onto the level of episode and episode cluster where events fall into the patterns of traditional tales, of longer or shorter adventures.

V and VI. EPISODE AND EPISODE CLUSTER

Object	Topos	Theme
The events of these episodes	1. Young men travel abroad to find adventure and to prove themselves.	1. Testing of the hero
	2. A feud is initiated and ended.	2. Successful coping with destructive forces

On this level the theme has broad cultural and psychological implications and may be sensed as referring back to mythic origins.
On these last five levels, and on the next, it is at times useful
to invoke the concept of displacement.[16] Very briefly, this as-
serts that the themes, characters, and narrative forms of literature first take shape in the sacred myth that gathers about ritual.
When myth loses its sacred function, characters and their en-
vironments lose their divine attributes and take on increasingly
realistic forms. As the power of characters to deal with their
environment is limited, the heavenly and hellish boundaries of
the story are no longer apparent. But the origin of these stylized
episodes, scenes, and motifs can be assigned not only to the
myth, but to the ritual upon which myth took shape. Since ritual
enacts patterns which relate to the activity of the human spirit,
which reflect the dynamics of the psyche, the effect of such patterns can still make itself felt even in displaced modes.[17] The
concept of displacement is more useful in explaining why certain
arrangements of events can arouse a strong subjective response
than in enabling one to establish specific objective interpretations of particular passages in literature.[18]

   The seventh level is that of plot.

VII. PLOT (in saga literature a story preserved by tradition or rep-
        resented as having been so preserved by the man who re-creates it)

Object	*Topos*	*Theme*
The world created by the work, e.g., Iceland as it appears in *Njáls saga*	A formal pattern organized in a traditional familiar fashion[19]	Disturbance and reestablishment of order; conflict and compensation (refers to archetypal pattern)

The overall structure of events focuses on the dominant concern
of this literature, which is the blood feud.

   The last level is the archetypal level. Here events in the
sagas, Iceland itself as it is represented in the sagas, are seen

to take their place in a universe inhabited by other literary worlds and peoples. Here the *topos*, the traditional image, is the curve itself of the plot; the objective referent is to all other works that possess this curve; the thematic reference is to spiritual patterns, movements of the psyche, abstract mental patterns which can be filled with images.[20] The hierarchy of levels thus bends back upon itself, for the images that can contain, symbolize the archetype, take us back to step one. The last chapter of this book will clarify the relevance of this archetypal level to *Njáls saga*. Its diagram, without explanatory examples and argument, appears thus:

VIII. ARCHETYPAL LEVEL (underlying curve of plot)

Object	Topos	Theme
All other works that possess this curve	The curve itself	Relates to abstract mental patterns that can be filled with images or symbolized by a single image

Because a work like *Njáls saga* is made up of typical units which possess a consistent thematic reference, certain aesthetic consequences follow. In much the same way the poetic formula can summon to mind all the other occasions on which it has been used,[21] the typical units of saga provide simultaneous access to all their other appearances. For an analogue in written literature, they function very much as simile and metaphor do in Shakespearian drama where the richness of the work is enhanced by the recurrence of similar images and clusters of such images that provide cross-references to events not only within the confines of a given play but also to all such events in other plays by Shakespeare. Perhaps one reason why simile and metaphor as such rarely occur in the sagas is that their function of providing associative links with other parts is fulfilled by the traditional images that are here called *topoi*.[22]

It follows that a given saga-man may achieve effects by departing from the standard image which has been fixed in the audience's mind by its familiarity with these images as they are repeated in the body of saga literature. When the vain and hasty Þorvaldr Ósvífrsson comes with his father to ask for Hallgerðr's hand, "they immediately announced their business and put forward a marriage proposal" (ch. 9, p. 31). This hastiness is unseemly and runs counter to the usual motif of polite delay proper on such occasions. It suggests that Þorvaldr through his impetuosity may be entering into a bad bargain—and indeed it is one that costs him his life. The saga-man cannot rely wholly on the audience's familiarity with other sagas, however; he must establish the norms within his own work. Part of the task of *Njáls saga*'s leisurely introduction, part of the task of these introductory sections which most sagas possess, is to set forth the stock material which the saga-man may later condense, expand, provide parallels for, and make changes upon.

As sagas progress each scene can look back to what has preceded it. In *Njáls saga* and in some others one senses that each event is connected with, is even the result of, all that has gone before. In consequence scenes and even motifs become laden with significance, with an ability to summon up associations with all prior events. At the heart of the saga are the great, vivid, thoroughly realized scenes in which very many of the saga's major themes come together and visibly appear. Gunnarr's last defense, Hildigunnr's incitement, Flosi's spurning of the pile of silver heaped before him at the Althing, the Burning, and the great battle at the Althing with its following reconciliation are some of these great scenes. And when the saga is reread or retold the early scenes take on a weight of association because they call to mind their later analogues; they forewarn of what is to come. Provided a work is bound together by large thematic interests, that is, provided one may, without excessive wrenching, naturally argue that most of the typical units from which it is made contribute to the weaving together of a few dominant themes, one can begin to perceive a pervading all-allusiveness in any part of the work.[23] Foreshadowing and back-reference are devices inherent in this type of literature, but their presence can be emphasized and directed by a skillful composer sensitive to their exploitation. At the Burning itself the numerous references to Gunnarr's death are surely not there by happenstance. They force one to brood over the fate and the complexity of human passions which have brought things to such a pass; they force one to contrast the essential decency of the men who attacked Gunnarr to the desperate solution that Flosi is determined to carry out. Njáll proposes to go inside, for Gunnarr was able to make a good stand from within his house:

> "That is not the way to look at things," says Skarpheðinn. "Those chieftains who attacked Gunnarr in his house were men of such quality that they would rather have turned back than to burn him within. But these men will attack us with fire, if they cannot win by another way because they will do anything to get the better of us." [24]   (ch. 128, p. 326)

The remark must have had contemporary force, reflecting as it does on the chieftains of the Sturlung Age who did not stop short of burning within; the celebrated burning at Flugumýr may well have been in the minds of the audience as it cannot help but be in ours. [25]   Such carefully placed effects are found whenever a powerful artistic mind imposes its imagination on the material out of which it constructs an entire work. The dominant interests of the saga-man will influence the arrangements and choices of these parts as they fall into shape. If a coherent vision controls the shaping of the work, this vision will be reflected in the parts themselves, in their relationship to each other and to the whole. Saga composition is an art of comparison and contrast, of significant repetition of parallel scenes and of significant opposition of thematically contrasting material. If the saga-man exploits the effects that are inherent in his genre, little of his material need be wasted, off the point, or superfluous.

In order to test this statement, it is instructive to take some of the early chapters of *Njáls saga* and show how they introduce and relate themselves to the major themes of the work. A certain

circularity here seems inevitable; one needs to know the whole
to fit the part to it, to make the initial act of critical generosity
that assumes a design which imparts meaning to the units of the
work. What I say about the opening eight chapters of *Njáls saga*
obviously is based on the experience of the whole work. Most
critics in this century and some in the last have sensed the deep
ethical concern of the composer which provides a thematic unity
to the events of *Njáls saga*. More than most sagas, it presents
its action through the collisions of opposing ethical forces:
greed against generosity, small-mindedness against magnanimity,
malice against good will, foolishness against wisdom—in short,
evil against good. This underlying opposition is clear enough
and pervasive enough to drive the saga's most recent translators
to say that "in the last resort of definition, we might call *Njal's
Saga* a homily." [26] And so it is, in the sense that all great literature conveys an abiding sense of ethics defining the human experience. Magnus Magnusson and Herman Pálsson in the introduction to their translation provide an excellent concise summary
of the major themes which *are Njáls saga* when they once become visible in our imagination and fixed in narrative time
through sequential scenes. Nevertheless, as Ian R. Maxwell
observes, the "grand moral unity" of *Njáls saga* seems to fall
apart whenever the saga is analyzed, [27] particularly if one demands the type of organic unity which simply does not obtain in
works belonging to oral modes of narration. For the editors of
Njáls saga in the late nineteenth and early twentieth centuries,
the work was disfigured by extraneous material and interpolations. It has been the task of later critics—and there have not
been many—to reverse this critical approach, which is self-
defeating, and to view the saga as a whole, as if it were indeed
Njáll's saga, as its name states, [28] and not the sagas of Gunnarr
and Njáll, interrupted by adventures of a number of other people
and digressions on a number of various topics. I hope that my
approach will clarify the reasons why readers do sense a unity
in *Njáls saga*. It is an analysis of the process by which similar
patterns are used in this saga to lead up to major scenes, scenes

which then stand as images of all that is at stake. Hence it is appropriate to begin at the beginning of *Njáls saga* to see how what seems to be remote to the central action is actually germane and to look at the sort of material with which the saga-man chooses to begin and which hence begins to determine the course and values of *Njáls saga*.

The saga begins with the introduction of Mǫrðr Fiddle. Although it is stated that he is a "powerful chieftain" (ch. 1, p. 5), his genealogy is not imposing. One learns only that he is the son of Sighvatr the Red. More importantly, Mǫrðr is "a great lawyer and so skilled in legal matters that no judgement was thought judged according to law unless he took part" (p. 5). Mǫrðr has an attractive and well-bred daughter named Unnr, thought to be the best match in the Rangriver plains. So much for that.

"Now the saga turns west to the Breidafjord Dales" (p. 6). The expression is not unusual except for the distance involved and its presence in the first chapter. It signals a jump of several hundred miles from the south of Iceland to the northwest. Most saga introductions, if they do shift from one family to another, confine their range to the local district. This is the first indication of the scope of *Njáls saga*, whose action is to embrace most of the districts of Iceland. By calling attention to itself, it also calls attention to the man controlling the saga, who chooses, or allows, the story to turn westward. As such, it is one of a number of such phrases that do call attention to the saga-man's choice of material. Finally, it introduces the first opposition of contrasting forces, an opposition of geography, of character, and of theme. Later, once the saga-man has established his polarities, he no longer needs explanatory phrases to shift his scene—in the feud between the women at Bergþórshváll and Hlíðarendi the audience comes to be shuttled back and forth between the two places with no apologies whatever.

In Breidafjord

> there was a man named Hǫskuldr, the son of Dala-Kollr. His mother was Þorgerðr and she was the

daughter of Þorsteinn the Red, the son of Óláfr the
White, the son of Ingjaldr, the son of Helgi. Ingjaldr's
mother was Þóra, the daughter of Sigurðr Snake-in-the-
Eye, the son of Ragnarr Hairy-Breeks. Uðr the Deep-
minded was the mother of Þorsteinn the Red, the daughter
of Ketill Flat-Nose, the son of Bjǫrn Buna. (p. 6)

Hǫskuldr has a half brother, Hrútr Herjólfsson. They share the
same mother and hence the same ancestry on that side. Their
genealogy, going through some of the most famous settlers of
Iceland back to the heroes of the early viking age, contrasts
with the modest lineage of Mǫrðr Fiddle. With no explicit comment the genealogies themselves put against one another the
man of law, who, it seems, has gained his eminence only in his
generation, with men who claim descent from renowned warriors
—in short, there is a preliminary setting against one another of
two codes, of two ways of looking upon life, the first through the
vision of law and the second through the vision of the warrior
and hero. At times these codes conflict, at times they complement one another, but they are distinct codes. The contrast is
repeated more forcefully in the juxtaposed introductions of
Gunnarr and Njáll (chapters nineteen and twenty).
     Nothing further is told about Hǫskuldr's character, but "Hrútr
was a handsome man, tall and strong, skilled in arms and gentle
in disposition, a very shrewd man, harsh with his foes, but a
good counsellor in important manners" (p. 6). This last detail
is important to keep in mind.
     One time when Hǫskuldr is feasting with his friends, he and
Hrútr are sitting together. Hǫskuldr has a daughter, Hallgerðr.
"She was playing about the floor with the other girls. She was
beautiful in appearance and tall, and her hair was fair as silk
and so long that it came down below her belt" (p. 6). Hǫskuldr
calls his daughter over to him and gives her a kiss. When she
has rejoined her playmates, he asks Hrútr what he thinks of her,
inquiring, " 'Don't you think she is beautiful?' " Hrútr is silent
and when prodded answers, " 'That girl is beautiful enough and
many will suffer for it; yet I do not know where thief's eyes have

come into-our family'" (p. 7). Hǫskuldr is angered and there is
coolness between the brothers for some time. The chapter ends
with the references to Hallgerðr's brothers that remind one of the
Laxdœla saga.

The power and economy of this scene cannot be appreciated
until the whole saga has been read. There are small touches
one wonders about—Unnr is said to be a handsome woman,
courteous and well-bred (*væn kona ok kurteis*, p. 5), with connotations of an aristocratic refinement carried by the adjective
kurteis. But the references to Hallgerðr refer only to her physical beauty. She is *fríð sýnum*, "fair of face," "beautiful in appearance." Is the silence about her manners meant to contrast
with the favorable details given about Unnr? The conjecture is
at least appropriate in the light of Hallgerðr's later behavior.

It is a peaceful and domestic scene with which the saga-man
has chosen to begin. Yet stretching ahead of the children's play
and the beauty of the young girl, obedient to her father, are terror and death. Who can hear of Hallgerðr's hair without immediately thinking of the great scene when Gunnarr, Hallgerðr's
last husband, fighting for his life, asks her for some strands of
hair so that he may refit his bow. "'Does anything depend upon
it?' she says. 'My life depends upon it,' he says, 'because they
will never be able to get at me as long as I can use my bow.'
'Then shall I now,' she says, 'remind you of the slap [you once
gave me], and I don't care if you fight on for a long time or not'"
(ch. 77, p. 189). It may seem startling to juxtapose these two
scenes, but that is, indeed, what is brought about by the apparently innocent reference to the girl's hair. And in making this
juxtaposition the audience tells itself, here, for the first time,
of the dread activity that lies below the surface of things in
Njáls saga. "And now all is quiet for a while," the saga-man
states from time to time, but enmity and hatred are only banked
for a time to break out anew when events provide the opportunity.
Such reflections occur on rereading the saga. When the saga is
read for the first time, it is Hrútr's remark about the thief's eyes

he sees in Hallgerðr that provides the ominous forewarning. Hallgerðr will indeed become a thief and Gunnarr will reprove her for it by that slap in the face. Finally, the scene as a whole seems to be an ironic reversal of a familiar *topos* in heroic and folk literature—the recognition of the young hero who proves himself by some distinctive feat before a gathering of elders or through some means gives a hint of his future prowess. Hallgerðr has, in a passive manner, given warning of what her potentialities are; they will lead, however, not to glory, but to shame. The two are dialectically connected in *Njáls saga*. The points of highest heroism and nobility—Gunnarr's last stand and the Burning—are also the points of the greatest shame and evildoing—Hallgerðr's betrayal of her husband and Flosi's burning to death of an old man and his wife and all their sons. It is ironic that Hallgerðr, a proud woman, fierce in her independence, who must stamp her personality on events, will live in men's thoughts chiefly as the agent whose malice made Gunnarr's last defense all the more memorable. She will be remembered not for what she did, but for what she did to Gunnarr. The saga-man carefully underlines this point. Rannveig, Gunnarr's mother, tells Hallgerðr when she refuses Gunnarr aid, " 'Evilly you are acting and your shame shall long be remembered' " (*ok mun þín skǫmm lengi uppi*, p. 189). Only a few lines later when all is over, the man who had led the attack tells Rannveig: " 'A mighty hero have we now laid even with the earth and difficult that was for us. His defense will endure in memory [*ok mun hans vǫrn uppi*] so long as the land is lived in' " (p. 191). The *skǫmm* of Hallgerðr, but the *vǫrn* of Gunnarr. The words are linked by their identical vowels and by their place in virtually identical phrases. If I have jumped a long way from chapter one, it is partly because it is best to let such associations come naturally, and partly to show that they do come naturally. The saga lends itself to associations with what has gone before or is to come and is enhanced when read with a willingness to make connections.

Chapter one has three parts: the introduction of Mǫrðr and Unnr, and of Hrútr and Hǫskuldr, and the scene with Hallgerðr. These three parts form, or at least hint at, the triptych of character types who give impetus to events in *Njáls saga*, the lawyer, the warrior, and the woman. The one has wisdom and craft, the second strength and magnanimity, the third beauty and malice. These three types will keep appearing throughout the saga.

In chapter two Hrútr becomes betrothed to Unnr and then sails to Norway with his uncle Qzurr to claim his inheritance, as has been seen. Chapter three presents a familiar *topos*, the reception of Icelanders at the Norwegian court. But here the mode of reception introduces a major theme of *Njáls saga*, that of men becoming subservient to and falling under the spell of powerful women whose wishes are not to be denied, no matter what trouble follows. This chapter gives us the witches' brew of female passion, whether sexual or vengeful, masculine yielding, and money, which in varying combinations is served up at critical moments in the saga. Here Hrútr, in order to regain his inheritance, has to apply to Gunnhildr, the queen-mother, who knows of his affairs and is eager to speed them in exchange for certain services. As soon as she hears that a ship has come in, she inquires about "what Icelandic men were aboard," and perhaps she comes down hard on the word *manna*.[29] When her steward tells her Hrútr and Qzurr are aboard, she sends him to offer them her hospitality for the winter. They receive this message in private and retire to think about the offer. Qzurr speaks what strikes me as a key line of the saga: " 'It seems to me, kinsman, that now we will have made up our minds' " (*Svá lízk mér, frændi, sem nú muni vit hafa gǫrt ráð okkat*, ch. 3, p. 12)—a delicately ironical phrase that means exactly the opposite—"it seems as if our decision has been made for us." If they refuse Gunnhildr's offer, he explains, she will drive them from the country and help herself to their property, but if they go to her, "she will confer upon us such honor (*sæmð*) as she has promised" (p. 13). Again there is an ironic flavor to this phrase—Gunnhildr has a notorious appetite for men and her *sæmð* is not such as is usually conveyed by the word. The men are in that classic northern dilemma—they have before them two choices, both of which are bad. Indeed, as Qzurr realizes, they have already made their choice. This is a major theme of the saga, for much of it is shaped by the yielding of men to the will of women, by their being forced to do so. At the climax of the saga, Flosi, who has been incited to blood revenge upon the Njálssons by his niece in such terms that he cannot evade or change his duty, also recognizes the dilemma when he perceives he cannot overcome the defending force at Bergþórshváll by conventional assault: " 'There are now two choices, and neither is good. The one is to turn back and that will be our death, and the other is to set fire to the house and to burn them within. And that is a great responsibility before God when we are Christian men ourselves. But nevertheless that is the course we will take' " (ch. 128, p. 328). But Flosi already had his choice made for him, long before he came to Bergþórshváll.

Hrútr and Qzurr are brought before Gunnhildr, who coaches Hrútr how to behave when he meets her son, King Haraldr Grey-Cloak. Hrútr makes a good impression and is turned over to Gunnhildr's care. Qgmundr, her steward, goes out with Hrútr and Qzurr and "led them to a stone-built hall. It was hung with the most beautiful tapestries and there was the high seat of Gunnhildr. Then Qgmundr said, 'Now that will prove true which I was telling you about Gunnhildr [that is, about her hospitality]; here is her high seat and you are to sit in it. And you may stay in this seat even when she herself is here' " (ch. 3, p. 14). A feast is served; Gunnhildr comes in and when Hrútr starts to rise she tells him to stay seated. "And in the evening she said, 'You shall lie beside me in the upper room tonight, we two together.' 'You shall decide such matters,' said he" (p. 15). Then they go upstairs and Gunnhildr "at once locked the room from within." Hrútr evidently passes muster, for "the next two weeks they slept together alone in the upper chamber." Gunnhildr cautions her attendants, " 'You will have nothing to lose except your lives, if you say anything about the affair between Hrútr and me' " (p. 15).

Now Queen Gunnhildr appears as a semilegendary figure in the
saga literature about whom dark tales are told,[30] and Hrútr is not
the only Icelander to be inveigled into that stone hall (an anachronism that spoiled some of the saga's plausibility for earlier
editors).   But there is something sinister about these scenes
which have both a ritualistic flavor to them and a slightly ludi-
crous touch, for Gunnhildr is considerably older than the man she
keeps. It is a saga version of the nursery rhyme about the spider
and the fly; the tune is amusing, but the conclusion unpleasant.
There is a reversal of proper order here that should ring an immediate alarm for a medieval audience and which is betokened by
Hrútr's occupation of the Queen's high seat.   The next time in
Njáls saga that a woman invites a man to take his place on such
a seat will be when Hildigunnr maneuvers Flosi into provoking
her terrible incitement.

Hrútr's involvement with Gunnhildr comes to its conclusion
when he has returned to the court, having won fame and honor
for his exploits.   He finds Gunnhildr has recovered his inheritance for him, and has had the man hanged who was trying to
keep it out of Hrútr's hands.   Hrútr gives her half of it, a reward
that was perhaps in Gunnhildr's mind from the beginning.   But
when spring comes, Hrútr grows silent, thinking of Iceland and
Unnr.   He admits to Gunnhildr that he wishes to return, but denies that he has a woman back in Iceland.   At his departure
Gunnhildr gives him a gold bracelet, a reminder perhaps of the
mixed motives of money and love that have brought them together,
and she gives him a curse.   With that woman in Iceland whom he
intends to have he may never have pleasure, although he may
work his will with other women: " 'And now neither of us have
prospered; you did not tell me the truth in the matter' " (ch. 6,
p. 21).   But Hrútr has had very little choice in this matter too—
had he admitted to Gunnhildr his betrothal to Unnr, he would
also have risked the Queen's anger. This is the start of the first
real trouble in *Njáls saga*.   Gunnhildr's curse will bring about
Hrútr's unhappy divorce from Unnr and her subsequent marriage
to the man who will father Mǫrðr Valgarðsson, a major mischief

maker. But Gunnhildr's curse hangs over *Njáls saga* less as a causal event than as a thematic darkening of the skies. Gunnhildr works her will on Hrútr—" 'if I have as much power over you as I suppose, then I lay this spell upon you' " (p. 21). With less magic but equal force Hallgerðr, Bergþóra, and Hildigunnr bend the men about them to their will and trouble is the only result. The theme first stated when Hrútr's will yields to Gunnhildr is not played out until many of the Burners lie dead upon the battlefield of Clontarf, a field and battle behind which move spellbinding women and a malevolent queen.

Hrútr's adventures abroad are the first of a series of parallel adventures which help give structure to the saga and link characters and theme. Hrútr is the first appearance of a type which is brought to perfection in Gunnarr and Kári, warriors who combine strength with magnanimity. Hrútr is the weakest of the three; he succumbs to Gunnhildr and later must give way before Gunnarr, but on his own ground in Iceland he is a worthy man. One of the themes of these adventures abroad is the testing of the hero. Njáll states it plainly when Gunnarr returns from his successful voyage: " 'You have been greatly tried, but nevertheless you will be tested more in the future because many will envy you' " (ch. 32, p. 84). The adventures themselves seem to belong to the larger theme of bride-wooing, as I have said. After each of them a marriage follows, Hrútr to Unnr, Gunnarr to Hallgerðr, Kári to Helga Njáll's-daughter, although in this last case, Kári, whom the Njálssons have met abroad, comes from the Hebrides to Iceland to settle. These three cases of faring out to prove oneself and coming back to marriage provide an example of the large type of traditional patterns which build the saga. [31]

Hrútr and Unnr are married, but there is a coolness between them the first winter they spend together. Obviously troubled, Unnr seeks out her father who consults with Hrútr and Hǫskuldr; the passage has been quoted in the previous chapter. The scene is not developed; in fact, the reader has to pause and imagine it to himself, an effort the sagas often demand of their audience. Two sides are there, men of good will who wish to reach an understanding, Hrútr and Hǫskuldr on one side and Mǫrðr on the other. The issue at stake, although no one mentions it, is Unnr's dowry—if matters should come to a divorce, Mǫrðr will be obliged to ask for its return, and trouble, which neither side wants, will follow. But the true cause that divides them, that underlies the difficulty, is not brought out into the open—it is the sexual incompatibility between Hrútr and Unnr. The girl is too embarrassed to speak up about it and she stands silent while the men of good will go about patching up the difficulty.

An abstraction of the scene gives us two sides of well-meaning men who reach a settlement that maintains the status quo, but which fails to take into account the woman on the edge of the scene to whom this settlement is unacceptable. The settlement suppresses the underlying cause of trouble only at the risk of a more violent return of this conflict at a later stage.[32] When the matter is thus generalized, it is possible to view this scene as the first illustration of a process that occurs over and over again in *Njáls saga*. Women for various reasons cause trouble. Men try to control it. An uneasy settlement is reached only to be undone by new trouble-making. The scene that gathers all these others to it is the scene in chapter 123 where Flosi and the Njálssons face each other over the pile of silver, which men of good will, desperately seeking a legal settlement to the quarrel, have heaped up. On top of the pile Njáll has placed a blue silk cloak, apparently meant as a clinching gift. The woman on the edge of that scene is Hildigunnr whose terrible incitement has committed Flosi to blood revenge. Just when the two sides seem on the verge of agreement, Flosi chooses to misinterpret the gift of the cloak, and the meeting is disrupted by an exchange of vicious sexual insults between Flosi and Skarpheðinn Njálsson, Flosi questioning Njáll's manliness and Skarpheðinn spelling out Flosi's intimacy with a notorious troll. The consequent breakdown of negotiations leads directly to the Burning, the best efforts of worthy men—it is clear that Flosi would prefer to settle—come to naught because they have ignored the woman behind the scenes whose lust for blood-revenge strangely mingles with the mortal imputations of sexual perversion.[33] It is again a long way from Unnr as she stands silent in the tent while the three men reach a short-lived settlement to the tense and crowded scene at the Althing 117 chapters further on in the saga. The one scene is quickly told, the other carefully and vividly realized. But the parallels are close enough for the two scenes to be associated.

The great moments in *Njáls saga* are vivid and dramatic scenes which incorporate and represent many of the saga's major themes. Because so much has happened prior to them and because they do exist in association with many other events, they thus bear a charge of meaning and seem symbolic of the entire action. The process is not unlike the one found in Greek drama, where major themes are presented to the eye in a culminating memorable event. When Oedipus puts out the sight of his own eyes, that, Whitman remarks, "is the active climax of a whole series of images dealing with the symbolic implications of sight and blindness." Other examples come to mind—the purple carpet Agamemnon treads, the net which traps him in the coils of death, Medea's fiery chariot. "Thus images become action; and the scene is an image dramatized."[34] Sagas use typical actions in place of images; the high moments of the sagas stamp the meaning of these actions upon one's mind. In a sense the great scenes may be considered images; as one pictures them they have a static vividness. The confrontation of the men across the pile of silver topped by the rich blue cloak is an especially memorable tableau.

After the settlement in chapter six, Unnr returns home. But the next spring she overcomes her modesty and privately tells her father just what the trouble is. She and Hrútr cannot consummate their marriage and when Morðr asks for details, the curious workings of Gunnhildr's curse are made plain. " 'Whenever he touches me, then he becomes so enlarged that he is not able to have pleasure with me, although we have both tried in every way to enjoy each other, but it is not possible. And yet before we draw apart, he shows that he is in nature as normal as other men' " (ch. 7, p. 24). Unnr's confession comes as somewhat of a surprise; readers probably will expect that Hrútr has been made impotent by the curse (Dasent, the Victorian translator of *Njáls saga*, modestly fudged the passage so as to force his readers to just that conclusion). But the punishment is appropriate, not only to Hrútr's name (which means "ram"), but to the theme of excess which runs through *Njáls saga*. People come to grief through greed, through hastiness, through revenge out of all proportion to the offense. Had Hrútr's difficulty been impotence, that fact would have served just as well to further the immediate plot. As it is, it advances the plot and becomes a component, a minor but a striking one, of an important theme.

Mǫrðr agrees to support Unnr in her divorce and the matter ends in his disgrace at the Althing when he is forced to leave Unnr's dowry unrecovered in the face of Hrútr's challenge to single combat. But this whole episode (chapters one through eight), which tells of the dealings between Mǫrðr and Hrútr, is brought to a close on quite a different note. Hrútr and Hǫskuldr ride home. On the way they shelter one rainy day at the home of Þjóstólfr, the son of Bjǫrn Gold-Bearer (not the Þjóstólfr who avenges Hallgerðr). They warm themselves before the fire:

> Þjóstólfr sat between Hǫskuldr and Hrútr. Two boys were playing about on the floor—they were in Þjóstólfr's care—and a girl was playing alongside them. They were very talkative because they were heedless. One of the boys said, "I shall be Mǫrðr and summon you to give up your wife and cite as my grounds the fact that you have not slept [*sorðit*][35] with her." The other boy replied, "I shall be Hrútr and refuse your claim for the dowry, if you don't dare to fight with me." They went on like this for some time, whereupon a great laughter burst out from the household. Then Hǫskuldr became angered and hit the boy who had called himself Mǫrðr with a stick. The stick struck him in the face and drew blood. Hǫskuldr said to the boy, "Get outside

and stop mocking us." Hrútr said, "Come over
here to me." The boy did so. Hrútr drew a gold ring
off his finger and gave it to the boy and said, "Go
away now and don't make fun of anyone again." The
boy went off saying, "Your noble-mindedness
[*drengskapr*] shall I remember ever after." For this
act Hrútr got high praise. Later they departed westward for home and now is finished the episode of
Hrútr and Mǫrðr. (ch. 8, pp. 28–29)

Note that the section closes as it opened with a scene of children at play. Many things come together and are foreshadowed
in this scene, which has analogues in *Gunnlaugs saga Ormstungu*
and in modern Danish folklore as Helga Reuschel has pointed
out. [36] It is a temptation to write at length on the one sentence,
"they were talkative because they were heedless" (*óvitrir*),
literally, not wise, stupid, lacking wit. Much Icelandic wisdom
is there. As is plain from many sagas and from the laws, an
open mouth can lead to big trouble. A good part of the machinery
of *Njáls saga* consists of gossip and rumors and secrets spread
from farm to farm by travelling parties—the children themselves
have heard of Hrútr's bedroom problems. Malicious chatter and
insulting verses bring about the deaths of men. It is clear from
other examples and from the scene itself that Hǫskuldr feels
himself and his brother gravely insulted and the blow he deals
the child is, under the circumstances, understandable. The deed
foreshadows the action of the next episode, where blows on the
face are atoned for by death. But the main significance of the
scene is in the way the insult to Hǫskuldr is finally settled.
There are two choices: by violence (the blow) and driving out
("Get outside," literally, "be outside," *verð úti*, a rejection)
and by atonement, even a self-sacrifice (the gift of the ring), and
acceptance ("come here to me"). These are the two ways of
settling disputes at all levels. The second way, as is heavily
underlined by the boy's praise for Hrútr ("Your noble-mindedness
shall I remember ever after"), is the better. And Hrútr is "a

good counsellor in important matters." His character reference in chapter one reinforces the validity of his words and deeds in chapter eight. The scene presents in miniature the two codes that mingle and conflict in *Njáls saga*: the heroic code which seeks to impose its way with inevitable violence, and a gentler code, one which becomes specifically Christian, which seeks to find peace through forgiving, through abstaining from violence. There are three counterparts in *Njáls saga* to this scene and they are highly important to the outcome and meaning of the saga.

In chapter ninety-four Njáll rides over to his son-in-law, Ketill of Mǫrk. Ketill has adopted Hǫskuldr, the son of Ketill's brother. Þráinn Sigfússon, whom Skarpheðinn Njálsson has killed for a number of good reasons:

> In the evening the boy came up to Njáll and Njáll spoke to him. Njáll had a gold ring on his finger and he showed it to the boy. Hǫskuldr took the ring and examined it and drew it upon his finger. Njáll said, "Will you accept the ring as a gift?" "I will," says the boy. "Do you know," says Njáll, "what brought death to your father?" The boy answers, "I know that Skarpheðinn killed him, but we need not bring that to mind which has been settled and fully atoned for." "That was better answered than it was asked," says Njáll, "and you will become a good man." (pp. 236-37)

Njáll then asks if Hǫskuldr will accept him as a foster-father and the boy agrees. This is a bold, even desperate gesture on Njáll's part, for he gambles that his new kinship with Hǫskuldr and Hǫskuldr's willing acceptance of it, which betokens a forgiving and absolving of Njáll from blame, will prevail over the deadly enmity growing between his sons and the Sigfússons. Njáll, who has foresight, knows this attempt is doomed, but it must be made, nevertheless. The motif of the older man giving a ring to the young boy is once more associated with themes of forgiving and acceptance.

Hǫskuldr grows up to be an almost saintly man. His murder, by his own foster brothers, is a crime that cannot be atoned for until Njáll and his sons are dead and the opposing sides have clashed in further bloodshed at the Althing. After that battle the situation once more seems incapable of settlement until Hallr of Síða offers to give up his claim for compensation for his son who was killed in the battle. This is a decision not easy to make. The whole saga has been filled with the actions of grieved men seeking compensation. To forego compensation implies a capacity to forgive, to make a virtue out of giving up that is rare in the Iceland depicted in *Njáls saga.*[37] It is a virtue, however, which has been strongly reinforced by the introduction of Christianity, a process to which *Njáls saga* devotes a number of chapters. Hallr has been an early supporter of the new religion and his action has been carefully prepared, as Ian R. Maxwell has shown,[38] so that we are ready for his statement:

> "All men know what grief I have suffered that Ljótr, my son, is dead. Many will think that he should be the most costly of those men who have died here. Yet to bring about a settlement I will offer to leave my son unatoned for and go nevertheless to offer both sworn pledges and peace to those who are my opponents. I ask you, Snorri the Priest, and others of the best men here that you so act that a settlement may be between us." Then he sat down and there was great and good applause at his speech and all praised highly his good will. (ch. 145, pp. 411–12)

Note how the saga-man each time shows what praise the forbearing man receives—communal praise in the case of Hrútr and Hallr of Síða, and Njáll's approbation of Hǫskuldr's tactful and generous reply.

The saga itself comes to an end on a prolonged note of forbearance. It is fitting that this work, where act builds upon act, where men and women will embroil themselves, will not let things lie, is brought to a conclusion by one man's decision not to act.

Flosi, who against his will gave grim assent to lead the Burners, imposes peace at the end, not through action, but through inaction in the face of the strongest provocation a man could endure —the repeated killing off of his followers, since Kári Sǫlmundarsson continues to take vengeance for the Burning. Flosi, it is true, is not legally bound to seek compensation for any of his men, and Kári, it is true, carefully avoids offending Flosi directly. Nevertheless, that is the kind of inflammable situation which has inevitably gotten out of hand in the earlier portions of the saga.

The two men confront each other in one of the most melodramatic scenes in the saga. Gunnarr Lambason, one of the Burners, is telling the story of the Burning to the court of Earl Sigurðr of the Orkneys who is hosting King Sigtryggr from Ireland. Flosi and others among his followers are there. Kári, who has followed in their path, catches up with them. Pausing outside the door he hears Gunnarr's boasting and shameful version of the story. It is too much for Kári. He leaps into the hall with his drawn sword, rips off an eight-line stanza, and then runs down the hall, "and struck at the head of Gunnarr Lambason. He swapped off his head so quickly that it flew up onto the table before the king and the earls" (ch. 155, p. 443). Earl Sigurðr orders Kári, his former retainer, seized and put to death, but no one obeys the order. Flosi pleads that Kári was only doing what he had to do. Kári is let go without pursuit. Earl Sigurðr has the tables scrubbed down and the body carried out, declaring, " 'When it comes to action, there's no man like Kári' " (p. 444). The point is that Flosi, even when Kári is within his power, has no wish to act and even intercedes for him.

At the very end, the two men, who have separately gone to Rome to seek absolution for their sins, come into a full reconciliation. Kári, who has received word of the death of his wife, Helga Njáll's-daughter, returns to Iceland and is shipwrecked in a furious snowstorm near Flosi's farm at Svínafell. "His men asked Kári what they should do, and he said it was his plan to go to Svínafell and put Flosi's hospitality [*þegnskapr*] to the test.

They went to Svínafell through the snowstorm. Flosi was in his
sitting room. He recognized Kári at once and sprang up to meet
him and kissed him and sat Kári in the high seat beside him"
(ch. 159, pp. 462–63). It is the final consuming act of acceptance and the strongest demonstration of the true nature of
þegnskapr, a word which has various connotations of the honor,
generosity, and allegiance of a loyal man. We look at Flosi's
warm hearth and welcome within and the raging snowstorm without and we remember Hǫskuldr's furious blow and exclamation,
verð úti, "get outside" (and into the rain), and Hrútr's gentle
gakk hingat til mín, "come here to me," and generous gift. The
whole curve of Njáls saga has been present in this little scene,
although we do not realize it until we return to it.

It would be possible to continue with this sort of analysis.
But a consideration of even these first eight chapters, which
form a convenient unit, is enough to show that most of the major
themes, in fact the overall pattern of the saga, are discernible
within them. Indeed, in discussing them in order, I have been
led, without at first fully realizing it, into discussing the major
events of the saga, more or less in order, from Gunnarr's defense
to the reconciliation of Flosi and Kári. The beginning foreshadows the end. Njáls saga begins way back from the central
events, and it is an unusual beginning, one that does not deal
with the direct ancestors of the saga's central figures but presents us with an action seemingly on the periphery of things,
with deeds of people who are "out of the saga" once they have
played their role. There is little direct causal linkage between
these early events and the death of Gunnarr and the Burning of
Njáll in the sense that these events absolutely determine Gunnarr's death and Njáll's burning. They do, nevertheless, lead to
them, in a pattern of choice, the range and freedom of which
diminishes the closer one gets to the central events. The reader
is justified in searching for a linkage, if only because he learns
"by experience that saga economy allows nothing superfluous."[39]
Andersson, whose remark that is, goes on to say that we must
make logical connections between a given episode and the climax

of a saga. But if the events in *Njáls saga* are to be held in
rigid connection with the climax, some will seem superfluous.
Events may be held up to the overall structure of the saga, or
they may be seen as thematically relevant to the main action.[40]
This is certainly the case in the first eight chapters of *Njáls
saga*. Events there "cause" the later action in the sense that
the forces of good and evil, of forbearance and wrath, of good
will and malice, first appear incorporated there in character types
who play conflicting roles throughout the saga. This congruence
between the early events and the action of the saga as a whole
has been sensed and recognized before. But I have tried to subject some of these beginning scenes to a closer reading than has
hitherto been attempted. For some this may appear as an over-
reading. Helga Reuschel, for example, finds that the scene between Hrútr, Hǫskuldr, and the children is "without constructive
value for the development of the story. All its charm and its
meaning for the saga lie in its liveliness and its realistic touch."[41]
The plot of *Njáls saga*, it is true, could go on its way unharmed
by the omission of the scene. But the meaning of the saga would
not; it would be less clear that the saga-man strongly intends his
audience to associate forgiveness with nobility of temperament,
with *drengskapr*. Much of the greatness of *Njáls saga* lies in the
balance of its parts and the richness of association that is built
up between them. This richness is attained because the composer of the saga has chosen, from all the narrative material at
his hand, those parts which consistently fit his pervasive and
controlling ethical vision.

4

The Rhetoric
of *Njáls saga*

The very last sentences of *Njáls saga* are: "These were the children of Kári and Helga Njáll's-daughter, Þorgerðr and Ragneiðr, Valgerðr, and Þórðr, who died at the Burning. And the children of Hildigunnr and Kári were Starkaðr and Þórðr and Flosi. The son of Flosi was Kolbeinn, who was one of the most renowned men in that family. And there I end the saga of the Burning of Njáll" (ch. 159, pp. 463–64). Here, as life moves on, in certain names of the children themselves are reminders of the past from which they spring, here is a final allusion to the most terrible event of that past (*Þórðr, er inni brann*), and then the saga-man steps forward to state through whose hands the story has passed.[1] He names his matter, the Burning of Njáll. The narrator here is the closest he ever comes to any direct appearance; more importantly, by naming his matter he directs attention to the central fact of this long narrative, so rich in episodes and spread out in time. The story is, as he says, about the Burning of Njáll. It is my purpose here to look at this narrator and his ways, to consider certain value-shaping techniques he employs in the saga to guide the opinion of his audience so that it may fully appreciate what manner of men and deeds led to the Burning, what significance lies in the events surrounding it, and by what means hearers of the tale may know, to put it simply, what is good and what is bad, what behavior men may praise, what acts they must condemn.   These techniques may be called the rhetoric of *Njáls saga*.   They include devices available to a reliable narrator; they include as well the ability to control point of view and the ability to shape the structure of the narrative so that one set of episodes may reflect and comment upon another.   A survey of these techniques will urge that the celebrated objectivity of saga narration is no obstacle to either the expression or the formation of moral and ethical judgements. The saga-man who tells his story need not take a neutral stand toward the events he narrates and he can provide his audience with sufficient means to interpret those events.

The sagas represented themselves to their audience as histories of the notable deeds of past generations.   The blood feud is the foundation for nearly all these narratives and, as such, forms an intrinsically dramatic structure.   Insult and injury lead to feuding and the killing of an important character.   This killing is avenged.   Eventually the surviving representatives of the opposing parties reach a reconciliation.   Recently Theodore M. Andersson has analyzed twenty-four of the major family sagas in terms of a six-part structure, the middle portions of which consist of the elements just described.[2]   An introductory section begins the saga; this introduction may present the opposing parties or tell of deeds in the generations prior to the main events.   An aftermath concludes the saga; it disposes of the later careers of important characters.   One may take issue with Andersson's analyses of individual sagas, but the pattern he has perceived does appear again and again, not only in the family sagas but in the episodes of *Sturlunga saga* and the terse anecdotes of the *Landnámabók*.

It is tempting to suggest that this pattern reflects a perception by the Icelanders themselves of those forces of law and custom which potentially at least could charge their daily acts with social and political significance.   This was a society where certain insults demanded compensation, where an offending party might pay for grave insults with death, where his kinsmen in turn were obliged to avenge that death or seek atonement for it. A body of law existed which recognized these obligations, codified them, and voluminously strove to keep order by sub-stituting fines of property and silver in place of deeds of ven-geance perpetuated by aggrieved persons. Given these condi-tions, it follows that the basic pattern of the histories reporting such events is determined to a large extent by the very structure of law and custom (see ch. 1, n. 55).

The family sagas, nevertheless, are distinguished from the barely realized incidents of the *Landnámabók* and from the welter of such patterns of conflict and settlement in *Sturlunga*, although that too has its great moments of finely wrought narrative. The composer of a family saga could elaborate the basic pattern by various means which enhance its worth as entertainment and enable an audience to judge events. The ways by which this pattern is elaborated constitute the rhetoric of the saga. By this definition, rhetoric will be closely bound to consideration of the form of the saga, for the rhetorical techniques become ap-parent when a saga in its entirety is set against the pattern of the blood feud which is its framework.

When the family sagas are set against other historical writings that relate the deeds of Icelanders, it is possible to distinguish four forces that have wrought them into their distinctive shape. In each of these four the control of a narrator makes itself felt. They may be termed: *reduction and elimination*, *expansion*, *commentary and guidance*, and *architectonics*. By the first of these, reduction and elimination, I mean that characters and facts not necessary to the narrative are not included. Material that may be available in traditional record appears only insofar as it contributes to the dramatic effect or to the logic of the narrative or to the illustration of a character. The sense that the saga-man exercises control over his material at every point can be a strong one. The comparison of the family sagas with the contemporary narratives in the *Sturlunga* compilation reveals how relatively unoppressed the former are with the mass of names, intricate kinships, and small detail, which, although they make *Sturlunga* a most valuable historical record, nevertheless obscure the main thrust of the story of the broils among the principle chieftains and bishops of Iceland.[3]　The process of reduction, of trimming from the tale what is not directly relevant, is also felt in the characteristic dismissal of persons when their role is done, when they are "out of the saga."　Similarly the allusions to other sagas at once call to mind the range and action of those complete narratives while at the same time re- minding the audience that this present story is keeping to its own track.

The second technique is one of expansion.　Suitable points of the narrative are developed into fully realized scenes.　A tendency to expand and polish inherently dramatic scenes is one natural to all historical writing.　But a look at the European histories suggested as inspirations for saga-writing[4] and at *Sturlunga*, which obviously preserves a number of authentic exchanges of speech, shows how much further the shapers of the family sagas went in exploiting the possibilities of their matter, fashioning vivid scenes that at once hold the attention of the audience and embody the thematic concerns of the saga.

Under the general term of expansion might also fall the tech- niques and conventions which slow down the action, set forth in detail the movements of opposing parties, and prolong suspense before climactic events.　Theodore M. Andersson has described these techniques and suggested a terminology for them, under the heading of "The Rhetoric of The Saga."　Andersson discusses other features as well which altogether comprise "some of the more prominent dramatic moments and techniques in the saga. They are designed to make the story tense and telling, to catch the reader's interest while the plot is being unraveled."[5] Andersson however discusses saga rhetoric chiefly as the means by which the emotions of the audience are raised and manip- ulated—how the story is made tense.　How it is made telling— how its values are articulated and made clear—is a matter that has not been dealt with.　This task is achieved principally through the means I have called commentary and guidance, and architectonics.   Architectonics refers to the positioning and structuring of the large episodes and divisions of the saga. Commentary and guidance refer to the pervasive assistance the audience receives about the values and judgments to be placed upon events as they occur one after the other.   I shall shortly suggest how these terms are applicable to *Njáls saga*.   But in order to do so some discussion of the "objectivity" of the sagas is obligatory.

It is a frequent statement that saga narrative is objective. The narrator himself seldom intrudes to make didactic commentary on events.   He reports only those facts, deeds, and speeches essential to the forward motion of the story.   The saga-man, moreover, restricts his viewpoint.   He is not an omniscient narrator.   Scenes are presented as they might be viewed by an alert observer close to the participants.   What these participants say and do may be heard and seen, but what they think and what moves them to act is left for the audience to decide.[6]   In this sense the art of the saga is objective, although it should immediately be evident that a subjective, authorial control is operative in what the saga-man chooses to show us objectively. Nevertheless, this use of a limited external point of view and the style itself, dense in fact and generally bare of ornament, which conveys the narrator's vision, have impeded critics wishing to approach the sagas.   It has been felt that the lack of overt general conclusions by the saga composers render their works uninterpretable in any large moral sense; that the sagas indeed come close to an ideal of "pure narrative" that is not concerned with the conveyance of ulterior didactic statements.[7] But it is doubtful whether any such thing as pure narrative exists.   Any fiction implies some relationship with an audience;[8] once two facts are set in some kind of order that fact itself requires evaluation.   Any plot needs a value system so that events do not seem to happen without cause, or, if they do, that in itself provokes comment.   Even in modern objective literature where all authorial intrusion is suppressed the very lack of overt commentary is in its own way a judgment on the world and in its own way depends upon a set of values in the reader. Presumably the saga-man could rely on a certain consensus of ethical and moral opinion in his audience so that events could simply be presented without his direct commentary. Nevertheless, even within the conventions to which the saga-men adhered there are ways to establish and articulate the value system of the story.

It is instructive to reflect that the audience must accept as true whatever the saga-man reports. That he is thus a reliable narrator is so obvious a fact that few have dwelt upon it, but the other conventions of saga-telling and their most effective deployment depend upon the saga-man's precise apprehension of his role and viewpoint. The values, moreover, of a teller of tales, even where traditional narrative is concerned, are revealed in the very choice of what he tells and the form in which he tells it.[9] It is thus of interest that the man who set down the longest of the family sagas and one of the most popular chose to arrange his story about four major events: Gunnarr's last stand, the introduction of Christianity to Iceland, the Burning of Njáll, and the great lawsuit that follows. The very juxtaposition of events seems significant. First a man who represents the very best of the old heroic virtues is hemmed in and brought to death; then the conversion, affecting an entire nation, opens to view the full range of Christian good and evil; the wise and good-willed Njáll is destroyed along with his family; and, finally, the law of the nation proves incapable of dealing with and containing the consequences of that event.[10] Whatever judgments this broad structure of the saga suggests are partly determined by these particular events that the saga-man has chosen for filling up the traditional saga matter of the blood feud.

Standing closer to *Njáls saga* one can see that the saga-man establishes his values both through his own commentary and through his control of point of view. Excluding for the moment the subject of character introductions and character relationships, I will first touch upon some of the other features of this commentary. Throughout the story the saga-man tells facts which may indeed be objectively true but which nevertheless either suggest what should be thought of a thing or limit the range of thought upon a matter. At one point before the Burning it appears that the quarrel between Flosi and the Njálssons will be submitted to arbitration. "It might so be said," remarks the saga-man, "that all the assembly was delighted at this" (ch. 122, p. 310). The saga-man has objectively reported that the men at the Althing are delighted at the decision to arbitrate. But since among the men who are so delighted are the principal chieftains of Iceland and since the Althing was an assembly of men of authority and of farmstead holders with their followers and thus reasonably representative, it seems safe to say that the saga-man is stating that arbitration is preferable to vengeance in blood, that settlement in the assembly is preferable to taking the law into one's own hands even though law and custom allowed, or at times even required, that this be done.

Under the guise of reporting popular opinion the saga-man may also indicate what is to be thought of such a matter. "The slaying of Gunnarr was spoken ill of throughout all the districts and he was greatly mourned by many men" (ch. 77, p. 191). This technique hardly needs commentary. An admirable use of it is found when the saga-man, doing nothing but his duty, reports a rumor about Hallgerðr in her later career. "Some said Hrappr and Hallgerðr were good friends and that he was sleeping with her, but others spoke against this" (ch. 88, p. 220). Whether or not the rumor is true, that it can even be considered shows how far Hallgerðr has fallen since the proud days of her first encounter with Gunnarr. It is a long way down from Gunnarr of Hlíðarendi to Killer Hrappr, an engaging but utter rascal, who has committed manslaughter unatoned for, reneged on his fare for his subsequent hasty flight to Norway, fathered a bastard on the daughter of the Norwegian chief who sheltered him, axed to death the steward who interrupted his illicit love-making, and plundered and then put to the torch a holy temple of Earl Hákon, the Norwegian king. When rumor reports, truthfully or not, that Hallgerðr has taken up with such a man as Hrappr, that report indicates and limits the range of what may be thought about Hallgerðr *now*.

At least once the saga-man is able to turn even a reported lack of information to advantage. In chapter thirty-four the seating arrangements of the main guests at Gunnarr's wedding are told with some care:

> Gunnarr sat in the middle of the bench and in from him [away from the entrance] were Þráinn Sigfússon, then Úlfr Aur-Priest, then Valgarðr the Grey, then Mqrðr and Runólfr, then the [other] Sigfússons; Lambi sat the furthest in. Next to Gunnarr on the outward side sat Njáll, then Skarpheðinn, then Helgi, then Grímr, then Hǫskuldr [Njálsson], then Hafr the Wise, then Ingjaldr of Keldur, then the sons of Þórir from Holt in the East. Þórir wished to sit the furthest out of the guests of honor because then each man would think his seat a good one. Hǫskuldr [the bride's father] sat on the middle of the bench [opposite Gunnarr] and his sons inward from him; Hrútr sat outwards from Hǫskuldr. (pp. 88–89)

And after telling this, the saga-man intrudes to comment, "But it is not said how the others were seated" (p. 89). Now there are a number of such disclaimers scattered about in the sagas, and some of them probably are genuine admissions that no knowledge or tradition was available about the matter. After surveying all such remarks Theodore Andersson concludes that "there is only one which is completely trivial, the passage [in *Njáls saga*] which disclaims further knowledge of the seating arrangement at Gunnarr's wedding."[11] But this very disclaimer of further information causes the reader to look again at the information that is given. And when he does he sees that it presents in tableau the sides whose strife will fill the second half of the saga, the Njálssons and their kinsmen, the Sigfússons and theirs. Valgarðr the Grey is at the feast who later with his son Mqrðr will scheme to bring death upon the Njálssons; Mqrðr indeed will join in the attack against Gunnarr himself. Men are present here who themselves or whose sons will ride to the Burning of Njáll. There is a pervasive dramatic irony at Gunnarr's wedding, for the audience knows as the characters cannot what will be the outcome of the divisions so neatly suggested by the seating arrangements.[12] By the little phrase, "but it is not said how the others were seated," the saga-man makes use of a conventional phrase to call attention to what he has chosen and not chosen to tell. And what he has chosen to tell turns out to be more significant that it appeared at first glance.

In addition there are various small touches, embellishments of actions, that contribute to the making of a value system. Otkell Skarfsson, a rather foolish and vain man, who is allowing himself to get drawn into a conflict with Gunnarr, is "not sharp-sighted" (ch. 49, p. 128). Not wishing to travel the Icelandic paths because of his poor eyes, he sends Skammkell, a trouble-making friend, to carry out an errand that Otkell himself should have performed. Skammkell lies about the outcome of his mission and the result is Otkell's eventual death at Gunnarr's hands. His shortsightedness has served to advance the immediate plot but it is also a small detail symbolic of Otkell's lack of wisdom. Gunnarr forces this first quarrel with Otkell to a settlement in which Otkell and his party are forced to back down. But new trouble follows. One day, when Otkell is riding past Gunnarr's farm, his horse bolts away from him and "Otkell now goes faster than he would wish" (ch. 53, p. 134). Gunnarr is out sowing in the field as Otkell, in a close repetition of the earlier phrase, "rides now faster than he would wish. ... And just as Gunnarr stands up, Otkell rides over him and his spur rakes against Gunnarr's ear and cuts a great gash which at once bled heavily" (p. 134). The spectacle of a near-sighted, short-tempered man on a runaway horse bearing down on the best man in Iceland stands for the uncontrollable will towards disorder against which the constructive forces of *Njáls saga* strive for so long a time.

Later one Sigurðr Hog-Head offers to spy on Gunnarr's movements and the death wound he receives from Gunnarr's arrow shot

is a swift judgment on what is fitting compensation for spies:
"Sigurðr threw up his shield when he saw the arrow flying high
and the arrow came through the shield and into his eye so that it
came out through the back of his neck and that was the first
killing" (ch. 63, p. 157).   One of Þráinn Sigfússon's troubles
has been a loose tongue, but Skarpheðinn Njálsson cures that
for him: "Þráinn was about to put his helmet on. Skarpheðinn
comes bearing down on him and hews at Þráinn with his axe.
The blow came upon his head and cleft it down to the back
teeth, which fell out upon the ice" (ch. 92, p. 233). Þráinn need
no longer worry that his impulsive words and swaggering manners
will lead him into difficult situations.[13] There are more examples
of this method of underscoring the values of the saga that could
be given.

But by far the most important ways through which values are
established and opinions controlled are through character relationships and point of view. Clearly if one set of characters is
introduced who have many of the qualities most admired by
Icelandic society and another set introduced who have qualities
generally admitted as undesirable, and if these two sets are put
in conflict with one another, this conflict will have moral and
ethical implications even though the events which comprise it
may be reported with admirable objectivity. This is the situation that prevails in the first half of *Njáls saga*. Another problem arises when two parties, both of whom possess admirable
qualities, come into conflict, and this is the situation that prevails in the second half of *Njáls saga*.

Because the saga-man is a reliable narrator, because there are
no grounds to doubt the information he gives about his characters, he can therefore effectively and economically endow the
plot with value through what he tells us of his characters. In
the forthright introductions of Gunnarr of Hlíðarendi and of Mǫrðr
Valgarðsson, one of the fundamental conflicts of *Njáls saga* is
established.   Gunnarr's is one of the most fully revealed por-
traits in the saga and he is the first whose features are fully
described:

Gunnarr was a large and powerful man and very well
skilled in arms. He swung a sword or shot with a bow
from either hand, if he wished, and he fought so
swiftly with his sword that three swords seemed to be
in the air at once. He was a very good archer and he
hit everything he aimed at. He leapt more than his
own height with all his armor on and as far backwards
as forwards. He could swim like a seal and there
was no game in which any might contend against him.
It has been said that no man was his equal.

He was a handsome man in appearance, fair-skinned,
with a straight nose which turned up at the tip, blue-
eyed and keen of sight, with red cheeks. He had
abundant yellow hair that hung well. He was the most
courteous of men, resolute, generous and even-
tempered, a fast friend, but careful in his choice of
friends. He was prosperous. (ch. 19, pp. 52–53)

This is a picture of a man who could be admired anywhere at any
time. By this description alone *Njáls saga* is lifted out of a
realm of specifically Icelandic social virtues. Mǫrðr, on the
other hand, is described in terms of qualities only—the saga
never says what he looks like—and these qualities are attributes
of evil:

Unnr and Valgarðr had a son who was called Mǫrðr,
and he is in this saga for a long time. When he was
fully grown, he behaved badly towards his kinsmen
and worst of all towards Gunnarr; he was a deceitful
man in his behavior and malicious in his counsels.
(ch. 25, p. 70)

This is repeated in chapter forty-six:

At that time Mǫrðr Valgarðsson lived at Hof in the
Rangriver plains. He was cunning and malicious....
He greatly envied Gunnarr of Hlíðarendi. He was
prosperous. (p. 119)

Prosperity is the only quality Mǫrðr shares with Gunnarr, perhaps as an indication that an active will, an ability to make things happen, is present in both.   Later events reveal that Mǫrðr, apart from his abiding ill will, is greedy, cowardly, and uxorious.[14]   Mǫrðr is an embodiment of an evil-seeking agency, evil whether considered in terms of Loki and pagan malice or of the devil and Christian envy (and the fire that destroys Bergþórshváll may be associated with them both). When such an agent as Mǫrðr acts against such a man as Gunnarr and when Mǫrðr brings the wise and gentle Njáll to his death by conspiring against his sons, the reader of the saga not only should but must view this conflict in ethical terms.

Thus the forthright statements of character, which the saga-man uses according to his position as a reliable narrator, can themselves establish the central and conflicting values of the saga.   Even what the saga-man sometimes does not tell us about his characters may indicate what is to be thought of them. In the following example silence itself, in place of an expected commentary, becomes functional: "Gunnarr and Hallgerðr had two sons. One was called Hǫgni and the other Grani. Hǫgni was capable and taciturn, slow to be persuaded and truthful in his words" (ch. 59, p. 150). When nothing is said of Grani, the reader may suspect that he lacks the virtues of his brother. This suspicion is confirmed later on, again in a most economical way, since Grani is described in terms of a person whose attributes by now are known all too well: "Hǫgni and Grani, Gunnarr's sons, were fullgrown. They were men unlike in disposition. Grani had much of his mother's temper, but Hǫgni was a good person" (ch. 75, p. 182). Both these strokes, which are not without humor, reveal a full understanding of the effects possible within the conventions of saga narrative.

Once a person's character is established, it can be exploited in other ways to indicate the implications of a situation and to suggest a judgment of it. The telling of who likes whom provides effective touches throughout the saga. In chapter thirty-

six a servant of Hallgerðr named Kolr (coal), "a great rascal,"[15]
at her behest kills a servant of Njáll and Bergþóra named Svartr
(black)—the names tell one what to think of their doings.
Bergþóra in turn hires a henchman named Atli who passes by one
day on a black horse. Njáll makes a wry comment on Atli's
promise as a workman, but, as the saga-man relates, "Skarpheðinn
treated Atli well" (p. 96). It is already clear that Skarpheðinn
is the most formidable and warlike of Njáll's sons and the little
comment here tells that at least one of Njáll's household besides
his wife is not loathe to join the game that Hallgerðr has begun.
Similarly in chapter ninety-one the saga-man comments that
Þráinn is well disposed towards Hrappr (p. 225) and the remark
immediately shifts some of Hrappr's unwholesome qualities onto
Þráinn.

Finally, the establishing of character allows for the presence
of reliable spokesmen whose pronouncements on events and
persons indicate what ought to be thought of them. On virtually
every important occasion in *Njáls saga* someone reliable is on
hand to point out just what the significance is of what has
happened. A minor example of this technique, which at times is
almost obtrusive, occurs in chapter eighty-nine when the blund-
dering Earl Hákon works himself into a rage over his failure to
find Hrappr's hiding place aboard Þráinn Sigfússon's ship. The
earl proposes to take out his anger on the Njálssons instead,
who are in the harbor; he wants to row after them and kill them
(pp. 220–21). His son Sveinn counsels restraint: " 'That is not
a good plan,' says Sveinn, 'to turn the charge on an innocent
party and to let that man escape who is guilty' " (p. 221). " 'I
shall rule in this matter,' " says the earl, who does not want to
listen to platitudes at this moment. And in the second half of
Njáls saga a series of trustworthy and important persons counsel
that Mǫrðr Valgarðsson has been noticed to cause more harm
than good.[16] These culminate in a scene where Kári, citing
Mǫrðr's father-in-law, Gizurr the White, as his authority, tells
Mǫrðr to his face: " 'You are behaving in this matter just as

Gizurr expected because everything about you partakes of badness since you are both frightened and faint of heart' " (ch. 135, p. 356). There is never any doubt over what is to be thought of Mǫrðr.

In chapter seventy-five Gunnarr decides to turn away from the path of exile that has been decreed for him. The momentousness of this decision and the degree to which it will estrange Gunnarr from the customs and fellowship of his countrymen are strongly emphasized when Kolskeggr, his brother, pleads with him in a speech that appeals to all that Gunnarr has held to in the past. It is death for Gunnarr to turn back; Njáll has predicted that, as he has predicted long life and prosperity for Gunnarr should he abide by the terms of his exile.

> "Do not give your foes cause to rejoice," says Kolskeggr, "that you are breaking your word because no man would think that of you. And you may keep in mind that everything will come to pass just as Njáll has said." "I will never leave," says Gunnarr, "and I would wish that you do the same." "That I shall not," says Kolskeggr, "I shall never act basely [*níðask*, a strong word] in this or any other thing that is entrusted to me, and so this will be the one thing alone that will divide us. Tell this to my kinsmen and to my mother, that I do not expect to see Iceland again because I will hear of your death, brother, and then nothing will bring me back upon the homeward way." (pp. 182–83)

It seems almost improper to subject this beautiful speech to analysis. It is the moment when the normal laws and customs of men urged so movingly by Kolskeggr no longer are sufficient to contain and define the realm towards which Gunnarr is now moving, a realm where the breaking of an agreement imposed on Gunnarr by the cumulative envy of lesser men than he is no base deed but rather an act of tragic nobility, freely willed and yet

necessary if Gunnarr of Hlíðarendi is to fulfill all that is potential in his being. But this act separates him from other men.
Gunnarr's brother, who has stood by him in everything else, must
part from him here and reproach him, and because it is Gunnarr's
brother the reproach is all the more forceful and sorrowful. The
strength of the bond that has been between them is shown in its
breaking. They ride apart to their separate ends, Gunnarr to his
lonely death in his house on the slope of the hill, Kolskeggr,
remaining in the world of men, to Constantinople, the great city
near the center of the world.

All these devices, the brief direct intrusions of the saga-man,
the dutiful reporting of public opinion, the small symbolic embellishments of the action, the establishments of relationships
between characters, and the pronouncements of reliable spokesmen, are, in the conventions of saga-telling, facts which may not
be doubted and hence they are devices of reliable narration
which may be used throughout the saga to control and guide
opinion and judgment. Their characteristic use in the sagas
results from the point of view of the narrator, who may closely
approach but who does not obtrude upon the scene. Thus there
is one major device left to describe before going on to consider
the formal structure which contains all these devices and which
in turn is illuminated by them. Control of the audience's
sympathy through control of point of view in a genre that professed to be objective and historical is one of the great achievements of the saga-men. In limiting their knowledge, in effacing
themselves and taking a stand, as it were, behind their characters
so that the audience beholds events as if it were itself trans-
ported to the scene, the saga-men thereby exploited the tendency
of any audience to identify and sympathize with the persons from
whose viewpoint the narrative unfolds.[17] The most celebrated
and obviously deliberate manipulations of point of view are not
found in *Njáls saga*.[18] For this reason the masterful handling of
point of view that is exercised in this saga may not be fully
recognized. There is space here only to indicate some of the

difficulties faced by the composer of *Njáls saga* and some of the ways in which he resolves them.

In the second half of *Njáls saga* and especially in that portion of it which gets under way after the conversion of Iceland, the narrator must solve the problem of distributing and controlling the audience's sympathies. His task is to strike a balance between the two parties, that of Njáll and his sons, who are burned, and that of Flosi, who burns them. To burn one's foes within their house was recognized as a desperate deed, a deed of last resort. This judgment is underlined within the saga itself. At Gunnarr's last stand, Mǫrðr Valgarðsson urges the use of fire:

> Mǫrðr said, "Let us burn him within." "That shall never be," says Gizurr, "even though I knew my life depended on it. It is easy for you to devise a plan which may work, such a cunning man as you are said to be. ... " Then Mǫrðr again said that they should burn Gunnarr within. Gizurr answers, "I do not know why you will keep saying what none of the rest wish, and that shall never happen." (ch. 77, p. 188)

One recalls that at the Burning Skarpheðinn, before he submits to his father's wish that they shelter inside the house, finds time to praise the noble qualities of Gunnarr's foes, saying that they, unlike Flosi's men, would never resort to burning (ch. 128, p. 326). Flosi himself recognizes the desperate nature of the act (ch. 128, p. 328). The problem for the saga-man then is to prevent the story of the Burning from becoming a melodrama (as the story of a burning becomes in the *Hœnsa-Þóris saga*), a story of good men who meet an evil death. The full tragic effect of this, the saga's central event, would be lost if Flosi were simply a malevolent (*illgjarn*) man like Mǫrðr. Flosi must be represented as an admirable man who is driven by circumstances beyond his control into taking a vengeance he rather would have avoided. At the same time it must be shown that the Njálssons (who are the foes Flosi seeks) have committed a deed that makes such a vengeance obligatory. And in this case that deed is the slaying of Hǫskuldr Hvitaness-Priest, their own foster-brother and the husband of Flosi's niece, Hildigunnr. The saga-man then must make it clear that the Njálssons have committed an irrevocable and evil deed and yet keep the sympathy of the audience with them; to show the Burning as the appalling and inevitable deed it is, and yet to establish the Burner as a man who is admirable in Icelandic terms. "Flosi was a very cordial man and most hospitable to visit, and it is so said that in most respects he had been endowed with the qualities of a true chieftain" (ch. 146, p. 419). It is a statement of high praise but nevertheless a qualified one, one of the few direct hints from the narrator that in his opinion a man who was a chieftain in all respects would not have resorted to burning within. In fact the great achievement of this narrator is to have composed a work whose comment is not on the men who slew their foster-brother nor on the men who avenged that slaying with fire but on the society in which such things could come to pass.

That Hǫskuldr's slaying is an evil deed is made quite clear, perhaps most effectively in the telling of the deed itself:

> Hǫskuldr Hvitaness-Priest woke at sunrise; he got into his clothes and threw over himself the cloak Flosi had given him; he took a seed basket and in the other hand a sword and goes out to the field and sows grain.
>
> Skarpheðinn and the others [his brothers, Kári, and Mǫrðr] had agreed that they should all inflict a wound on him. Skarpheðinn springs up from behind the fence, but when Hǫskuldr saw him, he wished to move away. Then Skarpheðinn leapt towards him and said, "Don't worry about running away, Hvitaness-Priest," and hews at him. The blow struck his head and Hǫskuldr fell to his knees. He spoke these words, "May God help me and forgive you!" Then they all

> ran at him and dealt him wounds.   (ch. 111, pp. 280–81)

This deed is thoroughly condemned.   Njáll realizes that it is terrible news; that it means death to him and his family:

> "Sorrowful tidings," says Njáll, "such bad news to know that it is truthful to say that so grieved am I that I would think it better to have lost two of my sons if only Hǫskuldr were alive. ...."   This was the only thing that touched Njáll so deeply that he could never speak of it without weeping.   (ch. 111, p. 281)

"The killing of Hǫskuldr became known throughout the land and was condemned," reports the saga-man (ch. 112, p. 283).   Flosi calls it an evil sowing and predicts an evil harvest (ch. 115, p. 288).   Skarpheðinn himself acknowledges to Guðmundr the Powerful that he understandably is blamed for such a deed (ch. 119, p. 302).   Even an unsavory character like Þorkell Braggart brands Hǫskuldr's death among the worst deeds that have been done; when Skarpheðinn in turns accuses Þorkell of an even worse crime he claims that Þorkell has raised his hand against his own father (ch. 120, p. 304).   The evil of the deed stands forth in Skarpheðinn's appearance which becomes twisted, baleful, and troll-like.   All the chieftains before whom Ásgrímr and the Njálssons go in supplication remark upon it.   (In passing one should note the care by which the onus of Hǫskuldr's death is mainly shifted to Skarpheðinn; Kári's share in the slaying is played down, probably because Kári's later role at the end will demand an intact reputation.)

But this very supplication scene, a famous one in saga literature, demonstrates how sympathy with Skarpheðinn and his party is maintained.   It is maintained chiefly because this supplication is told from their point of view.   The reader follows them around, shares their hopes that they will receive offers of help, feels the shock and fears the withering of those hopes when Skarpheðinn lashes out at the chieftains with his slanderous retorts. In other words, because the story is predominantly told from the point of view of the Njálssons' party, the reader identifies with the cause of that party. The good will, respect, and sympathy that have been established for Njáll and his sons by the end of the first half of the saga cushion and absorb the reproaches that must be made for Hǫskuldr's slaying. Furthermore this slaying is partially excused because through it the Njálssons have themselves become the victims of a long-range intrigue of Mǫrðr Valgarðsson.[19]

But if the supplication scene retains sympathy for the Njálssons because the narrator takes his stance beside them, then, above all, because the Burning is depicted at length from the point of view of those who are burned within, pity for Njáll and his sons and the binding of emotions to their side are permanently secured. Even the baleful spirit that has descended upon Skarpheðinn is refined and purged in the flames. He dies, loyal and fierce, and the reader follows him to that end:

> Then Skarpheðinn went to Grímr, his brother. They joined hands and trod upon the flames. But when they came to the middle of the hall, then Grímr fell down dead.   Skarpheðinn went to the end of the house. Then there was a great noise. All the roof fell in. Skarpheðinn was in between the fallen timbers and the gable-end; he could not move from there at all. (ch. 130, p. 333)

What comes to pass then must be judged from what the burial party finds in the ashes:

> There they found the body of Skarpheðinn. He had stood up against the gable-end. His legs were severely burned right up to his knees, but the rest of him was untouched. He had bitten down on his under-lip. His eyes were open and unswollen. He had driven his axe into the gable-beam with such force that half the blade had sunk in and the blade had not lost its

> temper. ... Then Skarpheðinn's clothes were removed
> because they were not burned. He had laid his hands
> in the shape of a cross with the right hand above.
> They found two marks on him, one between the backs
> of his shoulders and the other on his chest. The two
> of them were burned in the shape of a cross, and they
> guessed that he must have burned them there himself.
> All the men said that Skarpheðinn looked better in
> death than they had expected because no one was
> afraid of him.[20] (ch. 132, pp. 343-44)

After passages such as that—and they are but a small part of
the Burning, the tale of which is at once unflinching and full of
genuine pity—it becomes necessary that the staggering fears
and hatred which the Burning will arouse do not devolve on
Flosi himself.

Flosi at this point is in need of some rehabilitation. He has
from the first been represented as a capable man. His initial
introduction is quite short for a person of such importance.
Aside from the usual genealogical credentials, it speaks of his
strength and capacity for action: "Flosi lived at Svínafell and
was a great chieftain. He was tall and strong, a very vehement
man" (ch. 95, p. 238). This is in ethical terms a virtually
neutral description. Flosi's full character and capacity for good
and evil emerge only gradually. In a masterful way he is represented as behaving well in ugly situations whose ugliness nevertheless cannot help but reflect on him. Egged on to blood
revenge by his widowed niece in the most horrific fashion—
before his own men she scathingly insults him and flings about
him the blood-laden cloak of the slain Hǫskuldr—he then
passionately rebukes her:

> Flosi hurled the cloak back into her face and said,
> "Monster that you are, you wish that we should take
> up what will turn out the worst for all of us. 'Cold
> are the counsels of women.' " (ch. 116, pp. 291-92)

But from that moment on he is committed to taking that course. The blood from Hǫskuldr's cloak remains on Flosi's shoulders.

Shortly thereafter (ch. 117, p. 294) he gives an impassioned speech, cautioning and warning such vengeful and bloodthirsty men as Grani Gunnarsson and Gunnarr Lambason just what they are getting into when they undertake the prosecution of the Njálssons. Nevertheless he leads a party, in which there are many such men as Grani and Gunnarr, to the Burning. He conducts himself with resourcefulness and dignity at the court actions following the Burning, but his lawyer, although agile, is a vain and unpleasant man who has had to be bribed into conducting Flosi's defense. Ketill of Mǫrk, an honorable man, praises Flosi for his determination and wisdom (ch. 124, p. 316),[21] but Flosi is not above indulging in demeaning abuse of Njáll (ch. 123, p. 314) and goes out of his way after the Burning to provoke Ásgrímr, the father-in-law of Helgi Njálsson whom Flosi has killed with his own hands (ch. 136, pp. 360–61). Indeed Flosi is rebuked for this last action by his own father-in-law, Hallr of Síða (ch. 136, pp. 361–62). But on the whole it must be said that Flosi succeeds in obtaining respect, a respect reinforced by his generally decent conduct after the Burning. A certain self-disgust is perceptible in his retort to Módólfr Ketilsson who has made up a boasting verse about the Burning: " 'We will vaunt ourselves on other things,' says Flosi, 'rather than on this, that Njáll has burned within, because there is no fame in that' " (ch. 130, p. 336). And to one Geirmundr he concedes with a touch perhaps of weariness: " 'Men will call this both a mighty deed and an evil one. But now it can't be helped' " (ch. 130, p. 334). Flosi has carried out the Burning, but he has not been corrupted by it: "Flosi never boasted of his deed, nor did any man notice fear in him" (ch. 131, p. 342). Both Flosi's qualities of leadership and the respect in which the Eastern chieftains hold him are brought out during his trip up the coast in the dead of winter to seek help in the case that will be raised against him (ch. 134). And his generosity and eagerness to bring the long dragged-out feud to an end are revealed in his frequent praise of Kári, his refusal to act against Kári's vengeance on his followers, and his final warm embracing of Kári at the end of the saga.

It may seem obvious enough that Hǫskuldr's slaying is a bad deed and the burning of those slayers a worse one; that the sympathy of the audience is with Njáll and his sons because enough events and important enough events are depicted with the dominant (but not predominant) part of the showing devoted to Njáll and his party.   The well-proportioned and considered use of this last technique has been only briefly indicated here. The point is, however, that these facts are obvious, that the readers of *Njáls saga* are enabled to make the various judgments about them that they do.   Even the choices of what is shown and the placing of these choices along the total curve of the saga is part of the rhetoric of the saga.   The apparent self-effacement of the narrator in no way prevents the telling of a story whose values may be consistently, if complexly, related to a heroic and Christian vision.   These relationships begin to emerge clearly as one steps away from the individual episodes of *Njáls saga* and endeavors to behold the form of it as a whole.

One observation easily made is that *Njáls saga* divides into two halves.   It is less easy, however, to state without reservation just where this division falls.   The second half of *Njáls saga* is generally considered to begin after Gunnarr's death when the narrative picks up the tale of the Njálssons' journey abroad.   But a second important division occurs at chapters 100 to 105, which tell of the conversion of Iceland.   The intervening material looks both backwards and forwards.   The story of the Njálssons's entanglement and feud with Þráinn Sigfússon takes up a quarrel that has been prepared for in an earlier episode. The story of Njáll's adoption of Hǫskuldr Þráinsson and of Njáll's achievement in establishing a Fifth Court[22] looks forward to and provides for the happenings after the conversion, when events are set in motion that lead directly and inexorably to the

Burning. There is thus a certain overlap between the two halves of the saga. In turn, this overlap is a reminder that critics, although they find it easy enough to agree on the divisions between episodes. have greater difficulty in agreeing about the relationship between episodes. That is not to deny that the disposition of the parts within the whole is important, only to say that not all agree where the lines dividing the parts should be drawn. That each reader may make a somewhat different construction of the larger units of the saga testifies not so much to the vagaries of critics as to the overall unity of the saga and the wealth of relationships between its episodes.[23]

The way in which the history of the conversion is introduced strikes many readers as an awkwardly handled interruption of the main story. This is a judgment that will vary according to individual taste. Ian R. Maxwell has shown (and his demonstration is persuasive) how the saga-man has linked this episode with the main narrative and how he has altered and fitted his historical material to the purposes of the saga (for example, in the careful preparation of Hallr of Síða whose charitable behavior will be so decisive to the peacemaking after the battle of the Althing).[24] It seems to me too that this section is by no means extraneous to the whole of *Njáls saga*. The conversion of Iceland is properly emphasized and properly strikes one as a major pause because it marks a decided extension of the saga's range of values. With the establishment of Christianity the old values of pagan Iceland (as represented in the saga) are set within a frame of new values. They are not necessarily superseded or contradicted. What was noble in the old code had much in common with what is noble in the new, but the consequences of noble or ignoble actions become weightier. Fame becomes fame in heaven and hell as well as in heroic legend. Gunnarr lives on as a hero after death—indeed he is seen in his burial mound striking his harp exultantly and singing defiant songs[25]—but this scene represents the continuation of his fame in Iceland. It is not an uplifting of Gunnarr himself into realms beyond the

knowledge of men. The possibility of such realms is first
descried when the missionary Þangbrandr tells Hallr of Síða
what wonders follow in the train of the angel Michael: " 'Many,'
says Þangbrandr. 'He shall weigh everything you do, both good
and evil, and he is so merciful that he deems greater all that
which is done well' " [26] (ch. 100, p. 257).

Mercy can redress the old balance in which bad deeds were as
telling and in fact as memorable as noble deeds—one again
recalls Ranveig's rebuke to Hallgerðr, "Evilly you are acting
and your shame shall long be remembered." Gunnarr's heroism
is in part defined by Hallgerðr's treachery, even dependent on
it in that the full extent of his heroic qualities could not be
realized unless Hallgerðr had chosen to betray her husband
when he was fighting for his life. What that fame celebrates
which accrues to such heroic exertion is the extraordinary
prowess that reveals in the hero a close to superhuman, a
numinous energy. But the heroic acts themselves may be harm-
ful or constructive only within a tribal context. It is the fury
itself of some heroes which demands commemoration. In the
larger view their deeds are at once awesome and difficult to
judge; they are meant to be beheld, not moralized upon. One
sure thing about Achilles's wrath is that it leaves food for
vultures on the plains of Troy. The Icelandic poet of the
Atlakviða leaves Guðrún and her victims in the burning hall
and holds back comment at the end beyond the bare statement:

> Enough has been said of this.
> No woman in byrnie ever since so acted
> To avenge her brothers;
> The bright Guðrún brought death
> To three princes before she died.

The Burning of Njáll has some of the fascination which such
deeds of elemental and thorough destruction have. Even in a
work like *Beowulf*, which more nearly embodies an elemental
opposition of forces, where the hero takes upon himself the

defense of men against the threat of monstrous foes, even there
the good that resides in the hero must largely be measured by
the strength of the evil he opposes.   And to a considerable
degree this remark applies to men like Gunnarr and Grettir as
well.   They fight their fights against malice and ill-luck and
treachery, and the renown and glory of those fights provide men
with hope of fame and the will to endure and prevail.   And yet,
although they may prevail for a time, they nevertheless do fall,
and the world is left to lesser men who must look back to the
strength of men in former days.   But the message Þangbrandr
brings tells of a future world and throws open to the Icelanders
a way out of the dilemma faced by the old society where good
deeds must be weighed in terms of the base deeds they opposed.
Christianity offers a resolution of this dialectic.   Out of the
heart of the fire and grief of this world Njáll speaks these
words: " 'Act well and do not speak despairing words because
this one storm shall be, but it shall be long until such another.
And trust in this, that God is merciful and he will not let us
burn both in this world and in the next' " (ch. 129, pp. 328–29).

When Njáll's body is recovered from the ashes it is uncor-
rupted and untouched; his skin shines with a holy brightness.
This detail is surely not—even in the neutral sense—an
"excrescence"[27] on the matter of the story; it is a deliberate
contrasting of the different meanings, the changed possibilities,
surrounding death from Gunnarr's day to Njáll's.   Denton Fox
remarks:

> One feels that the world has changed since Gunnarr's
> death, so that it is now conceivable that a man could
> live a long and honorable life.   The change is not a
> large one, for the duty of blood revenge is still
> paramount, the law is still ineffectual, and Christianity
> is intermittent and superficial, but there is nonethe-
> less a distant glimpse of a rational and merciful order
> underlying the world.[28]

Perhaps then it is not entirely coincidental, at least it is fitting, that the two halves of *Njáls saga*, dealing as they do with different frameworks of values, differ markedly in their structure. The first half of the saga can be neatly marked off into separate episodes. As I have remarked, the gathering of these episodes into larger divisions is a subject upon which opinions differ. For example, all will agree that *Njáls saga* has a leisurely introduction. For Einar Ól. Sveinsson this introduction consists of the first eighteen chapters and includes the quite clearly marked episodes of Hrútr and Mǫrðr Fiddle and of Hallgerðr's early marriages. Thus *Njáls saga* proper would begin with the introduction of Gunnarr, one of its principle figures, and that is a sensible proposition.[29] Theodore M. Andersson extends the introduction all the way to chapter forty-six through the long feud between Hallgerðr at Hlíðarendi and Bergþóra at Bergþórshváll on the grounds that nothing comes of this feud and that Gunnarr's ultimately fatal involvements with his neighbors begin with the first feud between Gunnarr and Otkell.[30] And I would take the middle ground along with Ian R. Maxwell and maintain that the introductory portion of *Njáls saga* covers the first thirty-four chapters.[31] Gunnarr's marriage is the high point of a series of episodes dealing with adventure abroad and marriage at home and it is the end of a section in which nothing truly drastic has yet happened that will put events on the path towards Gunnarr's death and Njáll's Burning. There have been forebodings enough, a curse, one disappointed romance (Gunnarr's at the Norwegian court), three marriages—two of which have ended in death and the other in divorce—so that even without Njáll's gloomy predictions one might suspect that Gunnarr's marriage to Hallgerðr will end badly. But it is only at this marriage that the outlines of the conflicting parties are first seen clearly and only after it that the chain of killings begins.

But however one defines the introduction to *Njáls saga*, the episodes within it are easily distinguished. This episodic structure is maintained through Gunnarr's portion of the saga and up to the conversion. Gunnarr becomes involved, provoked really, against his wishes into a succession of feuds, each one of which in turn leads to graver and more nearly irrevocable actions and each one of which embroils more and more Icelanders on either side. Gunnarr's very magnanimity, restraint, prowess, and honorable reputation attract men of opposite qualities who *will* try Gunnarr to the limit. His very victories generate more foes. At length he loses control over his situation; his sense of honor obliges him to place himself at the advantage of his enemies and he is ultimately killed by, be it noted, honorable foes, Gizurr and Geirr, who themselves have had their hand forced by little men to lead an attack on the man who embodies all that is most admirable in his society.[32] The impossibility that Gunnarr might have found a way out is shown in his statement to Kolskeggr: " 'I would like to know,' says Gunnarr, 'whether I am a less manly man than other men since killing seems to me a weightier matter than it does to other men' " (ch. 54, pp. 138–39). When Gunnarr has to think of manliness in terms of a readiness to kill, there is little chance that he can avoid the feuds that bring him down. Gunnarr's death, Fox states, is an indictment of such a society "whose only non-materialistic value is a narrow concept of honor (largely something as simple as the imperative: 'a man must revenge injuries')."[33] That statement may be too sweeping, but certainly Gunnarr's death indicates that something is wrong; that there is a destructive undertow sweeping at the foundations of the finest achievements of this society, an undertow which, in the Icelandic idiom, will drag a man to death (*at draga til dauða*).[34] The episodic structure of the first half of *Njáls saga* suits this conclusion. At the beginning each feud is unconnected with those that have gone before, but ties soon establish themselves, one by one the avenues are closed to Gunnarr and he is hemmed around with foes.

The second half of the saga, at least that main part of it which takes place after the conversion, is gathered into a much tighter structure.   Although strands of the plot are clearly marked, as the narrator shifts from one side to the other, there are no new episodes such as are arranged around Gunnarr.   From the time Mǫrðr Valgarðsson and his father scheme to raise mortal hatred between the Njálssons and their foster-brother, the plot unfolds along a path that leads directly to the Burning and its inevitable reprisals.   Gunnarr had almost to the end a choice before him, the choice clearly foreseen by Njáll.   He could leave Iceland, serve his exile, and return to a prosperous and lengthy life; or else he could stay and die (ch. 74, p. 181)—the choice is not unlike the one offered to Achilles.   But once Hǫskuldr has been slain the vengeance that must be taken is unavoidable and Flosi is obligated to it, however much he would like to settle.   After a certain point is reached in the affairs of men a not-to-be-overcome drive towards destruction begins.[35]   A tragic undertow pulls at the fates of these Icelanders and the very measures that Njáll and other men of good intentions take to avoid, or at least to postpone, the final conflict only make the ultimate breakdown of order all the more severe when it comes.   One set of events which incorporates this process is the intensely cultivated love and friendship between the Njálssons and Hǫskuldr Hvitaness-Priest.   The bond is all too consciously and willfully imposed over a deep, if hidden, hostility.[36]   Mǫrðr's success in turning the Njálssons against Hǫskuldr depends in part on their unstated reluctance to believe that Hǫskuldr can in truth forgive their slaying of his father, Þráinn.   When the relationship fails, it fails completely and disastrously.   Skarpheðinn then has on his hands, as Gunnarr came to have on his, the slaying twice in the same family, of father and son.

Comparison of the two halves supports the observation that the Burning of Njáll is indeed the great climax about which the entire saga is arranged and towards which events, even the distant events of the beginning of the saga, have somehow moved.   I make this statement because it is still all too easy to think of this saga in the old terms of a *Gunnars saga* and a

Njáls saga which have been merely hooked on to each other. The events leading up to Gunnarr's death are, of course, brilliantly realized and Gunnarr's last stand is one of the high points of the saga. But the Burning is a still greater event, and the matters surrounding it, both the gathering of powers that precedes it and the suits and vengeance that follow, are presented at far greater lengths than are the similar processes around Gunnarr's death. In the light of Andersson's descriptions of the narrative techniques that are manifest around the climax of a saga, such as thickening of detail, more extended and fully realized scenes, a slowing down of the time scale,[37] it is evident that the weight of the saga's concern rests in its second half. The time scale is slowed greatly in this portion of the saga. The events of the first 107 chapters from the scene of the young Hallgerðr playing near her father's side to Mqrðr's decision to work for the destruction of the Njálssons cover roughly fifty-eight years (c. 950–1008); events in the remaining chapters (a little more than 40 percent of the saga) cover seven years.[38] The amount of time covered shrinks to a point, to a single intense moment, while the amount of space devoted to presenting events greatly increases. The technique produces an effect of prolonged impending disaster. Although a similar treatment of the time scale is certainly noted in the narration of Gunnarr's last acts, its much more emphatic use as the night of the Burning draws near strongly affects the last half of the saga. Yet when these two halves are considered as one unity what becomes really important is not only that the Burning is, as Fox says, "the crest of the second and higher wave of the saga,"[39] but that there *are* two waves, that the full implications of what kind of deed the Burning is are made explicit only because it is preceded by Gunnarr's brave and lonely death. Without Gunnarr's death the Burning might seem melodramatic; it might seem, if not senseless, perhaps unacceptable. But a society in which the force of circumstances is such that it could destroy a man like Gunnarr of Hlíðarendi is a society in which such a force is capable of going on to destroy the farm and family at Bergþórshváll, to consume the wise and gentle Njáll. Looked at in another way, *Njáls saga* might be seen as an attempt to explain, to make comprehensible, the horror and ineluctability of this central disaster, as an attempt to cope with these facts, the Burning of Njáll, the death of Gunnarr, which—as tradition states and other evidence supports—did actually happen.[40]   The form crystallizes upon the event. But the event itself then acquires significance through the shape of the form. Perhaps this longest of sagas has to start so far back from its climactic event because only in that way can the disaster of the Burning be comprehended and made tolerable.

The line along which the plot of *Njáls saga* moves need not then be viewed as a horizontal one distinctly divided in two halves by the death of Gunnarr. It may better be looked at as a spiral—the events leading to Gunnarr's death take the reader in an ascending curve and reach a certain pitch; then very much the same process is repeated on a still wider curve and higher repetition of the curve.[41]   Whatever the image one wishes to use, it should illustrate that the two halves of the saga comment on one another and that the function of a particular episode may not be fully apparent until one steps back to view it in its whole setting. Two episodes that must be seen from such a stance are the feud between Hallgerðr and Bergþóra, where step by step the working off of a grudge between the two women leads to the death of eight men, and the adventures of Kári with Bjǫrn of Mǫrk. Andersson has said of the first episode that the

> rivalry between Hallgerðr and Bergþóra has ultimately
> no function in the plot, but is simply a bit of un-
> attached prefatory matter. The fact that it is so
> elaborately worked out actually misleads the reader
> into seeking some function for it which it does not
> possess. It does not even contribute anything es-
> sential to the characterization of the two women;

> Hallgerðr is fully delineated elsewhere and Bergþóra's
> character does not play an important part in the saga.[42]

It is true that this episode does not contribute to the succession
of events leading to Gunnarr's death. But the main point of the
episode is exactly that nothing comes of it. It shows how Njáll
and Gunnarr, who bring together strength, wisdom, restraint, and
good will are barely able to overcome and force to a halt the
serious trouble stirred up by haughty, and in Hallgerðr's case,
deliberately mischievous women. When this union of qualities
is lacking, when Gunnarr has to cope with little men who succumb
to the behests of Hallgerðr and who are not willing to settle
differences with generosity and restraint, he is embarked on the
course that will lead him to his death. This episode is important
to the large theme, that of the efficacy and limitations of good
will, which is of such importance in this saga. And something
does happen at the end of this episode that is crucial to the
story, for Þráinn Sigfússon is implicated in the death of Þórðr,
the Njálsson's foster-father. The Njálsson-Sigfússon feud is
the central feud of the saga,[43] and this is where it begins.

At the far end of the saga the episode of Kári and Bjǫrn of
Mǫrk balances this escalating feud between Hallgerðr and
Bergþóra. That first quarrel accustoms the audience to the
process of killings that lead step by step into ever deeper and
bloodier waters; the last also presents a series of killings, but
here both the results and the manner in which they are accom-
plished are in contrast to the former feud. Each vengeance that
Kári takes diminishes the burden of retribution he has shouldered
upon himself. A whole set of typical themes and actions that
were developed to sinister effect in the former episode are in
this latter altered in tone and made to contribute to the sense of
lightening and relief that enters the saga towards the end. Kári
enlists the help of Bjǫrn, the free grandson of a thrall who once
belonged to Njáll's mother.[44] Bjǫrn is the coward without
malice, the boaster without viciousness, and as soon as these

terms are applied to him they must be qualified, for Bjǫrn does stick by Kári and he does help him. Even in the midst of killing, Kári's fights take on a certain slapstick tone as Bjǫrn assists from behind the shelter of Kári's back. Verbal abuse, which has led to dire events earlier, now becomes comic as Bjǫrn bravely threatens and rails at the men whom Kári has put to flight. Even Bjǫrn's spying errands and reports of rumors now work to bring the saga nearer to its peaceful close whereas in prior episodes rumor had worked to stir up new conflicts. Kári himself refuses to start any more interfamily feuds and is careful to spare Ketill of Mǫrk, a Sigfússon who, although married to Njáll's daughter, has been honorably obliged to join Flosi's party.

At the end of their adventures Kári restores Bjǫrn to his shrewish wife (she has had some cause for her complaints) and sees to it that he brings her back a changed man for a husband:

> Then Bjǫrn spoke to Kári, "Now in front of my wife you must be my true friend indeed because she will not believe anything I say, and now, for me, everything depends on this.[45] Repay me for the good backing I have given you."
>
> "So I shall," says Kári. Then they rode home to the farm. Bjǫrn's wife asked for the news and received them hospitably. Bjǫrn answered, "Troubles have rather increased, woman." She said little in return and smiled. Then she said, "How did Bjǫrn turn out for you, Kári?" Kári answers, "'Bare is each man's back unless he has a brother.' Bjǫrn turned out very well. He coped with three men and he is, moreover, wounded himself. He was most useful to me in every way he could be." (ch. 152, p. 436)

"She said little in return and smiled." In terms of the whole saga this is unusual and encouraging behavior. The hard-tempered woman is mollified; the henchman is rewarded with new prosperity instead of death; enmity and desire for vengeance are quenched rather than inflamed. There is now light on the road ahead. The two episodes, the first the earnest feud near the beginning between the two haughty women, the second the increasingly comic pursuit of vengeance near the end, are pathmarks along a story that moves first into a growing darkness, one that will be at its deepest lit up by the glare of Njáll's Burning. Then, gradually, the story moves away from this darkness and out again towards an exhaustion of enmity and a restoration of peace. Viewed within the form traced by this movement the two episodes have become endowed with a significance and function which by themselves they would not possess. This movement raises questions about the genre of the saga form itself and the abiding significance of the events which that form contains. It is to these questions that I shall now turn.

5

Form and Theme

It is possible to derive underlying themes of *Njáls saga* from the form of the saga itself as it appears in perspective, a perspective distant enough to comprehend certain other works. The main curve of the saga suggests comparisons with other works and suggests as well the patterns of the human spirit which inform these works. As the themes emerge they are seen to comprise a polarity of forces, at times hostile, at times complementary to one another. Clusters of symbols (events, figures, sayings) align themselves in the direction of one pole or another. Belonging to these clusters are the so-called inserts (the chapters about the conversion, the Battle of Clontarf) and a supposed fault (the excessively long passages of law). Without them the fundamental themes of the saga would fail to be delineated clearly.

At the farthest distance from *Njáls saga* the events that remain impressed upon the memory are Gunnarr's last stand and the Burning. Each presents the image of men defending what they have inherited, and made, and held together, their families and their farmsteads, against foes determined to bring them down. Standing a little closer, one can perceive the outlines of the two great law processes that flank the Burning, the one where Flosi spurns the settlement offered him, the other where the suits of

the Burners and of Njáll's supporters break down into general
conflict. Gunnarr's last stand is also preceded by law processes and followed by violence, but on a lesser scale. In
terms of the excitement which the saga generates it is natural
to speak of events leading up to Gunnarr's death and Njáll's
Burning,[1] but in terms of the whole structure of this saga it is
useful to think of events as leading down through stages of
violence and disorder and attempted settlements to the baleful
vision of the flames and ashes at Bergþórshváll. The Burning
must have been a truly spectacular event, visible for miles
around the flat and sandy plain where Bergþórshváll stands. As
a vision it was all too real, and it stamped itself on the minds of
the Icelanders as a most memorable event in a stirring age. As
the central vision of the saga it seems a symbol for the failure
of law and for a destruction of order which men have not been
able to prevent.

Such symbols are the center of other heroic works. The destruction of Troy by fire and plunder is apparently the nucleus
of fact about which a whole epic cycle accrued. In a later
heroic age the Germanic peoples had no cities of their own to
burn, but their principal legends preserve memories of kingly
halls destroyed by fire. The *Beowulf*-poet, even as he tells of
the building of Heorot, broods over its coming destruction in
flames. From his allusions it appears that Heorot burned because well-meaning plans, intended as in *Njáls saga* to lay old
feuds to rest, only worked to awaken them to greater fury. The
old poem, the *Bjarkamál*, and the late *Hrólfs saga Kraka* call up
the heroic defense of Hrólfr's warriors within his burning castle
at Leire, where Heorot had stood.[2] The various strands of the
story of the Volsungs, as it was remembered to the north and
south in Germanic lands, have as main events the overwhelming
of men in their halls, often by fire: "Guðrún Gjúki's daughter
avenged her brothers, as has been told. First she killed the
sons of Atli and then she put Atli to death and burned the hall
and all the retainers. About that is said this poem." These

words introduce the *Atlakviða* and the sons whom Guðrún kills are of course her own sons too. The figure of the vengeful woman who will be satisfied by nothing less than complete and, indeed, insensate revenge appears in these tales. They find a final expression in the *Nibelungenlied*.[3] There the drive towards the utter destruction of men cannot be controlled. It rages unchecked—mighty kings and heroes are helpless to prevent or stay it—until the "she-devil" (*vâlandinne*),[4] Kriemhild (the counterpart of Guðrún above), sees her brothers and the Burgundians annihilated along with the best part of Etzel's and Dietrich's men as well. This version of the story above all others expresses the fear (but the dreadful longing too) that has fascinated the Germanic peoples—the fear and yet the desire to behold the catastrophic end of all things. The *Vǫluspá* is the poem that gives mythic expression to this concern with the fate of the world which man inhabits. It tells and foretells the course of the world, of its creation from primeval chaos, of its dissolution into flames and darkness in the great battle between the gods and their foes from hell, of the mysterious rebirth of the world into a green land waiting to be peopled. The potency of these images has remained undiminished to the present day— their recent notorious association with the doom of the Third Reich was all too real.[5]

It has been remarked that the heroic legends of the Germanic peoples celebrate defeats and never victories.[6] Even in historical times the two most famous Norwegian kings, Óláfr Tryggvason and St. Óláfr Haraldsson, were appreciated as much for having met their ends in properly spectacular debacles as for any of their other achievements. But a defeat worthy of celebration also implies a resistance heroic and sustained enough to live on as an example to later men. If in *Njáls saga* Gunnarr's death and the Burning of Njáll represent notable victories for forces of disorder, as the slaughter of tens of thousands at the end of the *Nibelungenlied* certainly does, nevertheless the poem and the saga (and other poems and sagas remembering the defeats of men) are victories of another sort. Out of destruction they create; they begin to make the memories of disaster understandable and endurable even in the act of preserving them. Those wrought with the greatest art (and *Njáls saga* belongs in that company) are triumphs of narrative organization, enduring achievements of the human will.

Gunnarr's defeat in defense of his house—it is actually pulled apart about him—and the reduction of Bergsþórshváll to ashes are the central images of that saga which, more than any other, deals with the efforts of men to rule themselves by law and their own good will.[7] That these events did happen shows that the efforts failed. But in the structure of the saga as a whole they by no means stand for a complete failure—indeed, the recuperative powers of men are defined in this saga by their ability, finally, to cope with these events. The men of Iceland, as represented in *Njáls saga*, go a long way into the darkness. The Burning itself threatens to lead to outspreading and uncontainable conflicts. But these are purged in the great battle at the Althing and there is hope they will not accumulate and fester anew. The settlements that are finally reached remain unbroken because men, willing good in God's name, follow Hallr of Síða's example and intercede to temper the old code. From this point on the course of the saga emerges, gradually, from a world of strife to the final peace of Kári's reconciliation with Flosi, a peace made firm by his marriage to Hildigunnr, the very women who incited Flosi to the Burning. At a very great distance, the curve of the saga resembles that of the mythic poem, *Voluspá*, where the world of gods and men falls apart into the blaze and extinction of *ragnarǫk* only to reemerge into a new light.[8] The curve of *Njáls saga* is shallower. Neither Gunnarr's death nor the Burning destroys the society pictured in the saga, although both shake it. The order that appears at the end is not the emergence of a newly born society but a restoration of the old society, scarcely transformed by but at least now open to the new light and revelation of Christianity.

I have meant to suggest by my phrasing and examples that into *Njáls saga* are displaced the patterns associated with myths of creation and the night journey.[9] It is true that many distinctive motifs of these patterns, even as they may occur in displaced form, do not appear. These patterns stand far back from the realistic and semihistorical genre of the saga and this original statement will be modified in the course of discussion. But it is here where such a discussion must begin. These patterns are associated with (and in myth they signify) the establishment, growth, and maturation of the human consciousness, with the concomitant development of individual will and capacity for creative ordering.[10] In heroic myth where the emerging awareness and will senses itself threatened by a return to or upheaval of those regions whence it came, the interplay between forces is portrayed as a struggle. It is a struggle between dark, bloody, engulfing forces from a chaotic realm, forces represented as belonging to a female chthonic side of nature, against powers with a masculine signature, often incorporated into a single hero, a figure of light, with will and strength to dare overcome and rule his opponent. The presence of this struggle (the delineation and explication of which is important to the development of the human spirit), although it is displaced into a realistic narrative, is one reason for the power which a work like *Njáls saga* can exert even through translation. The pattern of such a fundamental narrative structure appeals to and awakens counterparts in the psyche (archetypes) that are themselves charged with feeling. Since a single event or symbol belonging to an archetype may awaken the entire pattern, or contain it, brief moments, even phrases, in narrative may become the focal points of all the intensity and significance of that narrative.

But the sagas are a long way from the myths briefly touched upon above, a long way with respect both to their mode of presentation and to the state of man's consciousness that they reflect. Creation myths, with their theme of the dividing of heaven and earth from a primordial female chaos (or monster), and the night journey, with its descent into darkness of the hero who fights the dragon and emerges with greater wisdom, are myths that represent man and mankind at a youthful and adolescent stage of awareness and capacity for self-rule. In these stages men, and the heroes who represent them, are not only assaulted but are often overwhelmed and defeated by the forces that threaten what they have built up. Beowulf rids Heorot of the fear of Grendel; with God's light to show him the way he overcomes Grendel's dangerous mother, but he cannot avail against the dragon and the dragon's fire in his final fight. His death is the end of his people. *Vǫluspá*, the *Vǫlsunga saga*, and the *Nibelungenlied*, which in spite of the late date of their final preservation and recomposition in widely separated lands may be considered to have evolved from matters and concerns shared by the Germanic peoples, demonstrate the appeal of narrative processes that drive on to complete and terrible destruction. In *Njáls saga*, the reminder that Hallgerðr is descended directly from Sigurðr the dragon-slayer calls up into the saga the complex of emotions associated with the old poetry and legends.[11]

But the sagas show man with a firmer grip on himself than is reflected in the older tales. Things do get out of hand, of course, again and again, but the process is checked before an utter breakdown is reached. G. R. Levy has remarked that the sagas present a "mature vision of the human will resisting calamity."[12] The pattern that informs *Njáls saga* is implicit in this remark. It is a sustained effort of men, mindful of their origins and history, to maintain their society against whatever threatens to disrupt it, an effort by men whose race had the courage, will, and confidence to explore, conquer, and settle the lands from the North Cape to Sicily, from the Volga basin to North America. The vision of the saga is twofold here, for it comments not only on the men of Iceland's saga age but on the Icelanders of the thirteenth century. In commemorating the men of the past it warns and sustains the men of the present. Much has been written to say that the sagas are a continuation and final expression of the Germanic heroic age. But the sagas do not represent a continuation only of the old heroic spirit, the willingness to choose between the evil choices, to embrace defeat for the sake of fame, to die well and by dying well to live in fame which never dies.[13] Certainly, the sagas do glow with that light shifted from the legendary poems into the prose histories of Icelanders.[14] The old heroic celebration of man's unyielding will was noble and remains noble in the sagas. But what is equally impressive, and new, is the increased capacity of men to absorb disaster, to continue the story after the hall has burned and the heroes have fallen. The sagas show that man's ability to cope has grown stronger and this strengthening is an altering of, a coming to terms with, the fears and powers that shaped the earlier myths and legends.

The old fears of failure remain. But disheartening as Gunnarr's death indeed is and disastrous as the Burning is, the society depicted in *Njáls saga* has the strength to respond and carry on. Njáll's cause is taken up by his kinsmen; the following suits involve and embroil most of the island's mighty men and their followers. But even then, Hallr of Síða, with his willingness to forego compensation for his son Ljótr, pulls men back from the brink.

That men realize, early in the saga, what may eventually be at stake is seen in Gunnarr's immediate response to Hallgerðr's mischief-making. Invited to Bergþórshváll she has been insulted over a question of seating arrangements which Njáll's wife, Bergþóra, has provocatively established. Hallgerðr taunts Bergþóra with Njáll's beardlessness; Bergþóra insultingly replies. Hallgerðr appeals to Gunnarr:

> "It will be little use to me," says Hallgerðr, "to have married the man who is the most valiant in Iceland, if you will not revenge this, Gunnarr." He sprang up and leaped across the table and said, "I will go home, and it is most suitable that you should bandy words with your servants, but not in another man's household. Besides I am deeply obliged to

Njáll and I will not be made a fool by your incitements.'' (ch. 35, p. 91)

The two women, however, egging on lesser men, do stir up major
trouble, and it is perhaps difficult now to appreciate the extent
to which Gunnarr and Njáll must labor to keep the peace and
maintain self-control. The wise, older lawyer and the vigorous,
attractive hero working together are barely able to ward off the
first major threat to their peace, a threat insistently brought to
bear by proud and intemperate women. This is an image which
is presented in its purest form in these first series of ''escalations''[15] in which Gunnarr is involved, but it may be discerned
throughout the saga.

In *Njáls saga* women align themselves with those forces which
drag men to death, which disrupt their agreements and their
daily lives, which press them on to the narrow path between
shame on the one side and death on the other which so many
saga heroes walk. And because the saga-man's vision, although
centered in a realistic narrative, embraced a wider spectrum
than has been open to recent realistic narrative, other powers of
the forces of order and disorder come into view in the glimpses
and more-than-glimpses *Njáls saga* gives of the apocalyptic and
demonic realms. Discussion of the women and discussion of the
wonders in *Njáls saga* belong together, but they must be put off
until one more approach is made to the central experience which
underlies this work.

The problems which the Icelanders had to cope with were both
within and without them. Their primary experience and task was
the settling of the land itself—of imposing on an unpopulated,
remote, and volcanic island, rich enough but not overflowing
with natural resources, the forms of human culture.[16] But these
forms could not be successfully established and maintained unless men imposed order upon themselves, unless they could find
means to contain within certain limits the vigor, the rashness,
the aggressiveness, and the malice which were within them (as
they are within all men) and which were (malice excepted)
qualities expressive of the will and confidence of the Norsemen.

The need to control these qualities is recognized in Njáll's famous remark, which repeats an ancient legal proverb. " 'With laws shall our land be built up, but with lawlessness destroyed.' "[17] It is important to understand that Njáll is not as much invoking a concept of legal justice as a concept of the forms which are needed to guide the actions of men. It is the tragedy of Gunnarr, and of the lawyer, Njáll, that the law to which they try to submit their hopes and passions is inadequate to contain them.[18] In fact the original law of *Njáls saga*, the secular law untempered by the ethical commands of Christianity, cannot possibly bring about the building up Njáll speaks of so long as it is principally an elaborate substitute for blood revenge and so long as it is buffeted and misused by little men who are motivated by envy and malice and who must be opposed on their own terms.

The weapons men have at their disposal to effect the settlement and building of the land—and these are self-control and the system of laws—are two-edged. Gunnarr and Njáll go to great lengths to hold themselves in check and for both men the extent of their efforts is tragically defined by the magnitude of the fate which overtakes them when these efforts fail. Gunnarr wonders if something is not the matter with him because he is more reluctant to kill than other men. The result of this admirable reluctance—the saga represents it as admirable in the saga's own terms as well as ours—is simply to goad Gunnarr's enemies to further attempts to provoke him. When these attempts ultimately succeed—for Gunnarr is bound by the code of honor of the times—better men of good will are dragged in against Gunnarr and the result is that the man who represents all that is best about the old heroic society is outlawed from it and put to death by men who acknowledge their admiration for him. *Gísla saga* and *Grettis saga* present a similar pattern.

Njáll's story may similarly be seen as a lifelong striving, courageous and doomed, to avert the fate he sees before him. But each step he takes, settling quarrels, concluding alliances, adopting potential enemies, contracting worthy marriages, only ensures that the eventual collapse of his efforts will be all the more thorough. As long as men have only two courses of action by which to follow up an insult or injury—monetary settlement (either through legal judgment or arbitration) and blood revenge—the building up of the land through law will always threaten to devolve into violence and disaster. What is needed is a sanction that will permit men honorably to cease to seek revenge.

As I have suggested, it is not entirely accurate to read *Njáls saga*, or to summarize its major themes, as one of law striving against lawlessness. The saga makes it all too clear that the law itself can be used and misused as an aggressive and personal weapon. Njáll himself is introduced as a man "of sound and benevolent counsel and all advice which he gave men turned out well" (ch. 20, p. 57). But he is not above manipulating the law for his own family's benefit, although it may be argued that the nation also benefits from his maneuvering. Njáll has sought to marry his foster son, Hǫskuldr, to Flosi's niece Hildigunnr. She is a proud woman who does not wish to marry any man who is not a chieftain, and Flosi respects this wish. Njáll tries to buy a chieftainship for Hǫskuldr, but has no success.[19] He then embarks on an intricate scheme to induce his countrymen to establish additional chieftainships:

> Summer now passes until the Althing. That summer there were great disputes at the Thing. Many men came to consult with Njáll as was their wont. But he gave counsel in men's suits in an unlikely manner so that the pleas of both defense and prosecution came to nought. From this arose a great strife, when suits could not be brought to a conclusion, and men rode home from the Althing unreconciled. (ch. 97, pp. 241–42)

At the next Althing the situation is the same and men say they prefer to settle their quarrels with weapons. Njáll expresses dismay at the thought and acknowledges the responsibility which the great chieftains and wise men like himself have when complaints must be satisfied.[20] He proposes a Fifth Court to be established over the four existing Quarter Courts to function as a court of appeals. This plan is accepted; the court is established and with it additional chieftainships, one of which goes to Hǫskuldr. Njáll stipulates that " 'in this court it shall so be, that if one side pleads correctly and the other incorrectly, the judgment shall go to that side which proceeds correctly in its plea' " (ch. 97, p. 244). This is a point that is to be crucial to later events and which again reveals that the justice of the decision which may be reached through the forms is not the primary concern of the great lawyer. In the saga the establishment of the Fifth Court, a highly important development in Icelandic history, is represented as having come forth from Njáll's desire to get a good marriage for his foster son (see ch. 4, n. 22). It is a large reshaping of the Icelandic constitution for the sake of a personal aim, although the reshaping is a useful one and the aim (to erase the enmity between Njáll's kin and Hǫskuldr's) is by no means a selfish one.

But Njáll here does use his knowledge of the law as a personal weapon to manipulate the chiefs who are more powerful than he. In other contexts, it is possible to see that the law cannot only be used aggressively, but that it is indeed agression itself in a sublimated form. The last statement is virtually self-evident when one examines the wergild provisions of Icelandic law, which appear prominently in *Njáls saga* and which are similar to fines established for the slaying of men in Germanic law.[21] Here a man's death is simply equated with so much money (or goods), depending on his rank. For a man of any standing the standard compensation in *Njáls saga* is two hundred ounces of silver, the equivalent of the value of sixty-four milk cows.[22] The force of this equation is made clear in an example cited by Hakon Melberg of the father who refused compensation for his slain son, saying he did not wish to carry his son around in his purse.[23] The executive authority had an obvious interest in the institution of wergild, not only because it helped dampen and control feuding between clans but because it provided money for the state as well—in Norwegian law the king partook of any fines levied at the assemblies and in Iceland the Law Speaker received a half-share of any fines levied at the Althing.[24] Power can be seen as taking form around the institutions set up to deal with manslaughter cases and other disputes, and James Bryce has noted the unique course this process took in Iceland: "Of Iceland, indeed, one may say that so far from the State creating the Law, the Law created the State—that is to say, such State organizations as existed came into being for the sake of deciding lawsuits."[25] This statement too embodies some of the meaning of "With law shall our land be built." But it is important to remember that no central authority existed in Iceland for enforcing the decision of the law courts. That was left to the parties concerned.

Since a great deal of the law (and all of it that is represented in *Njáls saga* as being the law of the land) is concerned with defining the occasions when one may feel insulted or injured by another and with outlining the procedures to be followed in law suits, it is possible to say that the law is aggression projected outward and codified.[26] The more complicated its structure, the more potential violence it contains; the more elaborate its provisions for appeals and the more extended its capacities for dealing with complicated quarrels, the more extensive the violence that will be released if these procedures break down, as they do break down in *Njáls saga*. This process and the one-to-one equivalence of law and money to aggression become plain in the vivid confrontation between Flosi and the Njálssons which takes place before the Burning.

This scene has already been partly discussed, for it is the scene where Flosi, who has brought suit against the Njálssons and Kári for the slaying of Hǫskuldr, faces them over the great heap of silver which the arbitrators have pledged as an extraordinary compensation. Indeed Snorri the Priest, in announcing the decision, has asked the entire assembly, from the great chieftains to the farmers in their followings, to contribute, " 'for the sake of God' " (ch. 123, p. 312), something to make up the six-hundred ounces of silver that has been set as the atonement for Hǫskuldr. The pile of money thus symbolizes the stake and interest the whole national assembly has in bringing about a peaceful settlement through established legal means and it is associated with the might and interest of the Christian God.

After it is collected, Njáll takes a silk cloth and a pair of boots and places them on top of the pile. He then goes back to his booth, announces the satisfactory conclusion of the case, and pleads with his sons not to spoil it. Skarpheðinn grins. The critical scene then gets under way as both parties line up opposite one another in the Court of Legislature with the gifts and silver between them:

> Flosi entered the Court of Legislature to behold the money and said, "This sum is great and good and well paid out, as is to be expected." Then he took up the cloak and asked who might have given it, but no man answered him. Again he waved the cloak and asked who might have given it, and laughed, and no man answered. Flosi said, "Is it that none of you know who owned this garment, or do you not dare to tell me?" (ch. 123, p. 313)

Flosi, as noted earlier, is trapped. He desires to accept this settlement but he is bound to blood revenge by his niece's incitement. The cloak offers the opportunity. Not only might it remind him of the bloody cloak of Hǫskuldr which Hildigunnr in her passion flung about him, it may also suggest a slight to Flosi's manliness because such valuable garments were worn for show by man and woman alike. There is perhaps a suggestion that he is being overpaid, almost bribed by the anxious men not to take up arms. His irritation may be further stirred by the thought that the Njálssons have gotten off relatively easily in the amount which they personally had to contribute.[27] There is, moreover, an undercurrent of feeling here that somehow it is unmanly to agree to a peaceful settlement. It is one of the concerns of *Njáls saga* to show that manliness can be embodied in restraint as well as violence. But here restraint is no longer possible—it is obvious from what follows that if Flosi does not act to break the settlement, Skarpheðinn will. And, partly because of the unspoken anxiety that such peaceful proceedings are somehow less manly than open hostilities and partly because there was one sure way to provoke men beyond endurance, the agreement is shattered by an exchange of sexual insults:

> Skarpheðinn said, "Who do you think gave it?"
> Flosi said, "If you want to know that, then I will tell
> you what I think—this is my guess, that your father
> gave it, the beardless man—because many who see
> him do not know whether he is a man or a woman."
> Skarpheðinn said, "It is ill done to taunt him in his
> old age when no manly man has done that before. You
> can know this, that he is a man, because he has
> gotten sons with his wife. Few of our kinsmen have
> so lain unatoned for beside our house that we have
> not avenged them." Then Skarpheðinn took back the
> silk cloak and tossed a pair of blue breeches to Flosi
> and said that he'd have more need of them. Flosi
> said, "And why will I need them more?" Skarpheðinn
> said, "Because of this—if you're the bride of the
> Svínafell Troll, as they say, and every ninth night he
> uses you as a woman." Flosi then kicked the money
> and said he would not have a penny of it and said that
> now one thing or the other would be—that Hǫskuldr
> should remain unatoned for, or else that for him they
> would take blood revenge.[28] (ch. 123, pp. 313–14)

The pile of silver has represented, or rather, it *is* in palpable form the most complex agreement yet seen in *Njáls saga*. It is intended to contain and control the long chain of passion and violence that has slowly linked itself together and grown in strength ever since Njáll's wife, Bergþóra, insulted Gunnarr's wife, Hallgerðr; ever since Þráinn Sigfússon took part in the murder of Þórðr Freedmansson, the Njálssons' foster-father. Flosi's mocking words to Njáll, "the beardless man," rake up the old insult first composed by Hallgerðr and repeated by her in her last appearance in the saga (ch. 91, p. 229). By using it Flosi associates himself with the pride and spitefulness of Hallgerðr. By using it, and thus by ensuring that Hildigunnr's desire for blood revenge will be fulfilled, he becomes an agent of these women and for the forces that these women harbor. When he kicks the pile of silver all the hopes and painfully constructed agreements of the men are broken down. One could not ask for a more concrete or vivid symbol for the relationship between money and aggression. The structure he spurns lapses back to its primal form which is violence. Just as the pile of silver embodied the most far-reaching settlement attempted in the saga, so its kicking apart leads directly to the most terrible event of the saga, the Burning.

The men of good will in *Njáls saga* have struggled to keep a hold on the matters that so closely affect their lives. Underlying this effort to maintain order—and such is its force in the saga that through long episodes its time units may best be defined in terms of the yearly cycle of events that are brought to focus and judged upon at the Althing—underlying this effort is the Icelanders' own experience in settling and maintaining their land. This experience, this participation in bringing the world of man to a land where none before had dwelt,[29] was preserved in the *Landnámabók*, celebrated in the sagas, and made visible each summer in the gathering together at Thingvellir, the impressive site of the Althing. Here suits were decided upon, laws made or altered, news exchanged and stories told. The assembly helped maintain a cultural and linguistic unity in an island whose geography and difficult communications might otherwise have led to a drifting apart of the settlers.

Perhaps the very view of things as they appear from Thingvellir may have imparted to the men gathered there a sense of the issues involved in the making of a nation. It is not possible to say what conscious effect this view worked upon the medieval Icelanders, although it is certain that the man who composed *Njáls saga* was thoroughly familiar with Thingvellir[30] and could perhaps expect his audience to provide their own landscape from their own knowledge. But for men today the landscape at Thingvellir can awaken feelings that are not altogether dependent on the wealth of history and heroic saga that pass in review. It is a proper intuition and critical sense that leads Einar Ól. Sveinsson to begin his book, *Á Njálsbúð*, with an evocation of this landscape and with an appeal to the memories it calls up, for this is where a book about *Njáls saga* should begin.[31] But even apart from the memories, the landscape itself is meaningful, as Ari Bouman has noted,[32] for by itself it is a vast image of the situation in which civilized and civilizing man has ever found himself. From the cliff above the assembly plain one's gaze meets the snow-covered mountains to the north and east that reach into the astonishingly bright and clear, or else, in the shifting clouds and weather, glowingly colored or greyly luminous skies of the Icelandic high summer. From the mountains the eye moves down along a sprawling mass of lava, the Thingvallahraun, poised like a frozen and menacing slide on the eastern slopes, and then the view sweeps on past ridges cleft with deep water-filled rifts to the fast-running river and grassy flats along which and near to which the booths, Law Rock, and Court of Legislature of the Althing were. Across the river a small church stands that seems helplessly small in the wide vision.[33] And then at last the eye moves on to the deep waters of Thingvallavatn, the largest lake in Iceland, and one which has taken shape in the basin formed by the collapse of what was once a prodigious outpouring of lava and volcanic substances. The lake's level has risen now since its southern outlet has been dammed; the water has submerged many of the sharp and grotesquely shaped outcroppings of volcanic rock that used to stand along the shores. In this traverse the eye travels from the heavens above to the deep lake resting in the bed of lava welled up from infernal regions below.[34] In between are the small buildings and grassy patterns which remain where men once met to decide the law that should build the land, the land that stretched out before them from the high plateau in which Thingvellir is seated. The outward objective vision corresponds to man's own vision of his inward self-predicament as he has expressed it in dreams, myth, and heroic literature—of his defensive stand in the fields he has cleared and ordered for himself from where he may look upward to the hills and light for help against the threats that emerge from the caves and meres and chaotic heaped-up rubble of the outpourings of the earth itself.[35]

The land itself is no passive thing, but felt to be alive, inhabited by a variety of spirits, both friendly and unfriendly, trolls, giants, apparitions, and the animated dead that live on in their barrows and venture about the countryside.[36] The land itself contains forces that can destroy all man has built up— devastating flash floods, the result of volcanic activity beneath glaciers, and volcanic outbursts, some of which are among the greatest ever recorded.[37] It is a tribute to the steady nerves, even obliviousness, of the saga-men, that these phenomena are scarcely noted in the family sagas.[38] Perhaps they had to be accepted as a portion of fate, for absolutely nothing can be done to avoid or resist them. Indeed a laconic reminder of the indifference shown towards men by the gods responsible for such activity is said to have helped persuade the Althing to forsake them for Christianity. As the assembly debated and was at the point of rupture over whether to maintain the old pagan ways or to adopt the new religion,

> a man came running and said that the earth-fire had come up in Qlfus and would overrun the farmstead of Þoroddr the Priest. Then the heathen men spoke up, saying, "It is no wonder that the gods become angry

at such debates." Then Snorri the Priest said, "What
were the gods angry at when the lava burned on which
we are now standing?" After that men went from the
Law Rock.[39]

But dry and sensible as Snorri's remark is, it recognizes that
the very ground on which the Althing met had originated in some
form of preternatural convulsion. In *Njáls saga* an incident occurs that similarly links the vulcanism of the land to the resent-
ful powers of the pagan gods. On his mission of conversion,
Þangbrandr is stalked by one Galdra-Heðinn, a wizard of sorts:

The heathen men struck a bargain with him that he
should contrive the deaths of Þangbrandr and his
company. Galdra-Heðinn went up onto Arnastakk
Heath and there performed a great sacrifice. Then
when Þangbrandr was riding westwards, the earth
burst apart beneath his horse, but he leaped from the
horse and came up safely on the edge of the brink,
but the earth swallowed the horse with all its gear
and they never saw him again. Then Þangbrandr
praised God. (ch. 101, p. 259)

If the saga-men kept a stiff upper lip about the natural perils of
their land, other Icelanders must have been more talkative, for
Saxo Grammaticus passes on reports of malignant springs,
mountains that belch forth flames, tumbling glaciers, pestilent
floods, and moaning spirits of the damned.[40] The thirteenth-
century Norwegian work, *The King's Mirror*, remarks in one passage that the fruitful earth must be called living[41] but as for
Iceland, the fires there which feed upon the stones must be the
fires of hell itself and the ice and cold of the land the cold of
hell itself, made visible to men as a divine warning: "But now
no one can deny what he sees before his own eyes, since we
hear exactly the same things about the tortures of hell as those
which one can see on the island called Iceland: for there are

vast and boundless fire, overpowering frost and glaciers, boiling springs, and violent ice-cold streams.''[42]   But, since God rules over all, the ''devil can, therefore, injure no one to such an extent that he is consumed either by the fires of death which he has kindled and continues to maintain by means of dreadful earthquakes, or by such other fiendish enmity or malignity as he delights in. For he is allowed to do nothing more than the task at hand.''[43]   In such a context Mǫrðr's wish to burn Gunnarr within, the fire Flosi sets to Bergþórshváll, and the words of Njáll, ''and trust in this, that God is merciful and he will not let us burn both in this world and the next'' (ch. 129, p. 329), link themselves to the much greater drama contained in the Christian vision.[44]

It is probably not necessary to pursue further the point that the land harbored powerful spirits and was itself alive, although Snorri's patriotic tale in *Heimskringla* should be mentioned where the mountain giants and animal spirits of Iceland frighten away the warlock emissary of King Óláfr (these guardians are incorporated into the present-day Icelandic national emblem). One might also recall the myth in Snorri's *Edda* in which the gods fashion the heavens and the earth from the body of the frost giant Ymir.[45]

To sum up, *Njáls saga* embodies and is built about an experience fundamental to the life of the Icelanders, that of governing their behavior by formal (if not always rational) procedures, of imposing law upon their actions. This experience became visible for a representative body of the population at the district assemblies and especially at the yearly great assembly at the Althing. In its turn the experience recapitulates and is analogous to the building up of the Icelandic nation. It reenacts the moment in their history when this people undertook in separate groups and by separate decisions to settle on the empty land, to press upon it the pattern of their culture. And this process in turn is analogous to the fundamental human experience, which each culture and each individual undergoes, of a coming to self-

awareness, of a building up and a maintaining of a conscious
integrity against whatever works to tear apart and dissolve that
structure.

The myths, symbols, and motifs associated with the complex
of patterns shaping the polarity that develops between this
integrity and its adversaries align themselves with powers
represented as belonging to masculine or feminine realms.[46]
The land and sea with their capacity to absorb and give rebirth
take on a feminine valence; so also do the threats that come from
the land and the sea. That which tills the land and builds upon
it and seeks to wrest the shape of the land to its will falls on
the masculine side. In *Njáls saga*—a saga which as it goes
along more and more clearly presents a dialectic between conserving and destroying forces—it is therefore at least appropriate that those forces which fall on the destroying side should,
in general, line up with elements belonging to the female world
and that those forces which fall on the masculine side are those
which strive to maintain order. Njáll and Gunnarr, Kári at the
story's end, and the great men of good will, chieftains like
Snorri the Priest and Hallr of Síða, even the turbulent Þangbrandr
who brings tidings of the might of God the Father, all act to
strengthen the society in which they move and to ensure its
continuance, either through actual legislation that affects the
entire country or by endeavoring to settle the quarrels set in
motion by women, or by both. In back of the smaller men who
oppose them and in back of the events that overtake them may
often be discerned the figures of vengeful women and other
powers, supernatural, associated with the land itself. Even
Skarpheðinn's love of battle and Flosi's vehemence, which are
kinds of a male pride of force, join to satisfy Hildigunnr's wish
for blood revenge. Gunnarr has few faults, but one of them is an
occasional hastiness of decision, an impulsive rashness which
offsets his usual self-control. This impulsiveness plays a large
part in two of his fateful decisions where, in effect, he hands
himself over into the power of present or future foes. In the one

this impulsiveness is called forth by Hallgerðr; in the other by the beauty of the land itself.

Gunnarr's courtship of Hallgerðr is a hasty one indeed. It begins when Hallgerðr, in a reversal of the custom, makes the first move:

> One day as Gunnarr went from the Law Rock, he passed below the Mosfell booth. Then he saw some women coming from the opposite direction and they were well dressed. She who was in the lead was the best arrayed. And when they met, she at once greeted Gunnarr. He took her greeting well and asked who she was. She said her name was Hallgerðr and that she was the daughter of Hǫskuldr Dala-Kollsson. She spoke boldly to him and asked him to tell about his travels; he said he would not deny her that. They sat down and talked. She was dressed so that she wore a red tunic which was handsomely decorated; she had over this a scarlet cloak trimmed with lace-work down to its hem. Her hair fell to her bosom and was both rich and fair. Gunnarr was in his princely clothes which King Haraldr Gormsson had given him. He had the ring on his arm which was the gift of Earl Hákon. They talked aloud and at length. It came about that he asked whether she was unmarried. She says that that was so—"and there are not many who'd risk it," says she. "Do you think there's no match good enough for you?" says Gunnarr. "It's not that," she says, "but I will be particular about my choice." "How would you answer if I ask for you?" says Gunnarr. "You won't have that in mind," she says. "But I do," Gunnarr says. "If such a notion has occurred to you," Hallgerðr says, "then go and talk with my father." Then they ended their talk. (ch. 33, pp. 85–86)

The scene is a fine one, with both figures dressed to play their roles. Gunnarr, home from his triumphant adventures, wearing his noble garments and the gold ring of the Norwegian ruler, is virtually a prince, or as near to it as an Icelander can become. Hallgerðr by now is a fully mature woman—the description again dwells on her remarkable hair and perhaps suggests the strong element of sexuality residing in her. Such vivid patches of color remain in one's memory precisely because they are infrequent. Gunnarr, even Gunnarr in his princely robes, will become a victim of this woman's pride and it is tempting to see in the color of her dress the red naturally associated with blood and, in some instances of Norse lore, with falsity.[47]

Gunnarr goes "at once" (*þegar*) to ask his old foes, Hǫskuldr and Hrútr, for Hallgerðr's hand. Hrútr tries to warn Gunnarr of Hallgerðr's mixed nature. When Gunnarr suspects that their former enmity is affecting his description, Hrútr replies, "It is not that; it is more that I see you cannot prevent yourself." And when Gunnarr says that Hallgerðr seems willing, Hrútr comments, "I see that this must be, because this is a marriage of desire for you both, and you two will risk the most, whatever happens" (ch. 33, pp. 86–87). Although Hrútr spells out to Gunnarr all her faults, they end by sending for Hallgerðr and letting her declare her own betrothal. Njáll, when he hears the news, is greatly displeased. "From her will come great trouble when she comes here to the east," he predicts (p. 87). Hallgerðr has brought out in Gunnarr an unexpected hastiness—it belongs to the larger theme of excess that runs through the saga. Hrútr's remarks show that he regards Gunnarr as a man not in control of himself (Hrútr, thanks to his experience with Queen Gunnhildr, has some knowledge of such matters). Gunnarr has given way to impulse and desire and he will bring to his home at Hlíðarendi a woman who in Njáll's words will be a continual source of trouble, of "all the trouble" (*allt it illa*) if Njáll's words are translated literally.

After this, it is not a complete surprise when Gunnarr, once

more at a crucial moment in his life, suddenly yields to impulses that perhaps have been stirring ever since a sentence of
exile has been passed upon him. Gunnarr bids farewell to his
people and rides off from Hlíðarendi, bound away from Iceland.
But his horse stumbles and Gunnarr has to jump from the saddle:
"His gaze was turned towards the hillside and the farmstead at
Hlíðarendi and he said, 'Fair is the hillside, so that never has it
seemed so fair to me, the bright fields and the mown meadows,
and I will ride back home and never go away'" (ch. 75, p. 182).
So at the last moment Gunnarr is led by fate (the omen of the
horse's stumbling)[48] and by his own inner desire to turn back to
the land which in its way has created Gunnarr and defined him.
To him the land seems infused with beauty, a beauty that must
come from the projection upon it of his own desire to stay.
Never has it seemed so fair to him; it is as if the land lures him
back, and, indeed, that is all the explanation we get from him in
life.[49] The close bond between the heroes of the sagas and the
very land itself appears at this moment and is given expression.
It is a rare, almost isolated, revelation in the sagas that this
attraction existed and was felt.[50] The fascination and compelling force of the scene is acknowledged by its fame—it is
probably the best known and most frequently cited incident in
all of saga literature, and this fact partly obscures how unusual
it is. It is not adequate to say that the saga-man is here simply
adorning, disguising, and diverting attention away from the undeniable fact that Gunnarr is breaking his word and the law of
the land.[51] Nor is it simply a rationalization uttered by Gunnarr
to excuse his suddenly formed but long brewing resolve to go
back and face his enemies, although that is part of the explanation for his speech.[52] Neither explanation accounts for the force
of the scene, for the fascination it exerts, and for the arrest of
attention it compels.

This force is one of archetypal potency in two senses, both
because it awakens thoughts of other heroes in similar predica-
ments[53] and because it presents a picture in itself highly signifi-

cant. Gunnarr in turning back turns back to face his enemies as
all heroes must—no hero can run away. Gunnarr himself says
so, for after his death his son and Skarpheðinn see him awake in
his burial mound, exultantly singing that "rather will he wish to
die than yield, rather die than yield."[54] One thinks of Roland
turning back from the shelter of the pass at Roncesvalles to face
the pagan host, proudly refusing to summon help and dying at
last on the slopes overlooking the lands his king had conquered.
(Gunnarr sends his men away to finish the harvest; it is possible to see reshaped in the pair of Gunnarr and Kolskeggr the
lineaments of Roland and Oliver). In a later tradition, Melville's
Ahab comes to mind as he brings the *Pequod* up into the wind
blowing away from the White Whale and sails back to face that
great foe. Gunnarr's action belongs to all heroic literature. The
image the saga-man's point of view provides at this moment
shows in a static picture the same pattern, the hero turned around
to face the region where he knows he will have to fight, here the
hillside and the house of Hlíðarendi. Gunnarr's return to the
land raises, contains, and satisfies unspoken but profound feelings because it reunites polarities—the hero with his masculine
will and strength turns back to the fair land, the alluring land,
which attracts him as Hallgerðr did when he first saw her, the
land from which he came and in which he will be buried. Ari
Bouman even suggests that Gunnarr returns because he cannot
give up Hallgerðr,[55] and although on the surface this seems
highly unlikely—there is little love lost between Gunnarr and
Hallgerðr at the end of their marriage—in another way Bouman's
observation is true, for Hallgerðr and the land belong to the
same complex of forces and they exercise over Gunnarr an
identical allurement. The hero fulfills himself by urging himself back to his home, his wife, his mother, and his land, all of
which are by him in his last fight, one of which betrays him.
Denton Fox sees that Gunnarr would not be himself if he went
away. Although fame and fortune and a long life are prophesied
for him should he abide by his sentence of exile, overseas he

would be just another man. But in Iceland he is Gunnarr of Hlíðarendi, and his true fame and his real identity rest in that[56] and in the defense he will make of his home, the last stand of the hero becoming a highly compact symbol of the defense of order and the settled land that is the major concern of *Njáls saga*.

Although Gunnarr is declared an outlaw at the end, he has stood for restraint and good will. When these become outraged beyond endurance, his defense becomes a retribution to those who worked to undo him and his best hopes. It is a famous defiance. It stands as a warning to future men and women who wish to raise strife against strong men and stir up trouble in the land. " 'His defense will endure in memory so long as the land is lived in' " (*byggt*) merges with and uses the same verb as " 'With laws shall our land be built up' " (*byggja*). At the same time Gunnarr fulfills the other half of the saying, " 'and by lawlessness destroyed,' " for he does break his word and in going back dooms himself. The situation thus attracts to itself values and themes of great complexity, but they complement, rather than contradict, one another.

In these two scenes, that of Gunnarr's meeting with Hallgerðr and that of his turning back to Hlíðarendi, there may be discerned the polarities of *Njáls saga* which at once attract, struggle with, and define each other. They emerge far more sharply, however, in the wonders and the furious women as the appearances of the former and the wishes of the latter come to be more and more bound together. Female trouble-making, turbulent men, pagan mischief, strange wonders, and hostile terrain first come together when Hallgerðr sends Þjóstólfr, her foster-father, to seek safety with her maternal uncle, Svanr. Þjóstólfr has just killed Hallgerðr's first husband. Svanr is the uncle who is "well skilled in wizardry...and an extremely difficult man to have dealings with" (ch. 10, p. 32). When Svanr hears the news of the killings, he exclaims, "Such I call men, who do not shrink from anything..." (ch. 12, p. 36). In Svanr's exclamation is that equation of vehemence with manliness which the saga en-

deavors to modify. The kinsmen of Hallgerðr's unfortunate husband send a raiding party after Þjóstólfr, but Svanr baffles the
attackers by conjuring up a magic fog:

> Ósvífr said, "Svanr will have caused this, and it
> would be well if nothing worse follows." A little
> later a great darkness came before their eyes so that
> they saw not, and they fell off their horses and lost
> their horses and stumbled into swamps, and some into
> the woods so that they came near to suffering injury.
> They lost their weapons.[57] (ch. 12, p. 38)

This happens three times before the men give up and ride away
to seek compensation from Hallgerðr's father. It is tempting to
see in the men benighted by the wizard's fog and gone astray in
the morasses and woods a symbol of the predicament of men in
pagan Iceland unable to avail against this combination of vengefulness and magic, in a plight where the land itself seems
against them.[58]

Svanr's close connection with the land can be seen in the
manner of his death, which the saga-man reports in his best
neutral style:

> The news became known from north in Bjarnarfjord,
> that Svanr had rowed out in spring to go fishing, and
> a great east wind had come upon the crew and driven
> them up at Veiðilaus and there they perished. But
> those fishermen who were at Kaldbak thought they saw
> Svanr going into Kaldbakhorn Mountain and he was
> well received there. But others denied the story and
> said there was nothing to it. But all knew this, that
> he was never seen again dead or alive. (ch. 14, p. 46)

The dark side of pagan Iceland stands behind Svanr. Þjóstólfr,
whom he shelters, is the first of the malicious little men, hard to
restrain and swift to carry out the urgings of proud women, and,
in fact, there is something peculiarly close in his attachment to

his foster daughter, Hallgerðr, and in his evident jealousy of her husbands.

The side of lawful dealings and good will obtains powerful re-inforcements when it is strengthened with the power of the Christian God whom Þangbrandr brings to Iceland. He tells Hallr of Síða of the angel Michael who in his mercy lets the good weigh more heavily than the bad (see p. 118 above). This is a crucial and new idea, one that can liberate the Icelanders from the bloody cycles of revenge to which their customs have committed them. Þangbrandr brings off a number of miracles to demonstrate the might of the new God. In them can be seen what Christianity is overcoming—shrieking heathen women casting spells, malicious ambushers, berserks unstoppable by fire or sword, wizards like Svanr, all that darkened the older days with sorcery, blood, and vengefulness. But once the force of Christian-ity is placed behind the men of good will and wisdom (Njáll is one of the first converts),[59] the conflicts in the saga intensify. From here on the conflict is no longer one between desirable and undesirable tendencies in a society of men. It becomes a widening one in which events in Iceland and elsewhere become specifi-cally linked with a conflict of good with evil. This conflict is made visible in the wonders. In the part of *Njáls saga* following the conversion they become spectacular unveilings of the apoca-lyptic and demonic realms. The use of them to underlie the conflict of men and to reveal a struggle of good against evil is unusual in the context of saga conventions. Although there are some parallels (such as the succession of good and bad dream women who appear to Gísli in his saga), marvelous happenings in saga literature often function to provide local color or appear as folklore elements routinely associated with given situations. They are part of the normal experience of the men and women who inhabit the sagas. But the happenings to be discussed here are no ordinary wonders; they are forcefully shaped and related; they endure in memory; and they gather up and symbolize major themes of the saga.

Unusual portents often accompany the climactic events of sagas. But the one that portends the Burning is extraordinary indeed and strikingly reveals what powers Flosi is committed to once he has resolved that "we shall ride to Bergþórshváll with our entire company to attack the Njálssons with fire and iron and not turn away before they all are dead" (ch. 124, p. 318). Time then passes.

> At Reykir in Skeið lived Runólfr Þorsteinsson. His son was named Hildiglúmr. One Sunday night Hildiglúmr went outdoors; it was twelve weeks before winter began. He heard a tremendous crash and to him it seemed that both earth and heaven shook. He looked westward then; he thought he saw a ring and a fiery glare about it and in the ring a man on a grey horse. The man passed over swiftly and he was riding hard. In his grasp he had a burning brand; he rode so close to Hildiglúmr that he could plainly see him. The rider was black as pitch. Hildiglúmr heard him speak these words with a great voice:

> > I ride a horse,
> > with icy mane
> > and dripping forelock,
> > the evil-working mount.
> > Fire at the brand's tip
> > and poison in between;
> > so fares Flosi's plan
> > as this burning brand;
> > so fares Flosi's plan
> > as this burning brand.

> Then the rider hurled the brand eastward towards the mountains and a great fire leapt up to meet it so that Hildiglúmr felt he could not see beyond to the mountains. He thought the rider held on eastwards beneath

> the fire and vanished out of sight.   Then Hildiglúmr
> went in and to his room and there lost consciousness
> for a long time, but finally came out of his faint.   He
> remembered all that had happened earlier.   He told his
> father and his father told him to tell Hjalti Skeggjason.
> Hildiglúmr went and told him.   "You have seen a
> witchride," says Hjalti, "and that ever comes before
> great events."   (ch. 125, pp. 320–21)

The nightmarish apparition speaks for itself; the black rider with
his horse at once icy and fiery is a rider from demonic realms.
The ominous pronouncement and the vision of the land convulsed
with fire and poison awaken thoughts of the *ragnarǫk*, the whelm-
ing of the created world by supernatural foes and monsters from
hell as it is told in Snorri's *Edda* and the *Vǫluspá*.   In Christian
commentary the figure of the horse and rider gathered to itself
similar associations; the rider was equated with the mind and
soul of man, the horse with the body, with appetites and passions, with woman.[60]   The rider who lost control of his horse
would be carried headlong to damnation.   Such commentary would
well fit Hildiglúmr's remarkable vision, which reveals that the
headlong course of Flosi's plan, driven as it is by Hildigunnr's
urgings, can no longer be headed off or stayed.   Finally the
vision recalls the earlier times in the saga when horses played
their part in letting loose the passions of men.   Gunnarr first re-
sorts to killing after Otkell on a runaway horse has ridden him
down (ch. 53, p. 134); his next great feud begins when matters
get out of hand at a horsefight (into which another Hildigunnr
has incited the Kolsson brothers, ch. 58, p. 148).   The significance of the careering horse bearing its rider along has thus
partly been established within the saga itself.   All these things
may be kept in mind as Flosi sets out to take fire and iron to
the Njálssons at Bergþórshváll.

The bodies of Njáll and Bergþóra are unburned when they are
recovered from the ashes, for which miracle (*jartegn*) all praise

God. And Hjalti Skeggjason speaks for all when he says that "Njáll's countenance and body seem so bright to me that never have I seen a dead man's body so bright" (ch. 132, p. 343).[61] This phenomenon, of course, frequently surrounds and preserves the bodies of martyrs and holy men. Flosi and his band have burned to death a saintly man; nor is there any reason to suppose that this episode is an interpolation or is out of harmony with the rest of the saga. What is best and most memorable about Njáll—his good will, generosity, and lifelong effort to uphold the orderly conduct of life—is associated with the Christianity that has begun to play its part in the island's affairs.

It is not surprising then that the Burners are summoned to retribution by a more than human power. Flosi dreams at Svínafell one night that a man who calls himself Iron-Grim comes out of the cliffs of Lomángúpr, calling out the names of men. In the list are many Burners and other men besides. When Flosi asks Iron-Grim where he is going, Iron-Grim replies that he is going to the Althing, where " 'First I shall clear [*ryðja*] the jury, and then the courts, and then the field for battle.' " Then, as Flosi tells it to Ketill of Mǫrk, he " 'struck his staff downwards and there was a great crash; Iron-Grim then reentered the mountain but I was filled with dread.' " Ketill does not have to ponder long before he can tell Flosi, " 'It is my foreboding that they will be doomed men who were summoned' " (ch. 133, pp. 347–48). Flosi's dream has been adapted from the *Dialogues* of Gregory the Great, as Einar Ól. Sveinsson has shown, and adapted well.[62] Iron-Grim is another figure from the demonic world, accompanied like the witch-rider with appropriate sound effects, swallowed up like Svanr by the mountain. He is a spirit of battle and strife and he is travelling to the Althing where his presence will soon be felt. In his words one hears the actual lapsing of the procedures of law back to the primitive strife from which they arose; the technical phrases *ryðja kvið, ryðja dóm*—"to challenge a jury or judge"—merge with the primal force of the verb, to clear, to strip away, even to conquer.[63] Iron-Grim will strip the facade from the forms of law to lay bare the field for slaughter. Yet at the same time he is under some constraint, for in summoning the men who are doomed to die, Iron-Grim is announcing the judgment of God who now rules the fates. His summons looks forward beyond the battle at the Althing to the great event which dominates the close of *Njáls saga*, the Battle of Clontarf. And there the hand and might of God are made manifest.

The Battle of Clontarf was fought near Dublin on April 23, 1014, a Good Friday. The Irish were led by Brian Boruma, the Irish High-King, against forces commanded by King Mælmordha of the Leinstermen and by King Sigtryggr Silkbeard, ruler of the Norsemen who controlled Dublin. As *Njáls saga* represents it, Sigtryggr's ambitions are inflamed by his mother, Queen Kormlǫð. "She was a very beautiful woman and well endowed in all those natural gifts not hers to determine, but it was a saying of men that she was completely evil in all things which were within her power to determine" (ch. 154, p. 440). Kormlǫð was married to King Brian, but divorced him, and now she is filled with hatred for him (ch. 154, pp. 441–42). The issue at stake in the Battle of Clontarf was really the Leinstermen's determination "to maintain their independence against the high king," but the victory of Brian, even though he was killed, also put an end to the ambitions of the Dublin Norse.[64] But in memory and tradition the issues became much wider. The battle became a decisive clash of the free and Christian Irish against hosts of the enslaving Northmen, an outright victory of Christianity over the heathen foes who had so long tried to usurp the Irish lands. An epic tradition grew up about the event and it is evident that *Njáls saga* drew on a lost saga about Brian or Earl Sigurðr for much of its material in these chapters (ch. 154–57).[65]

The presentation of this battle near the end of the saga gives rise to a curious effect. The saga is driving to its close—Kári has almost exhausted his missions of revenge, and both Kári and Flosi with his men are travelling by separate ways to Rome to be absolved there. But as the saga nears its close and as one

senses that the various strands are being brought together, at
the same time the scale of events widens immensely. There is a
strong tension generated between the compressive, concluding
drive of the narrative and the sudden expansion of the saga's
vision which now embraces the clash of nations and supernatural
powers. The reader's concern with the quarrels of Icelanders is
led on to an involvement with this great battle where the forces
that have clashed behind and through the actors in the saga emerge
and battle with one another on a much vaster scale.[66]

Flosi has been taken into Earl Sigurðr of Orkney's retinue.
When Sigurðr joins King Sigtryggr a number of the Burners follow him, but Sigurðr insists that Flosi make his pilgrimage to
Rome (ch. 157, p. 448). Sigurðr sails to Ireland and there
"fifteen men from the Burners fell in Brian's Battle" (ch. 157,
p. 453). But as accompanying portents have shown, Brian's
Battle was a triumph of Christianity over its foes. Its signifi-
cance is announced in terms that suggest comparison with
Judgment Day itself. When one viking, Bróðir, once a Christian
but now a relapsed and most cunning sorcerer, asks his brother,
Óspakr, the meaning of frightful omens that have bedeviled
Bróðir and his men (ch. 156, pp. 446–47), Óspakr answers:

> "When the blood rained upon you, that means that you
> will shed the blood of many men, both of your own and
> others. And when you heard the great din, it means
> that the world's shattering will be revealed to you;
> you will all die suddenly. And when the weapons
> attacked you, that means battle will come. And when
> the ravens attacked you, they were those demons whom
> you once believed in and they will drag you to the
> torments of hell." (ch. 156, p. 447)

Not one to ignore his own predictions, Óspakr embraces Christianity and goes off to join King Brian. Bróðir joins the Norsemen and it will be he who takes King Brian's life. The fall of
the saintly king before such a foe shows what forces have met

on this field. The saga-man feels no need to state the unspoken parallel between the King of the Irish and the much higher King who also died on Good Friday.

When the Burners fall, fighting on the wrong side, in such a battle as this, an absolute judgment is made of the Burning. In Icelandic terms to resort to burning was a shameful and desperate act, one of the acts to which the strong term, *níðings-verk*, was applied.[67] The death of fifteen of the Burners in the Battle of Clontarf implies that it was an evil act as well, at least implies that they met their proper deserts in a battle where there is no doubt whose side the God of Battles favors.

The Clontarf episode, far from being a clumsy digression for the sake of its own interest, an interpolation that disrupts the end of the saga by its expansion of a tradition about the fate of the Burners there, is instead a clear discovery in more-than-human form of the powers that have used men as their agents. The final shaping of this strife into a powerful image is presented in the *Darraðarljóð*, the poem which is the great coda to the tale of the Battle of Clontarf. In this, the powers that have men in their grip appear as the Valkyries who weave a frightful web. The rule that gives shape and order to men's lives is seen in the metaphor of the war-weaving loom as an interplay of bloody and opposing pulls driven together by force. If God rules the final outcome, nevertheless these powers out of an older pagan world still preside over the fates of individual men. Christianity has provided men with a vision that at once encompasses and surpasses these powers but it has not destroyed them, and thus it is not inconsistent that they are allowed to have the final say.

> On Good Friday it so happened at Caithness that a man named Dǫrruðr went outside. He saw that twelve riders rode together up to a certain bower and there they all disappeared. He went up to the bower and looked in a window which was there and saw that there were women within and that they had set up a loom. Men's heads were used for weights, and men's

guts for weft and warp, a sword for the beater, and an arrow for the shuttle. They were chanting verses.[68] (ch. 157, p. 454)

The poem they chant is in an old heroic meter although some of its phrasings resemble the glittering diction of the skalds. Two stanzas will suffice to give an idea of its substance:

> Hildr goes to weave the warweb,
> Hjǫrþrimul with her,
> Sanngríðr and Svipul,
> And with swords unsheathed.
> Spear shall clash,
> Shield shall break;
> The battle-axe shall bite the shield.
>
> . . . .
>
> And sorrow will await the Irish,
> Sorrow that will never
> In men's memories grow old.
> Now the web is woven
> And the field is reddened.
> Sorrowful tidings of the fall of men
> Will go about the land.[69] (ch. 157, pp. 455
> and 457, sts. 3, 9)

It is obvious that the Valkyries (for so they are revealed to be in their singing) are determining the outcome of the battle and of separate events within it by weaving their "web of war," for this phrase, if it is not the actual meaning conveyed by *vefr darraðar* (a kenning for the banner on a battle standard),[70] is what is certainly implied by their activity.[71] When they are finished the women tear the cloth from the loom and each keeps a piece of it. "They mounted their horses and rode, six to the south and six to the north" (ch. 157, p. 459). The action suggests the polarity of contending forces that have been woven together to make the battle.

As aftershocks following an earthquake, the weaving of this web and the battle this weaving fashioned are accompanied by lesser marvels. In some of them the motif of the engulfing earth or sea appears:

> At Thvattriver the priest saw on Good Friday a deep sea gulf beside the altar and he saw therein many dreadful things and for a long time afterwards he was not able to sing the holy services.
> This occurrence happened in Orkney, that Hárekr thought he saw Earl Sigurðr and some men with him. Hárekr took his horse and rode to meet the Earl and men saw that they met and rode beneath a certain hill. They never appeared again and no trace was found of Hárekr. (ch. 157, p. 459)

The deep anxieties of men rise to the surface here and take shape. The priest by the monstrous gulf opening before him, unable to sing the services whose words form appeals to the power and mercy of God, is a good symbol for the predicament of man awed and terrified by what he sees within himself. Man needs the forms and laws he himself creates; he needs the power of the heaven-dwelling God within him to hold back what threatens to sweep him away.

The *Darraðarljóð* completes and underscores the shift of modes that occurs in the Clontarf episode of the saga, the shift from a narrative centered upon the realistic actions of men to a narrative still so centered but whose boundaries have been flung wide open to admit the vision of the great powers that have informed the action of the saga. The poem is a confirmation of this shift. In form it contrasts with the stanzas of skaldic verse which have appeared elsewhere. In style its heavily stressed phrases and the characteristic alliterations intensify those same qualities that do indeed resound in the regular prose rhythms and word linkings of this saga. The *Darraðarljóð* is in auditory terms a climactic resolution of the heroic and preternatural themes that are suggested in the very sound itself of the prose instrument that is commanded by the composer of *Njáls saga*. And the inclusion of such a poem brings *Njáls saga* closer to the realm of the legendary sagas where other poems in Eddic meters are found along with abundant manifestations of the supernatural. This broadening of vision at the end of *Njáls saga* is not unlike the process in Aeschylus's *Agamemnon* to which Maud Bodkin refers:

> In the choral odes of the play, when the visible action and conflict of individual wills is suspended, we become aware of an action "lifted out of time and space on to the plane of the universal." On the invisible scene, "as though on a higher stage, uncurtained in the choral part," appear Hybris and Peitho, Nemesis and Ate, mythical shapes representing the forces concerned in the human drama.[72]

In the *Darraðarljóð* the wondrous is brought together with the women weaving the web of strife. Sinister queens stand at both the beginning and the end of the saga. Women begin the trouble in *Njáls saga* and they continue to incite it. Into them are displaced vaster destructive forces that in an impersonal way are sensed by the myth-making mind as feminine. Having looked at some of the wonders of the saga, one must turn to the women, since they go together.

Images of women as troublemakers and as creatures keenly aware that insult and injury to their men and kindred must be paid for appear often, not only in *Njáls saga* but in other sagas and other records as well. There is undoubtedly an historical base to such images. Tacitus gives us a picture of the German women whose heroic pleadings rally their men from the edge of defeat.[73] It is not too far a step from that to the image of a single woman furiously inciting men to avenge a fallen kinsman. Such is the image preserved in the Eddic poems where such vengeance was "felt as a vindication of the fame of the deceased.

We can deduce this by noting that the emphasis is always laid on the slain, not on the slayer."[74] Women are more mindful, perhaps, of the fame and reputation of the family that has been born out of them, of the plight they are left in when the protectors of the family are slain. For fame they are willing to sacrifice individual members. There is a certain sacredness about the duty of revenge and the task of whetting, of inciting men to the attack, is carried out with ritualistic care. Terror, fear, and awe accompany such moments, especially when men become overwhelmed by the force speaking through such a woman. The *Nibelungenlied* does not surpass the portrait of a fury-possessed woman such as is beheld in Fredegund in the pages of Gregory's *History of the Franks*. The awe inspired by a woman dedicated to revenge is still detectable in the admiring remarks made at the end of *Harðar saga ok Hólmverja* where Hǫrðr's fame is assured because

> Four and twenty men were killed in revenge for Hǫrðr.
> For none of them was atonement offered. The sons of
> Hǫrðr and his kinsmen and in-laws killed some, and
> Hróarr killed others. And most of them were killed
> through the counsel of Þorbjǫrg Grimkell's-daughter. . . .
> After no other single man in Iceland had so many men
> been killed in revenge and all unatoned for.[75]

But there is a change from the situation found in the Eddic poetry to that in the sagas. The figure of the avenging female loses some of her numinous qualities. Along with and in place of a woman who fulfills a traditional role appear proud, touchy, and willful individuals, women who act out of a sense of personal pique and desire, not out of familial service to the "sacred duty of revenge."[76] The contrast between the older and the newer types is seen in *Njáls saga* between Hallgerðr, who wishes to use Gunnarr to glorify herself, and Hildigunnr, who uses Flosi as an instrument to avenge her fallen husband. Her concern is not with her own reputation but with Hǫskuldr's.

It is reasonable to believe that some of the examples of such women and some of the instances of whetting to revenge found in the sagas reflect historical truth. But with a motif as persistent as this one, central in the cycles of heroic poems, one which occurs frequently in the family sagas and which is a marked feature of the legendary sagas, it must be recognized that this motif has become a standard narrative component because it satisfied otherwise unexpressed concerns, that it may act as a screen which at once conceals and utters certain perceptions which cannot otherwise be articulated.[77]

One explanation is that the figure of the vengeful woman is an outward projection of man's own uneasy awareness of the divided state within him, that it is a mechanism whereby the blame and guilt for his failures to control his passions (and for his desire for such failures) can be shifted to an outside cause. Maud Bodkin has referred to "a sense of man's terror of that weakness in himself which he projects upon the type figure of women."[78] E. R. Dodds has described the process in more general terms and has pointed out that in Homeric poetry motivation and explanations for man's impulsive acts are provided for by an elaborate system of terms for forces which are felt to possess man from the outside: "When a character acts in a manner contrary to the system of conscious dispositions which he is said to 'know,' his action is not properly his own, but has been dictated to him. In other words, unsystematised, nonrational impulses, and the acts resulting from them, tend to be excluded from the self and ascribed to alien origin."[79] Men first perceive the structure of their own passions and desires thrown outward upon the world; they have to perceive them outwardly before they can again take them into themselves and thus become introspectively aware of what indeed resides in them.[80]

Thus the women in the saga, who are portrayed as characters in their own right, also fulfill an impersonal role. They embody the conflicting passions and social dilemmas that exist within the culture, the culture of which the sagas are a partial expres-

sion.   There is the conflict between the natural reluctance of
men to risk their lives (for life is dear) and their duty to avenge
their kindred.   There is the conflict between shame that follows
for not taking forthright vengeance and the disapproval that accrues about those who will break and not abide by the settlements of men.   The actions of Gunnarr and Njall and other men
of good will are designed to strengthen the system of laws, to
enhance the status of those who prefer to talk rather than to
kill.   But the law by which Njáll hopes to build up the land is
not strong enough to resist the pressures that are brought to
bear upon it from men and women whose pride, shortsightedness,
rashness, and sheer malice conspire against it.   Moreover, the
old system of atonements and arbitration was in itself, as has
been seen, based on a rationalization and sublimation of the
original violence it sought to govern and hence was apt, in
times of instability, to revert to its original state.   Halfway
through the saga, the desire of men to build up a land through an
ordered pattern of life (a pattern in terms of which the old recourse to feud and fighting is seen as lawlessness) receives
powerful reinforcement with the introduction of Christianity.
Mercy, forgiveness, and the thought that reward and vengeance
are the Lord's (" 'He will not let us burn both in this world and
the next' ") have a power in them that strengthens the hand of
men willing good.   And as a consequence, the women who represent and speak for the older order are thrown over to and linked
with the pagan world where powers of darkness and evil stir.   It
must be emphasized that this is an impersonal process of representing divisions and polarities within the human mind, divisions
which are, of course, made objective and all too real in human
deeds and the pattern of human culture.   When I speak of men
who wish to build up the land, I mean the men and women who
together did in fact settle Iceland and wrought the culture that
has, through great times and hard times and many changes, endured to the present day.   This is the culture that produced the
sagas and the sagas remember many deeds of ancestors, but they
cast these deeds into forms not untouched by the force of myth.

A distinction has to be made between these men as they appear as historical characters in *Njáls saga* and as their figures are used as representative types; between these women as the saga preserves their individual persons and as the saga manipulates them under cover of traditional motifs to embody forces. And it must be remembered that at times the myth and the reality did merge and could not be distinguished. Hildigunnr, the proud but cautious bride who wishes her husband to live with her in the land east away from his dangerous kinsmen (ch. 97, p. 241) grows easily into the Hildigunnr who with priestlike deliberation and long-considered savage passion incites her uncle to blood revenge.[81]

This great scene stands for all the other times women have stirred up trouble in *Njals saga* and it is the culmination of the theme. This moment is reached when Flosi and his men ride to visit Hildigunnr, his niece, after the brutal slaying of her husband, Hoskuldr Hvitaness-Priest. Flosi has been talking with his kinsmen and allies who have urged him to accept the generous offers of settlement that Njáll and the others are sure to make. Flosi is ill at ease when he comes to make the visit to the widowed Hildigunnr—he knows what is going to happen, that she will egg him on to blood revenge in such terms that he cannot shirk from that course. But custom and courtesy oblige him to submit himself to her passion. There is an atmosphere of compulsion and ritual inevitability in what follows.

Hildigunnr has ordered the house swept, the tapestries hung up, and the high seat set at the table for Flosi. She goes to meet him: " 'Be welcome, kinsman; my heart is rejoiced at your arrival.' Flosi said, 'We'll eat the noon meal here and ride on' " (ch. 116, pp. 289–90). Flosi's curt and nervous reply to Hildigunnr's formal greeting reveals his uneasiness. He walks into the room where the meal is set and throws the high seat away from him, which Hildigunnr had set there to remind him that he is the head of her family. Flosi says,

> "I am neither a king nor an earl, and there is no need
> to furnish a high seat for me and no need to mock

> me." Hildigunnr stood close by and said, "That is
> too bad, if you are displeased because we did this
> with sincere intentions." Flosi said, "If you have
> sound intentions towards me, they will declare them-
> selves if they are good and they will condemn them-
> selves if they are evil." Hildigunnr laughed a cold
> laugh and said, "This is still off the mark; we will
> come closer before things are settled." (p. 290)

The towel Hildigunnr gives Flosi is full of holes and one end
has been ripped away, a token, Sveinsson notes, of Hildigunnr's
abandonment and loss.[82] Flosi uses the tablecloth instead. But
the action so far, as Hildigunnr has hinted, has only been preliminary. The issues come out into the open as the men eat:

> Then Hildigunnr came into the room and stepped be-
> fore Flosi, brushed her hair from her eyes and wept.
> Flosi said, "You are low in spirits now, niece, since
> you are weeping. Nevertheless it is proper that you
> should weep for a good man." "What action now or
> support shall I have from you?" she says. Flosi
> said, "I will prosecute your case as far as the law
> permits or strive for that settlement which good men
> will see is honorable to us in every respect." She
> said, "Hǫskuldr would have taken blood revenge for
> you, if he had had this suit to take up on your behalf."
> Flosi answered, "You are not lacking in savageness,
> and it is clear what you want." (pp. 290–91)

Hildigunnr reminds him that Flosi's brothers had taken blood
revenge on Árnorr Ǫrnólfsson for an injury to their father less
grave than that Hǫskuldr suffered:

> Hildigunnr then went from her room and opened up her
> clothes chest. She took out the cloak which Flosi
> had given to Hǫskuldr and in that cloak Hǫskuldr had
> been slain. She had preserved it with all its blood.

Silently she went up to Flosi. Flosi was finished and the dishes had been cleared. Then Hildigunnr flung the cloak over Flǫsi; the blood poured down all about him. Then she spoke: "You gave this cloak to Hǫskuldr, Flosi; now I give it back to you. In this cloak he was slain. I call God and good men to witness that I conjure you by all the might of thy Christ and by thy manliness and by thy valor to revenge all wounds which he had on his dead body, or else be called a contemptible wretch [*niðingr*] by every man." Flosi hurled the cloak back into her face and said, "Monster that you are, you wish that we should take up what will turn out the worst for all of us. 'Cold are the counsels of women.'" Flosi was so shaken that at times his face turned red as blood, then pale as grass, then blue-black as death [*blár sem hel*]. (ch. 116, pp. 291–92)

These similes account for three out of the one hundred forty-eight to be found in thirty-two family sagas and the degree of Flosi's agitation may be judged from the fact that this is the only such triple occurrence in these sagas.[83] In the last there is a buried mythological reference, for Snorri tells us of the goddess Hel, the goddess of the dead, that "she is half blue-black and half flesh-colored, whereby she is easily recognized, and rather lowering and fierce."[84] Flosi's face is stamped with the colors of fear and death whose power he is now forced to serve. The epithet Flosi flings at Hildigunnr in his dismay and anger— "you are the greatest monster (*þú ert it mesta forað*)"—curiously fits the assertion that women, pagan powers, the land, and perilous places gather together in an archetypal cluster of symbols. For the primary meaning of *forað* was a dangerous place, a precipice, abyss, or swamp, meanings which it still retains in modern Icelandic.[85] Perhaps the meanings, "monster," "ogre," developed because unpleasant creatures often dwell in such places. So considered, the epithet here draws to it associations of the swamps in which Svanr's blinded foes stumble, the cliff-sides that open up to receive Svanr and Iron-Grim, perhaps the deep sea gulf (*sjávardjúp*) that appeared before the altar at Thvattriver. Whether such associations were intended by the saga-man or consciously made by his audience is another question; one doubts that they were, although the use of the word, with its double meaning, may have released certain affects. But the possibility is latent in the saga for such an association.

Hildigunnr's incitement has been a stirring up of the strongest appeals to old custom and man's sense of shame and it has been a summoning of more-than-human potencies. Covered with his nephew's blood, called *níðingr* to his face in the presence of his men, urged by the power of the strongest god Hildigunnr can think of, the new Christ, Flosi is committed to the course he knows is the worst for all. Hildigunnr's reference to Christ certainly seems an ironic touch. Flosi is urged on in Christ's name to avenge the man who died with a prayer on his lips that God forgive his slayers. That Hildigunnr refers to "your Christ" makes it reasonably certain that she still speaks and acts in the name of the older gods. In fact, the blood-drenched cloak she wrathfully flings about her uncle may even be intended to evoke the scarlet or purple robe that the Roman soldiers, who were also of the old order, fling about Christ in mockery before his crucifixion. Flosi is no Christ-figure, but he is struggling to understand the new religion—his reluctance and words show that, for under the old code his obligation to avenge Hǫskuldr was clear and certain. And Hildigunnr's passionate gesture is, like the mocking investiture of Christ, a condemnatory one as well; the course Hildigunnr dictates is a course that should surely bring death upon Flosi's own head in turn. But except for Hildigunnr's curious reference to Christ, there is no word or phrase to indicate whether or not the saga-man intended his audience to draw such a parallel or whether or not he expected that it could. That the parallel does suggest itself, however is an indication of how critical this scene is.

" 'Cold are the counsels of women' ''—that wisdom, uttered at one of the most dramatic moments of the saga, awakens echoes of its own.[86] Hildigunnr's whetting must lead to the Burning and the consequences of that threaten to break apart the system of law and ordered agreements which give form, sense, and security to the national life. In fact both sides recognize that whatever the decision is at the Althing, it is one that cannot possibly be enforced by legal means and the suit will break down into the violence it is attempting to contain. Snorri the Priest admits this in a pretrial agreement he makes with Ásgrímr Elliða-Grímsson whose men and whose son, the great lawyer Þórhallr, are supporting the suits of Njáll's kinsmen and friends against the Burners. Snorri predicts:

> "It is likely that you will be prosecuting the case vigorously while they will defend themselves in a like manner, and neither of you will concede the other's right. Then you will not be able to bear them and will attack them. And that will be the only way left because they wish to repay your loss of lives with further shame and the death of your kinsmen with dishonor." It seemed to them that Snorri was urging them on somewhat. (ch. 139, p. 372)

And he can think of no solution but to set dead against dead. In the course of drawing up a battle plan he says, " 'and when you have killed as many of them on the other side as I think you can afford to pay atonement fees for and still retain your chieftainships and rights to residence, then I will jump in with all my men and part you' '' (pp. 372–73).

In a sense then the great law processes that follow are but an elaborate series of technical maneuverings over a foregone conclusion—that neither side will accept the decision. The law has become an inadequate instrument—the law that was designed not so much to determine the rights and wrongs of the issues it decided but designed rather to impose a correct form on the way settlements were to be reached. It is obvious in the suits that conviction depends on the correctness of procedure in the charge and not on whether the charge can be proven. There is no question that Flosi has led a party to burn the Njálssons within their house; the question is whether witnesses to the act can be correctly summoned and the jury correctly charged. Thus, when a verdict actually is given against Flosi, after a long series of technical quibblings and reversals themselves reversed by brilliant lawyering behind the scenes, the result is somehow irrelevant and hardly emphasized. Indeed the moment of victory for Njáll's party is quickly overturned, when Flosi appeals the verdict to the Fifth Court on the grounds of a procedural irregularity, a result of a carefully prepared scheme of Flosi's lawyer. The Burners in the climactic suit actually become the prosecutors for a brief moment until Þórhallr quickly institutes a counter-suit charging Flosi with bribing his lawyer to defend him. All this maneuvering is exciting and in its own way it is the analogue of the bloody escalations which have developed in earlier feuds, but it evades the central issue. The court and the law have failed, had to fail given the structure of the law, to make a satisfactory pronouncement on the tragic and terrible events of the saga—that Njáll and his sons were burned to death within their house after the brutal slaying of Flosi's nephew. The Burning above all has been a desperate and heinous act and the pronouncements the law makes upon it must have some relevance to the right and wrong of the matter if the law to which men submit themselves is to make any sense at all. If the law cannot cope with this central event, it must either be strengthened by new means or altered; otherwise, the land-destroying lawlessness that Njáll had feared will have prevailed.

The lengthy repetitions of the legal formulas work to stave off the issue in another fashion. They come to have a solemn, almost incantory effect, as if by their impressive phrasing and very sound they may ward off the trouble that is brooding over the assembly, as if through the sheer virtuosity of words they could sooth the violence at the same time that they summon witnesses to it. The effect is not unlike that of some of the magical charms and alliterative vows used to make pacts binding and to call down curses on oath-breakers.[87] At least, this is my conjecture why so much legal matter is present here and repeated verbatim at such length. For present readers many of these passages may become tedious and they are easily skipped over. It is obvious, nevertheless, that they are there by deliberation. Earlier trial scenes have prepared the audience for such procedures and made it familiar with the terminology. And when he wants to, the saga-man is perfectly capable of a summary:

> Ásgrímr and his men had the other suits for the Burning put in motion and they went forward. (ch. 143, p. 394)

> Then Mǫrðr named witnesses and stated those four charges which he had prepared against Flosi and Eyjólfr, and Mǫrðr used all the same words in his statement of the charge as he had previously used in his citation. (ch. 144, p. 398)

If extended passages of legal prose are present, the reason is that the saga-man wanted them to be. Perhaps his particular audience delighted in the full panoply of technicalities (no other saga so revels in such swathes of law)—and perhaps a truly skilled speaker could make all the matter of summoning and charging exciting and effective. There is, moreover, a certain satiric force and grim humor in the spectacle of all this frantic, windy, and death-laden lawyering. But I think the reason advanced above is also part of the explanation, that the law is used almost as magic in an attempt to ward off the inevitable conflict. In a saga so concerned with man's attempt to rule himself, it is appropriate that the law itself appears as a final barrier of words thrown up against the conflict that is rapidly approaching.

The conflict breaks into the open when Mǫrðr, who with

Þórhallr's backstage advice has skillfully conducted the case through all its stages, makes a final and fatal blunder, a blunder involving a technicality which Njáll himself had carefully stipulated at the time he established the rules governing the Fifth Court.[88] The way is open for Flosi's party to bring up their countercharges and have a sentence of outlawry proclaimed against their foes. Possibly Mǫrðr has deliberately blundered—he has been an agent for disorder all along and he has little love for the men whose suit he has been obliged to conduct. He disappears into the tumult which he has served so well. There is a glimpse of him pressing Flosi's men and then without any comment he is out of the saga just as Hallgerðr was allowed to vanish without any formal notice. This outbreak of battle is a striking scene where the procedures in the land's highest court suddenly revert to passion and war. The high feelings and hatreds and irreconcilable festering grievances hitherto pent in are purged and cancelled in the violence that follows. Their nature and this process of purgation are symbolized in the remarkable moment after Þórhallr, laid up in bed with an infected leg, hears the news of Mǫrðr's blunder:

> Now it should be told that the messenger comes to Þórhallr and tells him what had happened, that they would all be made outlaws and that the manslaughter suit was voided. And when Þórhallr heard that, he was so moved that he could not speak a word. He sprang up from his bed and seized with both hands the spear Skarpheðinn had given him and drove it into his leg. Flesh and the core of the boil were on the spear as he dug it out of his leg. Such a gush of blood and pus followed that it fell across the floor in a stream. Þórhallr went out of the booth without limping and strode so vigorously that the messenger could not follow him. He fared on until he came to the Fifth Court. Then he ran into Grímr the Red, a kinsman of Flosi. As soon as they met, Þórhallr laid out with

> his spear against Grímr's shield and cleft it apart.
> The spear went on through Grímr and came out be-
> tween his shoulders. Þórhallr cast him off the spear,
> dead. (ch. 145, p. 402)

The large clash of armed men which this act sets off is final
evidence that the old code has been broken down. The spectacle of so many men warring with one another on the plains
dedicated to the making and upholding of law shows what the
long chain of grievances and quarrels, begun decades before,
has led to. And although this battle may even accounts there is
no hope that the process will not begin anew unless some shift
of values is made. For the law, even when it worked by substi-
tuting itself for violence, never quite dispelled the shame and
anger roused by insult and injury. And because the law is a
substitute for violence, it is compromised, for violence is at its
base. Perhaps this is what Snorri the Priest alludes to when he
draws up his forces to halt Flosi's retreat. Flosi asks him why
Snorri is barring their way to a safe retreat: " 'I am not causing
your way to be barred,' says Snorri, 'but I know who is and will
tell you without being asked, that Þorvaldr Crop-Beard and Kolr
are bringing this about' " [89] (ch. 145, p. 406). The reference is a
somewhat confused allusion to an incident recorded in the
Íslandingabók. Þorvaldr had burned his brother Gunnarr alive in
his house; Þorvaldr's grandfather had murdered a thrall named
Kolr in the early days of the settlement. For this he had been
outlawed and the money from the land where Kolr's corpse was
found had been appropriated for the use of the Althing. Snorri's
reference may be a reminder that to the Althing itself a trace
still clings of these two base and contemptible crimes, that the
Althing is partly sustained by an outlaw's forfeit property. At
least it is an admission that the spirits of criminal and victim
still haunt the Althing.

But the old ways are not wholly restored after the battle is
ended. Hallr of Síða's generous offer to let his son lie unatoned
is the act that shifts the mind of the assembly. It is an act of

forgiveness, for Hallr a gesture of great sacrifice and for the
nation a new wisdom. Although foreshadowed in the gestures of
Hrútr and the good will Gunnarr and Njáll nurture between them,
it is here given public and dramatic sanction. It is the act that
shifts the saga itself onto an upward path that leads, eventually,
to the reconciliation between Kári and Flosi and to Kári's marriage with Hildigunnr. For the structure of *Njáls saga* is a structure that leads beyond the tragic events which are its points of
greatest intensity and deepest sorrow. The curtain does not fall
upon the figures of men mournfully praising the fallen Gunnarr,
or sorrowfully and wonderingly discovering the unharmed bodies
amid the ashes at Bergþórshváll. Such scenes bring to mind the
final scenes of dramatic tragedy. [90]

But it is perhaps well to remember that tragedy was once part
of a larger cycle that ended in comedy. Saga preserves this
larger structure. It is capable of focusing to a tragic point, but
it rarely ends there. Reports of vengeance and eventual settlement follow the death of major figures. These reports are nearly
always present, [91] although they can be shaped so as to give rise
to markedly different effects. Some sagas, as W. P. Ker and
Bertha Phillpotts have noted, avoid the fatal consequences towards which they seem to have been travelling, come to a rec-
onciliatory end, or else die quietly away. [92]   A saga like
Laxdæla saga ends with all passions exhausted and played out,
on a note of tragic regret, in Guðrún's famous admission to her
grandson,   " 'I was the worst to him whom I loved most.' " [93] In
Gísla saga the sections of revenge and aftermath are very sharply
curtailed and abortive. The saga's dramatic climax is the
heroic last stand and death of Gísli which comes very shortly
before the end. Grettir meets a fate very similar to that of Gísli,
but his saga yields to the impulse to continue onwards to a
lighter and more gentle ending. The adventure of Grettir's half-
brother in Constantinople and his happy marriage to the Lady
Spes comprise the story of a man of good luck. Here the saga
form breaks into the realm of romance. The generic contrast be-

tween the sections is obvious, but was not, I think, felt as a lapse of taste or artistic control. This upward swing seen so clearly in *Grettis saga* is visible also in *Njáls saga* and confirms a tendency of the saga form. It is a tendency towards an expanding action at the end. The saga hero dies alone, but his figure is not an isolated one. About the bodies of the slain gather friends and kindred. A man's death involved all men in Iceland, or could nearly do so, as *Njáls saga* illustrates. And the men that gather about the slain have come not merely to pick up the pieces. Life goes on; there is a healing vigor in the society that emerges in the saga literature. It was a society that was able to sustain great losses, to appreciate what had been lost, and that could yet go on. It is only in *Njáls saga* that the mechanisms of atonement and settlement fail to check the cycles of vengeance before they get so out of hand that a large disruption of much of the civil order is threatened, a disruption which the Battle at the Althing represents and portrays. But that threat too is finally contained. At the end Kári and Flosi are reconciled, and Hildigunnr married to Kári. The upswing concludes with a knitting together of the torn fabric of the island. It is a restoration of the old society, but in its restored form a society considerably changed and tempered, both by the experience it has endured and by the revelation of Christian mercy. There is an analogue here with the action of comedy which moves toward the birth of a new society and embraces old and new at the end in reconciliation and wedding.[94] It is tempting to say that saga as a genre contains the stuff of tragedy in a comic form, and, indeed, W. P. Ker comes close to such an observation when, after reviewing the *Bandamanna saga*, he says that heroic narrative in Iceland was "a form which proves itself equally capable of Tragedy and Comedy."[95] Perhaps one comes closer to an understanding of saga as genre if one considers that it developed after the breakdown of the epic synthesis but that it still remains close enough to this synthesis that it can contain in organic fashion much of the epic vision. It is a genre that, professing to be history, contains the adventure of romance, the fated course of heroes, the humor and self-criticism of comedy, all in a linear and self-restoring form. After fatal events, men could take measure of themselves and go on. The extent of the calamities they faced, the sternness with which they were expected to act, and the number of tales told about their heroic deeds were measures of the strength of their society.

At the end in *Njáls saga* the slowly rising curve along which Kári, Flosi, and Hildigunnr have made their way divides in two directions. The one direction goes with history and comes down to the listeners who are hearing the story. Curiously enough it is Kári, the striking heroic figure who first appeared upon the sea in his gleaming armor, whose line goes on into the world that the audience knows. By Hildigunnr Kári has children. A grandson, Kolbeinn, "was one of the most renowned men in that family" (ch. 159, pp. 463–64). The line goes on into the light of contemporary day. But for Flosi, whose strength served the destroying wrath of Hildigunnr, the line curves back into the realm of mystery and myth, back into that realm where all stories begin:

> Men say this, that such was the life's-ending of Flosi, that he fared abroad when he had become an old man to seek house timber. He was in Norway that winter. But in summer he was late in getting under way. Men told him that his ship was not seaworthy. Flosi said that it was good enough for an old and doomed man. He boarded that ship and put out to sea. Of that ship nothing was ever heard again. (ch. 159, p. 463)

"Of that ship nothing was ever heard again." As so often in the sagas a few words awaken memories of far-off times and the old heroic days. Flosi's last seafaring is not unlike the last voyage of the legendary Danish king, Scyld Scefing, when, given

to the ocean, he rides out in his funeral ship.   And the Beowulf
poet says:

> Men ne cunnon
> secgan tō sōðe   selerædende
> hæleð under heofenum   hwā þæm hlæste onfēng.[96]

[Men, the counsellors in the hall, the heroes
beneath the heavens, could not truly say who
received that ocean cargo.]

The treasure laden upon Scyld's ship is the tribute paid him by
men who will maintain Scyld's strong-handed rule.   Flosi, who
in his way and time served the old order, vanishes, without
praise, in a ship laden with timber for building anew.   Flosi the
old man disappears in the sea as all heroes must at sunset before they are reborn.   His end is a token to men that what they
have heard is not a history only.   His end is a token that what
they have heard they will hear again.

SELECTED ABBREVIATIONS
AND SHORTENED TITLES
NOTES
BIBLIOGRAPHY
INDEX

Selected Abbreviations and Shortened Titles

The following list includes those abbreviations which do not appear in recent *PMLA* bibliographies and the shortened titles for works frequently cited.

Age of the Sturlungs   Einar Ól. Sveinsson, *The Age of the Sturlungs*, trans. Jóhann S. Hannesson, Islandica 36 (Ithaca, N.Y., 1953)

BONIS   *Bibliography of Old-Norse Icelandic Studies* (Copenhagen, 1963–)

CCIMÆ   Corpus Codicum Islandicorum Medii Ævi

Family Saga   Theodore M. Andersson, *The Icelandic Family Saga: An Analytic Reading* (Cambridge, Mass., 1967)

Fornrit   *Íslenzk Fornrit*, 16 vols. (Reykjavík, 1933–)

History of Consciousness   Erich Neumann, *The Origins and History of Consciousness*, trans. R. F. C. Hull (New York and London, 1954)

Homer   Cedric H. Whitman, *Homer and the Heroic Tradition* (Cambridge, Mass., and London, 1958)

Nature of Narrative   Robert Scholes and Robert Kellogg, *The Nature of Narrative* (New York, 1966)

"*Njáls Saga* and Western Literary Tradition,"   Denton Fox,

"*Njáls Saga* and Western Literary Tradition," *CL*, 15 (Fall 1963), 289–310

Njálssaga (Jónsson)   *Brennu-Njálssaga*, ed. Finnur Jónsson, Altnordische Saga-Bibliothek 13 (Halle, 1908)

Origin   Knut Liestøl, *The Origin of the Icelandic Family Sagas*, trans. A. G. Jayne (Oslo, 1930)

Origins of Icelandic Literature   G. Turville-Petre, *The Origins of Icelandic Literature* (Oxford, 1953)

"Pattern"   Ian R. Maxwell, "Pattern in 'Njáls Saga,'" *Saga-Book*, 15 (Parts 1–2, 1957–59), 17–47

Problem   Theodore M. Andersson, *The Problem of Icelandic Saga Origins* (New Haven and London, 1964)

Rhetoric   Wayne Booth, *The Rhetoric of Fiction* (Chicago, 1961)

Sagnaskemmtun   Hermann Pálsson, *Sagnaskemmtun Íslendinga* (Reykjavík, 1962)

TAPA   *Transactions and Proceedings of the American Philological Association*

"Textual Evidence"   Theodore M. Andersson, "The Textual Evidence for an Oral Family Saga," *ANF*, 81 (1966), 1–23

Notes

CHAPTER 1

1. The word *saga* (pl. *sögur*) has a wide range of meanings and may refer to anything from a short report or anecdote up to extended written narrative (see Stefán Einarsson, *A History of Icelandic Literature* [New York, 1957], p. 122). It can be applied to virtually any prose narrative in the huge corpus of Icelandic literature, regardless of the matter or intent, whether fictional or historical. Literary historians, for the sake of convenience, may speak of, in secular literature, *fornaldar sögur* (legendary sagas of heroic Scandinavia prior to the settlement of Iceland), *konunga sögur* (the sagas of kings, Icelandic histories of Norwegian kings), *Íslendinga sögur* (family sagas, about the deeds of Icelanders in the Age of Settlement, 870–930, and the following century, 930–1030, the *söguöld* or saga age), and *riddara sögur* (knights' tales, Icelandic versions of Continental romance). The term *lygi sögur* (lying tales) should perhaps be reserved for adventure tales that border on folklore and fantasy, although the term can extend to *riddara sögur* and was applied by the medieval Icelanders to the *fornaldar sögur* as well. One should also mention the *Sturlunga saga*, a compilation of works dealing with the important deeds and outstanding men of Iceland in the late twelfth and thirteenth centuries.

2. The problem is acute for historians who wish to use the thirteenth century sagas to depict tenth century life and events. The broad outline the sagas give of the discovery and settlement of Iceland and of the growth of Icelandic society seems certain enough, but the closer one tries to focus on any given event, the less confident one becomes of

particular details of that event. Walter Baetke comments in *Über die Entstehung der Isländersagas*, in Berichte über die Verhandlungen der Sächsischen Akademie der Wissenschaften zu Leipzig, Philologisch-Historische Klasse, vol. 102, no. 5 (Berlin, 1956), 1–108: "Im übrigen bewegt sich aber Heuslers Beweisführung—auch abgesehen davon, dass sie die Geschichtlichkeit der Sagainhalte voraussetzt—in einem Zirkel; denn was wir über die Zustände auf Island zur Sagazeit wissen, wissen wir aus den Sagas; ob ihre Angaben 'echt' sind, könnten wir nur sagen, wenn uns andere Quellen eine Nachprüfung gestatteten, was aber nicht der Fall ist. Man hat das, was wir wirklich über das Island der ersten Jahrhunderte wissen, meist überschätzt" (pp. 60–61). ["In other respects Heusler's proof—apart from the fact that it presupposes the historicity of the saga content—moves in a circle; for what we know about conditions in Iceland during the saga age, we know from the sagas; whether their assertions are genuine we could only say if other sources afforded us a check, which is not, however, the case. What we actually know about Iceland in the first one hundred years of the settlement has been greatly overestimated."] On the other hand, few deny that in one way or another the sagas contain a core of more or less accurate tradition. Whatever the worth of the tradition, saga presents it to the audience as history, and the shape of a saga, its strictly chronological ordering, is partly accounted for by its mimesis of medieval historical writing. Knut Liestøl observes in *The Origin of the Icelandic Family Sagas*, A. G. Jayne (Oslo, 1930), p. 246: "If... we bear in mind the circumstances in which the Icelandic traditions grew up, and base our judgment upon the criteria afforded by the sagas themselves, we arrive at the final result that the family sagas have a historical foundation, that they claimed from the first to be history, and that they were looked upon as historical." And Sigurður Nordal has this to say about *Njáls saga*: "Whether the oral traditions about Njál have amounted to more or less [sic], and whether the writer felt himself more or less dependent on or bound by them, it has certainly been of no small consequence for his handling of the story that Njál was not his invention, but a historical person who had lived at a certain place and time and suffered a certain fate, and that the writer wanted his public to accept his Saga as history" (*The Historical Element in the Icelandic Family Sagas* [Glasgow, 1957], p. 25). In the same work Nordal warns that in the sagas "there is... a bewildering duplicity of purpose which goes far to explain the divergencies of opinion, and must be kept in view if we are to read the sagas to our full profit and do justice to them as literature" (p. 15).

3. See Theodore M. Andersson, *The Problem of Icelandic Saga Ori-*

gins (New Haven and London, 1964), pp. 83–84, for a convenient summary of and references to *Landnámabók* problems and scholarship, and pp. 93–94, for a revision of current views on the sagas' dependence on *Landnáma* as a source for genealogies.

4. Older views held that many sagas were put on vellum in the twelfth and early thirteenth centuries from fully developed oral versions. Modern opinions about the dating of each saga may be found in the introductions to the *Fornrit* series (see n. 7). Sigurður Nordal's "Sagalitteraturen," *Nordisk Kultur*, 8 B (1953), 180–273, provides a comprehensive survey of the dates and classifications of all the sagas. A number of books and articles discuss the shift in the dating of the period of saga composition and the implications of placing this period during and after the Sturlung Age (c. 1190–1262). These include Peter Hallberg, *The Icelandic Saga*, tr. Paul Schach (Lincoln, Nebraska, 1962); Einar Ól. Sveinsson, *The Age of the Sturlungs*, tr. Jóhann S. Hannesson, Islandica, 36 (Ithaca, N.Y., 1953), and "The Icelandic Sagas and the Period in Which Their Authors Lived," *Acta Philologica Scandinavica*, 12 (November 1937), 71–90; and R. George Thomas, "The Sturlung Age as an Age of Saga Writing," *GR*, 25 (February 1950), 50–66. In a collection of essays under the title *Höfundur Njálu* (Reykjavík, 1958), Barði Guðmundsson argues that events in the Sturlung Age may be so closely associated with some sagas as to allow their being read as *romans à clef*, an argument that he applies to *Njáls saga* in particular.

5. George Johnstone in "On Translation—II. A Comment," *Saga-Book*, 15 (pt. 4, 1961), 394–402, observes that "the cadences of Old Icelandic prose will translate into true English narrative which sounds abrupt, perhaps, but hardly affected" (p. 397). See also Ian R. Maxwell, "On Translation—I. A Review," *Saga-Book*, 15 (pt. 4, 1961), 383–93; Stefán Einarsson, "Eiríkr Magnússon and His Saga-Translations," *SS*, 13 (May 1934), 17–32; Randolph Quirk, "Dasent, Morris, and Problems of Translation," *Saga-Book*, 14 (pts. 1–2, 1953–55), 64–77; and J. N. Swannell, "William Morris as an Interpreter of Old Norse," *Saga-Book*, 15 (pt. 4, 1961), 365–82.

6. It is necessary to keep in mind that the Icelanders themselves were keenly aware of class status and that their important men considered themselves not unworthy to consort with kings. Einar Ól. Sveinsson notes: "The diffusion of the 'royal blood' [through traditional genealogies] among the Icelanders creates different conditions for their historical writing. Their sense of their own significance is high enough so that the reality around them, or the most memorable part of it, becomes sufficiently important in their eyes to serve as material for their

narratives. And in the case of native material they are not content with writing about nobility. For them, class or station count for nothing, so long as the protagonist is a man of great deeds" (*Age of the Sturlungs*, p. 28).

7. *Brennu-Njáls saga*, ed. Einar Ól. Sveinsson, *Fornrit*, XII (Reykjavík, 1954), ch. 1, p. 7. All future references to and translations from the family sagas will be taken from the *Fornrit* series, 16 vols. (Reykjavík, 1933–). References to *Njáls saga* will include chapter numbers when necessary in order to facilitate reference to other editions and to the latest English translation, in the Penguin Classics series, *Njal's Saga*, trans. Magnus Magnusson and Herman Pálsson (Baltimore, 1960).

This short quotation raises interesting questions. Hallgerðr's brother, Óláfr, is mentioned several more times. Gunnarr enjoys his support, visits him, and receives a watch-dog, Sámr, from him. These events are not found in *Laxdæla*. Did the composer of *Njáls saga* know *Laxdæla saga*? Did he expect his audience to respond to the allusion as readers today can? It seems very probable that he did know it (see *Fornrit*, XII, xxxix–xl, and Einar Ól. Sveinsson, *Um Njálu* [Reykjavík, 1933], pp. 106–20), but the assertion that he knew it very well and used it is vigorously refuted by Andersson in *Problem*, pp. 96–103.

8. Cf. Walter Baetke, *Entstehung*, p. 83: "Die Geschichten [of the family sagas] werden nicht in die Gegenwart, sondern in die Vergangenheit verlegt, aber nicht in eine unbestimmte, romantische Ferne, sondern in eine bestimmte, auch nicht allzu ferne Zeit der eigenen Geschichte." ["The stories (of the family sagas) were set not in the present but in the past, yet not in an undefined, romantic distance but rather in a definite and not too remote time of their own history."]

9. See *Fornrit*, XII, 283, n. 3 and 141, n. 4.

10. "Iceland's heroic age"—the *söguöld*, the period 930–1030 in which the major action of most sagas occurs. W. P. Ker remarks in *Epic and Romance* (1896; rpt. New York, 1957), p. 198, that "the theory of a conglomerate epic may be applied to the Icelandic sagas with some effect."

11. See Julia McGrew, "Faulkner and the Icelanders," *SS*, 31 (February 1959), 1–14.

12. The *Landnámabók* relates this incident between two newly-weds, Hallgerðr and Hallbjǫrn, whose marriage is not happy. Hallbjǫrn has prepared for a trip and enters the women's quarters to urge his wife to accompany him.

> Hallgerðr was sitting on the dais combing her hair. Her hair fell down to the floor; she and Hallgerðr Snúin-brók had the finest hair of all women in Iceland. Hallbjǫrn

bade her stand up and come away; she sat and was silent. Then he caught hold of her and raised her up, and it went thus three times. Then Hallbjǫrn stood still before her and said:

> The linen-veiled Love-Goddess of the ale-cask
> has me play the fool before her face.
> I shun that lady. Never shall I have atonement from her.
> Grief winds its way into my heart-roots.
> Trouble makes me pale.

He twisted her hair around his hand and wanted to yank her off the dais, but she did not stir. Thereupon he drew out his sword and cut off her head; then he went out and rode away. (Tr. from *Landnámabók Islands*, ed. Finnur Jónsson [Copenhagen, 1925], pp. 85–86)

The incident with its atmosphere of suppressed hatred, the attempt at first to solve the issue through a spoken appeal to the law as it were, to the obedience a wife should show a husband, the ritualistic thrice-repeated attempt to implement this appeal, and the resolution in sudden violence all most compactly represent the same kind of process that is spread out over hundreds of pages and decades of time in *Njáls saga*. It is not without interest that here is one of the few references to Hallgerðr Hǫskuldsdóttir outside of *Njáls saga*.

13. See *Njáls saga: The Arna-magnæan Manuscript 468, 4to (Reykjabók)*, ed. Jón Helgason, Manuscripta Islandica, 6 (Copenhagen, 1962), xi, and Einar Ól. Sveinsson, *Studies in the Manuscript Tradition of Njálssaga*, Studia Islandica, 13 (Reykjavik, 1953), 20–21.

14. Cf. George Johnstone, "On Translation—II," who comments: "These verses are frankly contrived, and their artificiality in contrast with the apparent artlessness of the prose, gives an effect which I have not seen elsewhere in the sagas. The poems are centres of emotion in the stream of events, made intense by the very strictness of the formal limitations" (p. 401). For analysis of many issues posed by the presence of such verses see Alois Wolf, "Zur Rolle der vísur in der altnordischen Prosa," *Innsbrucker Beiträge zur Kulturwissenschaft*, 11 (Innsbruck, 1965), 459–84. For a critique of the alleged parallels between Icelandic and Irish saga, see Andreas Heusler, "Die Anfänge der Isländischen Saga," *Abhandlungen der Königlichen Preussischen Akademie der Wissenschaften*, Philosophisch-Historische Klasse, no. 9 (Berlin, 1913), pp. 48–50, and summary in Andersson, *Problem*, pp. 58–60.

15. The passages of *Grettis saga* parallel to *Beowulf* are discussed and set out in R. W. Chambers, *Beowulf: An Introduction to the Study of*

the Poem, 3rd ed. (Cambridge, England, 1959), pp. 48–53 and 146–82. It is difficult to read them without feeling that these episodes must go back to a common Scandinavian source.

16. Sigurður Magnússon notes that "not many years ago a professor at the University of Iceland professed his firm belief in the existence of elves, and many prominent writers have made the same confession" ("The Icelanders," *Icelandic Review*, 5, no. 2 [1967], 21–26). There is an extensive literature on Icelandic dream-lore, past and present. G. Turville-Petre in "Dreams in Icelandic Tradition," *Folklore*, 69 (June 1958), 93–111, comments that modern Icelandic attitudes towards dreams still rely on medieval tradition and cites Margeir Jónsson, *Ráðningar Drauma* (Reykjavík, 1936), who speaks of dream books still in circulation in Iceland today. N. Kershaw Chadwick, "Norse Ghosts," *Folklore*, 57 (June and September 1946), 50–65 and 106–27, is valuable for an understanding of the activities of Icelandic ghosts and their mainland relations.

17. *Fornrit*, II, 212.

18. "Diese unwirkliche Welt ist mit der gleichen Sinnenfälligkeit und Nüchternheit des Stils beschrieben wie die 'reale.'" Siegfried Beyschlag, "Erzählform der Isländersaga," *Wirkendes Wort*, 1, no. 4 (1950–51), p. 224.

19. *Fornrit*, IV, 145.

20. See R. J. Glendenning, "Saints, Sinners, and the Age of the Sturlungs," *SS*, 38 (May 1966), 83–97, and Axel Olrik's comment in *Nordisches Geistesleben in Heidnischer und Frühchristlicher Zeit* (Heidelberg, 1908), p. 142: "In den bitteren Streitjahren der Sturlungen-kämpfe um die Mitte des 13. Jahrhunderts drückt sich die Angst der Seelen andauernd in Gesichten und Träumen aus." ["In the bitter years of strife during the Sturlung quarrels around the middle of the thirteenth century, the anxiety of the Icelandic spirit expressed itself continually in apparitions and dreams."]

21. This remark is intended only as a passing observation on the phenomenon of litotes in Germanic heroic literature. It may also be argued that understatement is in part the reflection of the boldness and self-confidence characteristic of the Norsemen during the centuries of viking exploration, conquest, and colonization. In Iceland today the habit of understatement seems to come from a sensible respect for, rather than an awe of, the situations that confront men there. Robert Scholes and Robert Kellogg in *The Nature of Narrative* (New York, 1966), pp. 166–67, regard litotes as inevitable, given the mode of narration and characterization in early literature. They conclude: "The narrative posture of understatement, associated as it is with the opaque

and static character, is simply a successful narrative formula, well suited to primitive narration, which develops in all cultures as the inevitable style in which heroic narrative is treated" (p. 167). The saga-men did, of course, recognize this "posture of understatement" and strove for it. The trait became an ostentatious mannerism in later *lygi sögur* (see Ker, *Epic and Romance*, p. 218). Lee M. Hollander classifies varieties of this figure in "Litotes in Old Norse," *PMLA*, 53 (March 1938), 1–33; see also his "Verbal Periphrasis and Litotes in Old Norse," *Monatshefte*, 30 (March–April 1938), 182–89, and Otto Springer, "The Style of the Icelandic Family Sagas," *JEGP*, 38, no. 1 (1939), 107–28, especially pp. 122–25 and further references, p. 123, n. 63.

22. The mechanism and significance of this kind of projection is analyzed by C. G. Jung in his essay, "Flying Saucers: A Modern Myth of Things Seen in the Sky," *Civilization in Transition*, tr. R. F. C. Hull (London, 1964), pp. 309–433.

23. Cedric H. Whitman, *Homer and the Heroic Tradition* (Cambridge, Mass., and London, 1958), p. 1. Whitman continues, saying "hence, literary criticism must make its peace with history, and the questions of date and authorship must look for solution not simply to logical or philological method, but also to real aesthetic responsiveness."

24. This style is by no means as stereotyped as some commentators would have it (see, for example, Liestøl, *Origin*, pp. 26–29). Each saga does have its own flavor and own characteristics, some of which survive in translation and others of which will be apparent only to native speakers. Some attempts to establish normal values and to analyze variations from them are Ari C. Bouman, "An Aspect of Style in Icelandic Sagas," *Neophil*, 42 (1958), 5–67, and *Observations on Syntax and Style of Some Icelandic Sagas*, Studia Islandica, 15 (Reykjavík, 1956), 1–72; Peter Hallberg, "Íslendinga Saga och *Egla*, *Laxdæla*, *Eyrbygga*, *Njála*, *Grettla*. Ett Språktest," *MM* (no. iii–iv, 1966 for 1965), 89–105, and "Några Anteckningar om Replik och Dialog i Njáls Saga," *Festschrift Walter Baetke*, ed. Kurt Rudolph et al. (Weimar, 1966), pp. 130–50; and Margaret Jeffrey, *The Discourse in Seven Icelandic Sagas* (Menasha, Wisconsin, 1934).

25. Almost all the discussions of oral composition which in the last three decades have proceeded from the discoveries of Milman Parry deal with poetry. Nevertheless much of this commentary, particularly when it discusses narrative units larger than the poetic formula, illuminates and clarifies many features of the Icelandic sagas. Among the studies in this field that I have found useful and suggestive are: Albert B. Lord, *The Singer of Tales* (Cambridge, Mass., 1960), and "Composition by Theme in Homer and South Slavic Epos," *TAPA*, 82 (1951),

71–80; Whitman, *Homer*; Eric A. Havelock, *Preface to Plato* (Cambridge, Mass., 1963); James A. Notopoulos, "Continuity and Interconnection in Homeric Oral Composition," *TAPA*, 82 (1951), 81–101, and "Parataxis in Homer: A New Approach to Homeric Literary Criticism," *TAPA*, 80 (1949), 1–23; John Finlayson, "Formulaic Technique in *Morte Arthure*," *Anglia*, 81 (1963), 372–93; Scholes and Kellogg, *Nature of Narrative*, esp. pp. 2–56. The recent state and future direction of this field of research are discussed and thorough references are given in Michael Curschmann, "Oral Poetry in Mediaeval English, French, and German Literature: Some Notes on Present Research," *Speculum*, 42 (January 1967), 36–52. Ann Chalmers Watts, *The Lyre and the Harp* (New Haven and London, 1969), is most valuable for its review of the subject, its new commentary, and its full bibliography. Demonstrations that works which are the products of literate writing men may retain features associated with oral compositions are found in Larry D. Benson, "The Literary Character of Anglo-Saxon Formulaic Poetry," *PMLA*, 81 (October 1966), 334–41, and Edward J. Wolff, "Chaucer's Normalized Diction" (Ph.D. diss., Michigan State University, 1966) (see summary in *DA*, 27 [March 1967], 3022a–23b).

26. See Liestøl, *Origins*, pp. 75–79, 99–100, 114–15, and passim; Axel Olrik, "Epische Gesetze der Volksdichtung," *ZDA*, 51 (1909), 1–12; J. H. Delargey, "The Gaelic Story-Teller, *PBA*, 31 (1945), 177–221; Richard M. Dorson, "Oral Styles of American Folk Narrators," *Style in Language*, ed. Thomas A. Sebeok (New York and London, 1960), pp. 21–51; and Jan de Vries, *Altnordische Literaturgeschichte*, rev. ed. (Berlin, 1964–67), II, 314–37.

27. Baetke, following Björn M. Olsen, notes in "Entstehung," pp. 59–60, that there is "in unseren alten Schriften kein Beispiel dafür, dass solche Sagaerzähler sich Isländersagas als Erzählstoff gewählt hätten" ["in our ancient writings no instance supporting the fact that such storytellers might have chosen family sagas as their narrative material"], and Hermann Pálsson in *Sagnaskemmtun Íslendinga* (Reykjavík, 1962), p. 40, also observes that no evidence exists for professional storytellers of family sagas. Any application, moreover, of the term *formulaic* to saga prose would involve a considerable loosening and redefinition of the term away from its usage in the criticism of poetry. Definitions of poetic formulae are based (with some adjustments for Germanic poetry) on Milman Parry's statement that the formula is "a group of words which is regularly employed under the same metrical conditions to express a given essential idea" ("Studies in the Epic Technique of Oral Verse-Making. I: Homer and Homeric Style," *Harvard Studies in Classical Philology*, 41 [1930], p. 80). Different syntactical

criteria would be needed to find in the cadences of saga prose and in their flexibility of expression—different phrases can describe the same motifs—a substitute for the metrical unit of the poetic formula. *Droplaugarsona saga* ends with a reference to one Þorvaldr who is said to have "told this saga" (*Fornrit*, XI, 180) on the basis of handed-down information, but Paul V. Rubow comments that this is simply the old formula found in romance and fairy tale from the earliest time (*Two Essays* [Copenhagen, 1949], p. 34). Rubow's observation can apply to many other frequently occurring phrases in the sagas relating to the mechanics of tale-telling. Concerning these Baetke remarks in "Entstehung," p. 29: "Auch in den Isländersagas haben wir es ohne Zweifel mit stereotypen Wendungen zu tun, die ihrem realistischen Erzählstil entsprechen; durch solche scheinbar objecktiven Hinweise suchen sie die Echtheit ihrer Geschichte zu beglaubigen." ["In the family sagas, moreover, we are dealing without doubt with stereotyped expressions, which suit their realistic narrative style; through such seemingly objective allusions they attempt to verify the genuineness of their story."] Theodore M. Andersson, "The Textual Evidence for an Oral Family Saga," *ANF*, 81 (1966), 1–23, classifies and discusses all such phrases occurring in the family sagas; some, he concludes, do seem genuine markers that the matter they introduce has come from oral tradition. Again, the issue is: to what extent do the family sagas in the manuscripts directly reflect the form and style of the oral traditions which almost all concede did exist about the Icelanders of the saga age?

28. I use the term *literate* in its neutral and technical sense. Often a single, not particularly emphasized detail in a saga will prove to be essential for a clear understanding of subsequent action. This characteristic implies that composer or audience could look back, if need be, to such details; it strikes me as a mark of bookprose. See Paul Schach, "The Anticipatory Literary Setting in the Old Icelandic Sagas," *SS*, 27 (February 1955), 1–13.

29. "Sturla the Historian," *Collected Essays of W. P. Ker*, ed. Charles Whibley, 2 vols. (London, 1925), II, 178.

30. "Die Anfänge," pp. 53–55.

31. Andreas Heusler, *Die Altgermanische Dichtung*, 2nd ed. (Potsdam, 1945), p. 213, cited and commented upon by Andersson.in *Problem*, p. 50.

32. "Nar man således indrömmer den mundtlige medelese (tradition) en overvejende betydning både m.h.t. indhold og dettes faste form— hvad jeg altid har gjort—kan den opfattelse dog hævdes, at nedskriveren ögsa kan have haft betydning, at han ikke har været en rent mekanisk skriver; han kan have lagt en vis farve over enkeltheder og formet ord og sætninger—ganske som enhver mundtlig meddeler kan

have gjort det" (*Den Oldnorske og Oldislandske Litteraturs Historie*, 3 vols. [Copenhagen, 1920-24], II, 206-07). Sigurður Nordal calls attention to this passage in *Hrafnkatla*, Studia Islandica, 7 (Reykjavík, 1940), 76. This important work has been translated by R. George Thomas as *Hrafnkels Saga Freysgoði* (Cardiff, 1958).

33. "Die Sprache unsrer Íslendingasögur vereinigt zwei Eigenschaften: sie ist ungewönlich gut (d.h. hier: klar, kernig, ausdrucksvoll in Wortwahl and Rhythmus), und sie ist ausnehmend natürlich, unpapieren. Beides zusammengenomen erklärt sich nur daraus, dass die Schreiber in ihren mündlichen Vorbildern eine geschulte Erzahlspräche vorfanden und ihr nach Kräften folgten. Bei vielen Sagas denkt man zuerst an ein Diktat: das Pergament fängt die gehörte Sprache des Geschichtenmannes mit der Treue des Phonographen auf. Aber die reichlichen Muster aus dem freien Vortrag setzen die Schreiber instand, neue Stücke in gleicher oder ähnlicher Frische hervorzubringen" ("Die Anfänge," p. 61).

34. Andersson defends these references as well as those in n. 27 as "at least culturally true.... If the institution of saga telling never existed, would a saga writer be likely to invent it? Baetke sees the allusions as so many efforts to substantiate the truth of an account, but the idea of inventing an institution, which everyone knew to be nonexistent, in order to allay doubts is hardly logical" (*Problem*, pp. 110-11). An important reference occurs in *Þorgils saga ok Hafliða* (part of the *Sturlunga* compilation), which speaks of saga telling as part of the entertainment at a wedding in Reykjahólar in 1119. The significance of the reference and earlier interpretations of it are discussed in Peter G. Foote, "Sagnaskemtan: Reykjahólar 1119," *Saga-Book*, 14 (pt. 3, 1955-56), 226-39. Hermann Pálsson brings together and discusses this reference and many others in *Sagnaskemmtun*. Pálsson, it might be said, argues (p. 52) that even as early as 1119 the entertainers Hrólfr and Ingimundr "had read out written sagas which they themselves had composed." Few others would agree with this. It must be added that it is not inconsistent for a bookprosaist to believe in the practice of saga telling. The issue remains the relation of the sagas in manuscripts to the oral tale.

35. *Um Njálu* (Reykjavík, 1933), p. 2.

36. *Dating the Icelandic Sagas* (London, 1958), p. 7.

37. This, and what follows, is an extreme condensation of the positions established by Icelandic and Scandinavian scholarship. These views have been made available to English and American readers in such books as Hallberg's *The Icelandic Saga*; G. Turville-Petre, *Origins of Icelandic Literature* (Oxford, 1953); R. George Thomas, "Studia Islandica," *MLQ*, 11 (September and December 1950), 281-97, 391-403,

which evaluates Nordal's work, and Thomas's translation of *Hrafnkatla*; and Sveinsson's *Dating the Icelandic Sagas*. The work of Lars Lönnroth, who has studied and emphasized the debt Icelandic writing owes to European influence and models, should also be mentioned. His monograph, *European Sources of Icelandic Saga-Writing* (Stockholm, 1965), summarizes his opinions and findings. Also see Peter G. Foote, "Some Account of the Present State of Saga-Research," *Scan*, 4 (November 1965), 115–26.

38. Reasons for considering Snorri the author of *Egils saga* are given in Nordal's introduction to his edition (*Fornrit*, II, lxx–xcv); and given further support by Ólafur Lárusson, *Ætt Egils Halldórssonar og Egils saga*, Studia Islandica, 2 (Reykjavík, 1937), and Peter Hallberg, *Snorri Sturluson och Egils saga Skallagrímssonar*, Studia Islandica, 20 (Reykjavík, 1962).

39. Among others, Axel Olrik observes: "Der Fall des isländischen Freistaats bringt das Aufhören der nationalen Sagadichtung mit sich. Man bevorzugt nunmehr die Märchensaga und wendet auf sie den ausgebildeten ästhetischen Sinn an; ihre phantastischen Elemente werden immer stärker, entfernen sich immer mehr von der Wirklichkeit" (*Nordisches Geistesleben*, p. 142). ["The collapse of the Icelandic republic brought with it the cessation of national saga. People preferred by this time the *Märchensaga* and applied to them a cultivated aesthetic sensibility. Their fairy-tale elements became ever stronger, removing them ever further from reality."] As Olrik implies, a number of these later works were fashioned with skill. Ian R. Maxwell remarks: "I did find that the mind retired in time before a new tale of the young *kolbítr* who trounces the berserk and breaks the spine of the king's negro wrestler. And yet, when the berserk actually swaggered up to the earl's high seat—although like Tiresias, I had foresuffered all—I always stayed to see what happened" ("Pattern in 'Njáls saga,'" *Saga-Book*, 15 [pts. 1–2, 1957–59], 17–47). An excellent study of later Icelandic romance is Margaret Schlauch, *Romance in Iceland* (Princeton, 1934). See also Sveinsson, *Age of the Sturlungs*, pp. 35–36.

40. Tenney Frank, "Classical Scholarship in Medieval Iceland," *American Journal of Philology*, 30, no. 2 (1909), p. 139.

41. For the dating of *Fóstbrœðra saga*, see the introductions to *Fornrit*, III, cxxxix, and *Fornrit*, VI, lxx–lxxvii; also Kemp Malone's review article, "J. M. C. Kroesen, 'Over de compositie der *Fóstbrœðra saga*,'" *Speculum*, 38 (April 1963), 366–68.

42. See *Hrafnkatla*. E. V. Gordon independently arrived at very much the same conclusion at the same time as Nordal in "On *Hrafnkels Saga Freysgoða*," *MÆ*, 8 (February 1939), 1–32.

43. *Problem*, p. 79.

44. "Fast alle machen, teils bewusst, teils unbewusst, der Lehre von der mündlichen Saga Konzessionen" (*Entstehung*, p. 70).

45. "So kam man zu einem tief unbefriedigenden Kompromiss: die schriftlichen Sagas, die wir kennen, stammen zwar nicht aus mündlicher Überlieferung, aber sie sind aus kürzeren Erzählungen aufgebaut, die ihre Verfasser der mündlichen Überlieferung entnahmen" (*Entstehung*, p. 77). ["So a deeply unsatisfying compromise was reached: the written sagas, which we know, surely do not originate from oral tradition, but they are constructed from smallish anecdotes, which their authors did gather from oral tradition."]

46. "Die Ereignisse der Sturlungenzeit gaben in vielem das Vorbild für die Sagawelt" (*Entstehung*, p. 83). ["The experience of the Sturlung Age provided in many respects the model for the saga world."] And, "Man hat daher unrecht, wenn man die Saga, wie oft in literargeschichtlichen Darstellungen, mit der Edda zusammen als Denkmäler altgermanischen, d.h., vorchristlichen Geistes betrachtet. Zum mindesten ist diese Betrachtung einseitig.... Aber die Saga ist, wie wir nun wissen, in christlicher Zeit enstanden und kann daher weder nach Form noch nach Inhalt als altgermanische Dichtung angesehen werden" (p. 86). ["One is therefore incorrect, if one considers saga—as often is the case in works of literary history—together with the Edda as monuments to the ancient Germanic, that is, to the pre-Christian spirit. At the least this way of thinking is one-sided.... But saga, as we now know, developed in the Christian period and can hence be viewed neither with respect to form nor to content as an old Germanic creation."] See also Baetke's remarks, pp. 97–98. These observations are not necessarily original with Baetke, but in view of the Wagnerian glow that has shimmered about so many studies of northern literature, he has probably felt it necessary to emphasize them.

47. For example, Rolf Heller, *Die Literarische Darstellung der Frau in den Isländersagas*, Saga, 2 (Halle, 1958). One must recognize that literary criticism of medieval literature strikes some Continental scholars as an uncertain adventure indeed. "There is unanimity between all in my generation," states F. J. Billeskov Jansen, "that structural analyses have to be able to stand up to an historical check. In the Anglo-American textual expositions there is danger that when concentrating on the text, you are, as it were, absolved from philological and historical verification" (quoted in Göran Printz-Påhlson, "Concepts of Criticism in Scandinavia 1960–1966: I," *Scan*, 6 [May 1967], 1–15).

48. "The Doctrine of Oral Tradition in the Chanson de Geste and Saga," SS, 24 (November 1962), 219–36; *The Icelandic Family Saga* (Cambridge, Mass., 1967); and "Textual Evidence."

49. *Problem*, p. 92.

50. *Problem*, p. 119. On p. 119, n. 63, Andersson adds that "there has been a natural tendency for the spokesmen of bookprose to achieve polemical effects by concentrating on the most doctrinaire and dated aspects of freeprose, especially the assertion of a rigid tradition.... However, the fundamental article of the freeprose theory, as I understand it, is not some unascertainable degree of fixedness in the oral transmission, whether it be 25 per cent, 50 per cent, or 75 per cent, but the assumption that the written sagas were preceded and preconditioned by oral sagas."

51. Scholes and Kellogg, *Nature of Narrative*, pp. 43–51 and 307–11, esp. pp. 44 and 50–51.

52. Curschmann, "Oral Poetry," p. 48.

53. For the effect of literacy on oral societies see Jack Goody and Ian Watt, "The Consequences of Literacy," *Comparative Studies in Society and History*, 5 (1963), 304–45, and Havelock's *Preface to Plato*. Marshall McLuhan's *The Gutenberg Galaxy* (Toronto, 1962) is about this subject, but is chiefly useful for its bibliography and copious extracts from scholarly works. Concerning the elements in primary epic, Rhys Carpenter, *Folk Tale, Fiction, and Saga in the Homeric Epics* (Berkeley and Los Angeles, 1958), p. 22, states: "Saga, which purports to be true fact and happening held fast in popular memory; fiction, which is the persuasive decking out of circumstance with trappings borrowed from contemporary actuality; and folk tale, which is utterly unreal but by no means utterly irrational—all these can be sewn together in the rhapsode's glittering fabric." Also see *Nature of Narrative*, pp. 12 and 48–49, where Scholes and Kellogg comment that "in some respects, the family sagas are epic poems in prose, with the mythic and fabulous element drastically curtailed and replaced by a strong emphasis on the historical and the mimetic. But this curtailment of myth and emphasis on mimesis is so nearly complete as to be at times more suggestive of the novel than the epic."

54. One of the limitations of the sagas as history is that they relate only what is *sögulegt* and omit much about which we would be curious. A good example of the Norseman's concern for making a good story out of a notable event is found in *Orkneyinga saga*. Earl Rǫgnvaldr and his crew have just captured a richly laden merchant vessel. "They were speaking about the event which had just taken place; each man was saying what he thought he had seen. And they discussed who had been the first to board, and they could not agree about it. Then some said that it would make less of an impression if they all did not have the same story about this great deed. And it came about that they all agreed that Earl Rǫgnvaldr should decide the matter and then they

should all support his version" (*Fornrit*, XXXIV, 227). Thereupon the Earl speaks a verse, declaring that Auðun enn rauði had the honor to be the first to board the captured vessel. Scholes and Kellogg discuss the relation between the forms of narrative tradition and history. They begin by noting that "if we should begin in the customary way, by considering an historical account of an event, the epic treatment of it will seem to involve the intrusion of imaginative distortion and contamination with obviously non-historical myths and *topoi*. If, on the other hand, we begin by reconstructing as clear a conception as possible of the oral tradition, we can see the historical event as intruding upon the traditional stock of myths and *topoi*, as requiring some sort of readjustment in the tradition to accommodate it, rather than the other way about" (*Nature of Narrative*, p. 40). Thus Nordal's comment (see n. 2), according to this conception, has matters reversed. What is important to the composer of *Njáls saga* is not that Njáll was a real person who suffered a given fate at a certain time, but that the fate which Njáll suffered was an extremely memorable one, one well suited to serve as a climax to a great narrative. "To write history is so difficult," says Erich Auerbach, "that most historians are forced to make concessions to the technique of legend" (*Mimesis: The Representation of Reality in Western Literature*, tr. Willard Trask [1953; paperback reprint, Princeton, 1968], p. 20).

55. This impression was strongly conveyed to me after reading in Norse and Icelandic law and I find my impression seconded by Scholes and Kellogg when they observe that "the intense cultivation of civil law in Iceland, at the expense of (or in lieu of) every other area of public life, itself necessarily imposed an almost artificial order on the lives of the Icelanders, presenting the saga-men with ready-made materials for narrative presentation, and producing inevitably a unique kind of narrative, tied closely to history and to the actualities of contemporary life" (*Nature of Narrative*, p. 48). Other authorities are more skeptical about the degree to which the Icelanders felt themselves constrained by the law in all clauses of its "artificial complexity." See, for example, Vilhelm Grönbech, *The Culture of the Teutons*, tr. W. Worster, 2 vols. (London and Copenhagen, 1931), I, 78–79.

56. Some idea of the degree to which given scenes or motifs belong to a typical stock is conveyed by the examples amassed and catalogued in Inger M. Boberg, *Motif-Index of Early Icelandic Literature*, Bibliotheca Arnamagnæana, 27 (Copenhagen, 1966); A. C. Kersbergen, *Litteraire motieven in de Njála* (Rotterdam, 1927); and Maarten C. van den Toorn, *Ethics and Moral in Icelandic Saga Literature* (Assen, 1955).

57. Hermann Pálsson's book, *Sagnaskemmtun*, assembles the evi-

dence for this practice, although many conclusions about its mode of existence in the thirteenth century must be based on evidence from later centuries. It should also be noted that the long house could accommodate a good crowd in its central hall. The hall at Flugumýr is estimated to have had space for 240 people; the great hall at the bishop's seat in Garðar in Greenland could accommodate a similar number (Helge Ingstad, *Land Under the Pole Star*, tr. Naomi Walford [London, 1966], p. 187).

58. Trans. from *Þorgils saga Skarða* in *Sturlunga saga*, ed. Guðni Jónsson, 3 vols. (Reykjavík, 1948), III, 351.

59. Þorgils was ambushed in the same house while he was asleep (*Sturlunga saga*, III, 353–54).

60. See *Óláfs saga Tryggvasonar* in *Konunga Sögur*, ed. Guðni Jónsson (Reykjavík, 1947), I, 3–4; *Þiðreks saga af Bern*, ed. Guðni Jónsson (Reykjavík, 1951), I, 3; and *Dunstanus Saga* in *Hakonar Saga*, ed. Gudbrand Vigfusson (London, 1887), p. 385. For the confusion or lack of distinction between hearing a book and reading it, see H. J. Chaytor, *From Script to Print: An Introduction to Medieval Vernacular Literature* (1945; paperback reprint, London, 1966), pp. 5–21. Chaytor makes the point that even solitary readers read aloud to themselves in order to apprehend the text.

61. Lars Lönnroth, *European Sources*, p. 7, notes that in many manuscripts the various saga genres distinguished today are there found side by side, even drawn up to make a continuous story, without concern for their veracity. M. I. Steblin-Kamensky, "On the Nature of Fiction in the Sagas of Icelanders," *Scan*, 6 (November 1967), 77–84, points out that all genres of sagas purported to tell of past events. Although we may divide them according to the distance between the event and their composition, that is, according to the degree to which they appear to be reliable histories, it is most likely, Steblin-Kamensky says, that the Icelanders made no such distinctions.

62. The extensive abbreviation in Icelandic vernacular writing is usually explained as a legacy from the beginning of manuscript writing in Iceland when vellum was scarce, but in fact the extent of the abbreviations increased as time went on, although the Icelanders came to have a plentiful supply of vellum, having a yearly surplus of calves to slaughter in order to maintain a balance between herd size and their limited pasturage. See Sigurður Nordal, "Time and Vellum," *Annual Bulletin of the Modern Humanities Research Association*, no. 24 (November 1952), 15–26, and Hrein Benediktsson, *Early Icelandic Script as Illustrated in Vernacular Texts from the Twelfth and Thirteenth Centuries* (Reykjavík, 1965), p. 86.

63. See Ian Watt, *The Rise of the Novel* (Berkeley and Los Angeles, 1960), esp. pp. 35–59.

64. See Chaytor, *From Script to Print*, pp. 115–37; and Ruth Crosby, "Oral Delivery in the Middle Ages," *Speculum*, 11 (January 1936), 88–110.

65. See Peter G. Foote, "On the Fragmentary Text Concerning St Thomas Becket in Stock. Perg. Fol. Nr. 2," *Saga-Book*, 15 (pt. 4, 1961), 403–50, esp. p. 445, n. 102. For the evolution and distinguishing features of the *sermo simplex*, see Erich Auerbach, *Literary Language and Its Public in Late Latin Antiquity and in the Middle Ages*, tr. Ralph Mannheim (London, 1965). Jan de Vries, *Altnordische Literaturgeschichte*, II, 318, comments on the difference between the Latin and the native style.

66. That the structures of heroic literature tend to incorporate material reflecting contemporary reality is argued, with varying degrees of insistence, by a number of scholars. The extreme position is held by Lord Raglan, *The Hero* (London, 1936), p. 37: "tradition never preserves historical facts." Rhys Carpenter in *Folk Tale* argues for the contemporaneity of Homeric epic with the eighth century Homeric world (see esp. "Saga and Fiction," pp. 23–44). Eric Havelock in *Preface to Plato* agrees, but rightly emphasizes the conservational function of epic literature. Whitman in *Homer* is more cautious (see esp. "The Memory of the Achaeans," pp. 17–45) and he emphasizes the "tenacity of oral poetry to its origins" (p. 27), a tenacity that is certainly documented (with, however, significant qualifications) in Denys Page's important *History and the Homeric Iliad* (Berkeley and Los Angeles, 1966). For sagas in particular, Sveinsson in *Age of the Sturlungs*, Baetke as noted (see n. 46), and Barði Guðmundsson in *Höfundur Njálu*, all see sagas as strong reflections of thirteenth-century Iceland. Van den Toorn in *Ethics and Moral*, p. 48, states that first "the sagas of Icelanders may contain several ancient elements, dating from the Saga Age itself, but their historical value as a whole must be regarded as pertaining to the Writing Time. Secondly, with regard to their ethics, it must be carefully kept in mind that these were *perhaps* governing in the Saga Age, *probably* valid for the Writing Period too, but have to be regarded *in any case* in the light of the latter" (his italics).

67. *Fornrit*, X, 58–59.

68. Margaret Jeffrey in *Discourse*, p. 27, also states that the saga teller would do some verbal mimicking to make clear to the audience who is speaking and how (see also p. 33).

69. Almost all speculation about the identities of the saga-men, who remain, like other tellers of epic tales, anonymous, points to the upper

layers of Icelandic society, to the chieftains and their relatives, many of whom received clerical training, if not ordination. The few cases where one can venture a good guess about the identity of the composer of a saga (e.g., Snorri Sturlusson for *Egils saga* and Sturla Þórðarson, who evidently had something to do with *Grettis saga*) bear out such speculation. See Pálsson, *Sagnaskemmtun*, pp. 94–104, for a recent opinion and summary of views on saga authorship.

70. Sturla Þórðarson, exiled from Iceland in 1263, made his way into the favor of King Magnus of Norway by reciting to him at length the *Huldar saga*, one of the *fornaldar sögur*. Pálsson argues (*Sagnaskemmtun*, p. 116) that Sturla told his version better and gained more applause than previous versions had because he was able to *read* it from manuscripts he had with him, an interpretation of this episode that is not likely to gain much acceptance.

71. *Hrafnkatla*, pp. 53–54. Sveinsson in the introduction to the facsimile edition of *Möðruvallabók* (Copenhagen, 1933), p. 11, notes "the brief and vigorous, but simple and graceful style which is not intended for silent reading, but is evidently designed for recital." And Auerbach cautions that "simplicity is an achievement, not a beginning" (*Literary Language*, p. 186). Andersson calls attention (*Problem*, p. 35) to Niels M. Petersen's *Historiske Fortællinger om Islændernes Færd* (Copenhagen, 1839) in which "Petersen traces the development of the written sagas as a gradual progression from the annalistic notations to a fuller imitation (but not reproduction) of the oral stories."

72. For a concise summary of earlier views on *Njáls saga*, see Sveinsson, *Um Njálu*, pp. 1–17.

73. Andersson calls attention (*Problem*, p. 51) to an early writer who perceived the thematic unity of *Njáls saga*, the Danish critic, Carsten Hauch, in "Indledning til Forelæsninger over Njalssaga og Flere med den Beslægtede Sagaer," *Afhandlinger og Æsthetiske Betragtninger* (Copenhagen, 1855), pp. 411–67. But eighty years later Sveinsson (*Um Njálu*, p. v) still saw it as his main task to show "that *Njáls saga* is an artistic whole, created by one man at a given time and place."

74. *Fornrit*, XII, pp. xxxvii–lx.

75. The composition of *Njáls saga* can be placed near to the year 1280 through its use of certain Norwegian legal codes which were introduced to Iceland after its loss of independence. Investigation into the legal material in *Njáls saga* and the use of such material for dating the work was first extensively carried out by Karl Lehmann and Hans Schnorr von Carolsfeld in *Die Njálssage Insbesondere in Ihren Juristischen Bestandtheilen* (Berlin, 1883); see *Fornrit*, XII, lxxv–lxxxiv, for this and other matters relevant to dating the saga.

76. Sveinsson writes in *Manuscript Tradition*, p. 28: "Apart from the [additional verses] there are no greater material differences between our manuscripts. Occasionally there are some slight discrepancies in the facts, but they are so few and insignificant that they might be detected only by collating the manuscripts." He suggests (p. 16) that this relative uniformity, pleasing to discover in a medieval work, may evince the respect of the scribes for the style of the author. Both main lines of manuscripts go back to a common archetype. Sveinsson conjectures that this may be the fair copy of a rather messy draft either written or dictated by the author and then recopied by a scribe (pp. 166–67).

77. In all, some fifty or sixty vellum and paper manuscripts of *Njáls saga* are extant (*Fornrit*, XII, cxlix). More vellum manuscripts of *Njáls saga* survive than of any other saga, a probable attestation to its popularity (Magnusson and Pálsson, *Njal's Saga* [Baltimore, 1960], p. 9).

78. Northrop Frye, *Anatomy of Criticism* (Princeton, 1957), pp. 246–47: "The basis of generic distinctions in literature appears to be the radical of presentation. Words may be acted in front of a spectator; they may be spoken in front of a listener; they may be sung or chanted; or they may be written for a reader.... The basis of generic criticism in any case is rhetorical, in the sense that the genre is determined by the conditions established between the poet and his public."

CHAPTER 2

1. The events of *Njáls saga* can generally be correlated with historical dates at the expense of some wrenchings and inconsistencies that are not sensed when the saga is read on its own. For a discussion of temporal problems and a chronology of events, see *Njálssaga*, Jónsson, xxxii–xxxvi, and *Fornrit*, XII, lxi–lxviii.

2. See Maarten C. van den Toorn, "Zeit und Tempus in der Saga," *ANF*, 76 (1961), 134–52, esp. p. 137.

3. See Maarten C. van den Toorn, "Zur Struktur der Saga," *ANF*, 73 (1958), 140–68, where one finds (p. 152) that *Egils saga* contains 93,828 syllables, 20,768 of which belong to direct speech, the other 73,060 of which hasten the plot along in an estimated reading time of 5 to 6 hours. Van den Toorn exclaims: "Über die Intensität der Raffung [time-compression] brauchen wir in diesem Fall wohl nicht mehr zu sprechen!"

4. Van den Toorn in "Zur Struktur" points out (p. 150) that saga mimesis includes passages of *Zeitraffung* ("time-compressed passages,"

distant imitation) and *Zeitdeckung* ("time-congruent passages," close imitation, speech), but none of *Zeitdehnung* ("dilation of time," such as interior thought).

5. I have followed the rendering in the Penguin *Njál's Saga* of *Án er illt gengi, nema heiman hafi*, a saying which also appears in *Gísla saga, Droplaugarsonar saga*, and *Hænsa-Þóris saga* (see *Gísla saga*, ed. Finnur Jónsson, Altnordische Saga-Bibliothek, 10 [Halle, 1903], 85, n. 12).

6. *The Discourse in Seven Icelandic Sagas* (Menasha, Wisc., 1934), pp. 16–17.

7. See Paul Schach, "Anticipatory Literary Setting in the Old Icelandic Sagas," *SS*, 27 (February 1955), 1–13, and Einar H. Kvaran, "Landscape in the Sagas: The Beginning of a Background," *TLS* (August 29, 1936), 685–86.

8. See Liestøl, *Origin*, p. 149.

9. In *Origin*, p. 217, Liestøl remarks that the presence of opinionated factions among the audience could also encourage the neutrality and lack of overt judgment of the saga-men.

10. King Haraldr Sigurðarson seems to have had it in mind that saga listening required an attentive audience, for in one famous anecdote he cautions an Icelander who is about to entertain his court at Christmas time that "there is heavy drinking at Christmas time and people will sit to listen to such entertainment only a short while" (see *Morkinskinna*, ed. Finnur Jónsson [Copenhagen, 1932], pp. 199–200). That the story was to be about King Haraldr's exploits may have heightened his concern for its reception.

11. "Other touches remind one of the techniques of the saga-men," e.g., "Gregory relates the whole incident without personal commentary, purely dramatically, shifting the tense and writing in the present as soon as he nears the decisive moment" (*Mimesis: The Representation of Reality in Western Literature*, tr. Willard Trask [1953; paperback reprint, Princeton, 1968], p. 86). "Gregory...gives us dialogues and similar brief utterances by his personages—words which break out in a moment and change the moment into a scene" (p. 87); "brief, spontaneous passages between human beings are dramatized in a most concrete fashion...the actors face one another breathing and alive—a procedure which can hardly be found in antique historiography" (p. 88). Saga readers will notice a familiar ring to such a passage of Gregory's as "immediately he put out the lights and split Sicharius' head with his blade. Sicharius uttered in the last moment of his life a little cry, fell down, and was dead" (p. 81).

12. William Whallon in "Old Testament Poetry and Homeric Epic,"

CL, 18 (Spring 1966), 113–31, criticizes Auerbach's distinction on the grounds that he is comparing two generally dissimilar modes of expression, Greek poetry and Hebrew prose. It may be, as Whallon concludes, that "the first chapter of *Mimesis* contrasts not two inherent attitudes of mind but two dissimilar provinces of literature" (p. 131), but surely that is the whole point. Auerbach is contrasting two modes of representing reality; that one mode is in meter and the other not is beside the point. Auerbach's choice of examples makes its case even in a modern English prose translation of both.

13. *CL*, 15 (Fall 1963), 289–310. W. H. Auden in a T. S. Eliot Memorial Lecture rebroadcast on the BBC Third Programme, January 9, 1968, "The Saga Hero, or Epic and Social Realism," makes use of Auerbach's description of paratactic narration. See also W. H. Auden, "The World of Sagas" in *Secondary Worlds* (New York, 1968). Peter G. Foote in "Some Account of the Present State of Saga Research," *Scan*, 4 (November 1965), 115–26, calls for an examination of the sagas in the light of Auerbach's definitions.

14. By lack of suspense, Fox presumably means that we know what is going to happen in *Njáls saga*, for the "plot" is given away by the title itself, *Brennu-Njáls saga*, the saga of the Burning of Njáll. There is, of course, a high degree of dramatic suspense, just as there is in the *Odyssey*, about how an event will be fulfilled.

15. *Fornrit*, VII, 261–62.

16. Flosi's dream in *Njáls saga* (ch. 133, pp. 346–348) is in part modelled on a source found in Gregory the Great's *Dialogues*, the dream of one Anastasius (Migne, *Patrologia Latina*, LXXVII, 185). Its adaptation by the saga-man is discussed in Einar Ól. Sveinsson, *Á Njálsbúð* (Reykjavík, 1943), pp. 8–13; and by G. Turville-Petre, *Origins of Icelandic Literature* (Oxford, 1953), pp. 136–37. Gísli's good and evil dreams obviously are of Christian inspiration. The Battle of Clontarf at the end of *Njáls saga* would seem to offer grounds for exegetical exercises. One wonders, too, if the events in *Njáls saga* prior to the conversion may not be regarded as taking place under a dispensation parallel to the Old Law of the Old Testament and the events afterwards under the New Law ushered in by Christ. Such a speculation could open the way to a quasi-figural linking between parallel events in those halves of the saga separated by the conversion.

17. See, for example, W. P. Ker, *Epic and Romance* (New York, 1957), pp. 181–83; and Andersson, *Family Saga*, pp. 65–93.

18. *Egils saga Skalla-Grímssonar*, *Fornrit*, II, 226 and 296–97.

19. For example, *Sturlunga saga*, II, 11–12.

20. Liestøl in *Origin*, pp. 156–57, speculates on the possible influ-

ence of the Bible on saga prose and Sveinsson detects some features
of clerical style in *Njáls saga* (*Fornrit*, XII, cxxxv), Fredrik Paasche's
introduction to *Homilu-Bók*, ed. Einar Munksgaard, CCIMÆ, 8 (Copenhagen, 1935), pp. 7–22, conjectures that some of the distinctive features
of Icelandic prose were derived from the example of Latin texts. See
also Jan de Vries, "Die isländische Saga und die mündliche Überlieferung," *Märchen, Mythos, Dichtung*, ed. Hugo Kuhn and Kurt Schier
(Munich, 1963), pp. 169–76, esp. p. 173.

21. Lars Lönnroth, *European Sources of Icelandic Saga-Writing*
(Stockholm, 1965), p. 24. Peter Hallberg criticizes Lönnroth's approach in "Medeltidslatin och sagaprosa," *ANF*, 81 (1966), 258–76.

22. The pervasive influence of European literature on twelfth century
Icelandic writing is clearly brought out in G. Turville-Petre's *Origins
of Icelandic Literature*.

23. *European Sources*, p. 11.

24. R. George Thomas remarks in "Studia Islandica," *MLQ*, 11
(September and December 1950), 400, that "the medievalist may find
here little that is familiar to his studies of Western Christendom, but it
is evidence that cannot be ignored of the way men in the thirteenth
century thought and acted when the influence of the church, supported
by the secular arm, was weak."

25. See Peter Hallberg, "Några Anteckningar om Replik och Dialog
i Njáls saga," *Festschrift Walter Baetke*, ed. Kurt Rudolf et al. (Weimar,
1966), pp. 130–50. Njáll in 150 speeches utters 4,725 words; Flosi in
115 speeches speaks 2,997 words; and Gunnarr comes in third with 150
speeches and 2,525 words (pp. 149–50).

26. In *Age of the Sturlungs*, Islandica, 36 (Ithaca, N.Y., 1953), Einar
Ól. Sveinsson sees the church as "bound to try to crush that which was
the heart of the Old Icelandic view of life" (p. 33). The sagas came
down on the side of what was good in the Sturlung Age. "And in this
changeable atmosphere grow the masterpieces of the age, the Sagas of
Icelanders. They have their root in the virtues that were fighting for
their existence, and are thus, as great literature so often is, a negation
of the principal elements in the life and manners of their age" (p. 75).
To R. George Thomas, the "best qualities of the Family Sagas suggest
a literature of retrospect" ("The Sturlung Age as an Age of Saga
Writing," *GR*, 25 (February 1950), p. 66). In *The Icelandic Saga*, tr.
Paul Schach (Lincoln, Neb., 1962), Peter Hallberg sees the virtues up-
held in the sagas as indeed those of an idealized pagan heroicism
(p. 108), but maintains (p. 113) that the old way of life with its virtues
and vices of "honor, self-assertion, and vengeance," endured through
to the Sturlung Age scarcely unaffected by any leaven of Christianity.

Yet the brawls of the Sturlung Age come nowhere near equalling the barbarities committed by "Christians" on the mainland of Europe.

27. For audience control on sagas, see Liestøl's remarks in *Origin*, pp. 31, 132, and 217.

28. I have not distorted or misrepresented Havelock's arguments by setting these two passages together out of order. That which follows on p. 171 is a conclusion similar to the material on pp. 167–68.

29. That epic poetry preserved and transmitted the information necessary for an oral culture is a thesis argued throughout Havelock's *Preface to Plato* (Cambridge, Mass., 1963), e.g., in assertions "that the warp and woof of Homer is didactic, and that the tale is made subservient to the task of accommodating the weight of educational materials which lie within it" (p. 61). See further, on p. 80:

> The boundary between moral behaviour and skilled behaviour in an oral culture is rather thin. This is inherent in the fact that so much of social behaviour and deportment had to be ceremonial, or had to be recorded ceremonially, which may amount to very much the same thing.
> Procedures have to be observed, and are recorded as operations made up of distinct acts precisely defined, which must follow each other in a certain order.... The ritual [reference is to a sacrifice in the *Iliad*] is an operation made up of distinct acts, precisely defined, which must follow each other in the order stated. The narrative requires that these be put into the past tense. But the series conveys the effect of a procedure carefully generalised so as to be easily imitable. It is a piece of preserved know-how.

30. An oral culture places a premium on intelligence. "We can hazard the guess, in short, that that specific and unique Hellenic intelligence, the source or cause of which has baffled all historians, received its original nurture in communities in which the oral technique of preserved communication threw power and so prestige into the hands of the orally more gifted. It made the competition for power, endemic among all human beings, identifiable with the competition for intelligence. The total non-literacy of Homeric Greece, so far from being a drawback, was the necessary medium in which the Greek genius could be nursed to its maturity" (*Preface to Plato*, p. 127). This remark throws light on the power and prestige of the Icelandic law-speakers and skalds (see n. 33).

31. When *Njáls saga* is viewed as a broad and authoritative summation of the written saga tradition, it is again illuminated by Havelock's remarks concerning the oral "great story."

> Finally, while the rhythmic memory can in theory accommodate a great range of short episodic stories, a sophisti-

cated oral culture demands a *paideia* which shall be coherent, a corpus of semi-consistent mores transmissible as a corpus from generation to generation. The tighter is the group structure, or the sense of common ethos shared by communities who speak a common tongue, the more urgent is the need for the creation of a great story which shall compendiously gather up all the little stories into a coherent succession, grouped round several prominent agents who shall act and speak with some over-all consistency. For the patterns of public and private behaviour, as recalled in a thousand specific episodes, are multiform and various, not reducible to a catechism, but nevertheless to be recollected and repeated at need. What shall be the frame of reference, the chapter headings, the library catalogue, within which the memory can find markers which shall point up relevant saws and wise instances? Only the over-all plot of a great story can serve, a plot memorised in thousands of lines but reducible to specific episodes which shall yield specific examples. (*Preface to Plato*, pp. 175–76.)

Cedric H. Whitman, in *Homer* (p. 80), makes the needed additional point that the introduction of writing and the final elaboration of the "great story" go hand in hand. "If one seeks the motivation for the transference of oral verse to written form it must lie in the disseminated knowledge of writing itself, in its disintegration of the belief that unwritten songs never change, and in the promise of real fixity. One ought, therefore, to associate the great epic, in contrast to the short epic song, not only with festival audiences, but also with writing, not because writing is necessary for its creation, but because the monumental purpose of the large epic is profoundly served by anything which bestows fixity of form."

32. On the level of literacy in thirteenth-century Iceland, see Einar Ól. Sveinsson, "Lestrarkunnátta Íslendinga í fornöld," in *Við Uppsprietturnar* (Reykjavík, 1956), pp. 166–92.

33. Norse and Icelandic culture was necessarily oral until the advent of Christianity and, even then, until well beyond the period of formal conversion. Cultural information was preserved in oral memory. Eddic poetry preserves heroic myth and much humble gnomic lore (see, for example, Lee M. Hollander, "The Didactic Purpose of Some Eddic Lays," *GR*, 1, no. 1 [1926], 72–79). Skaldic poetry (whose complicated tropes and figures largely derived from and depended on the stories told in the Eddic poetry) preserved history insofar as the deeds and battles of the kings whom the skalds served and memorialized can be said to be history. These poets were not merely court entertainers, but performed important roles as advisors and diplomats; many episodes in *Heimskringla* make this clear. In Iceland the law-speaker (*lǫgsǫgumaðr*), who filled the most important post provided for in the Icelandic constitution, was

required to recite *from memory* a portion of the law at each meeting of the Althing, three years being alloted for a complete recital.

The first great impetus to transfer important social statistics to the written record probably occurred at the end of the eleventh century in connection with the organization of Iceland into dioceses and the establishment of tithing laws (see Hrein Benediktsson, *Early Icelandic Script as Illustrated in Vernacular Texts from the Twelfth and Thirteenth Centuries* [Reykjavík, 1965], pp. 16–17). But the law-speaker was not eased in his task until 1117–1118, when, according to Ari Þorgilsson in the *Íslendingbók*, the most important portions of the laws, not surprisingly those dealing with manslaughter, were transferred to written codes, which later came to include the entire body of law. This was probably the first writing in the vernacular (*Early Icelandic Script*, p. 16).

It must be remembered that the availability of script, even of an alphabet, and the presence of literate individuals do not transform a society overnight, as Jack Goody and Ian Watt point out in ''The Consequences of Literacy,'' *Comparative Studies in Society and History*, 5 (1963), 304–45. The Mycenaeans used their linear B only for mundane inventory lists and there is no evidence that the later Greeks used it at all (see ''The Memory of the Achaeans,'' in *Homer*, pp. 17–45 and references). The Norsemen had a runic alphabet but reserved it for brief inscriptions and magical incantations. That fifth-century Athenians could scratch their names (or get someone to scratch their names for them) on potsherds used for ballots or that thirteenth-century Icelandic farmers could sign their names to parish records does not necessarily mean that a large portion of the community could read with ease or were at home in the world of letters.

It is true that no society since the Greeks has undergone their experience, which is unique. Here a highly developed and sophisticated oral culture under the impact of the introduction of the alphabet transformed itself, without overbearing outside influence, into a dynamic, literate, highly intellectual culture. The oral culture of the Germanic tribes was by no means as advanced and was no match for the assimilating powers of Western Christianity. But commentary on the Greek experience, if applied with due regard for differences, is relevant to the Icelandic experience as well. Iceland, of all the Germanic countries, developed furthest along the way open to an oral community before it met with Christian culture. And the extent of this development seems to have left its mark on the later evolution of written Icelandic literature.

34. The great amount of legal material in *Njáls saga* would seem to be an exception to the statement that narrative genres were freed from

their burden of cultural information. I argue below (see ch. 5) that the author of *Njáls saga* uses these swaths of legal technicalities for aesthetic and thematic purposes. Certainly the law as it is represented in *Njáls saga* is not an accurate reflection of Icelandic practice under the Norwegian monarchy or in the days of the republic.

35. "Narrative, oral or written, could move closer to entertainment." The decline of skaldic poetry and the rising popularity of ballads from the fourteenth century on is evidence for this statement. Even the *rímur*, which preserved much of the diction and metrics of skaldic poetry, more often than not derived their stories from the *fornaldar sögur*.

CHAPTER 3

1. In his notes for Kári's fight (*Njálssaga* [Jónsson], p. 184), Finnur Jónsson also calls attention to the similarity between the styles of Gunnarr and Kári. In the saga itself, Flosi, a reliable spokesman, heavily underlines the affinity between the two men. When he learns that Kári has escaped the Burning, Flosi says, "You have told us that which will bode no easy peace for us, for that man has now escaped who most nearly approaches Gunnarr of Hlíðarendi in all respects" (ch. 130, p. 335).

2. Gunnarr appears in all his finery in ch. 33, p. 85; Kári in ch. 84, p. 203.

3. In *The Icelandic Saga*, tr. Paul Schach (Lincoln, Neb., 1962), pp. 32–33, Peter Hallberg describes the execution of Sturla Sighvatsson, who, felled by exhaustion and wounds at the battle of Örlyggsstaðir, is set upon by the vengeful chieftains, and he comments:

> One seeks in vain in the Sagas of Icelanders for anything remotely approaching these revolting details. Here in *Sturlunga* the fighting is more petty, but at the same time more cruel. No powerful death-dealing blows are exchanged, no heads are split down to the shoulder at a single stroke. The assailant picks and pokes cautiously with his weapons, and his courage rises in proportion to his adversary's defenselessness and seems to reach its climax when he is dead [cf. the scenes of Grettir's death quoted in ch. 2 above].... When one reads this authentic contemporary report by an eyewitness, one has a strong impression that the battle descriptions in the classical sagas must have represented something belonging to the far distant past for the Icelanders of the Sturlung Age. And at any rate one at least has the right to raise the question whether the sagas' heroic ideals and warrior-ethics were not in es-

sence the fond dream and idealized fiction of a later epoch rather than the depiction of a once-existing reality.

4. "Unnr was extravagant [*ǫrlynd mjǫk*] and short-sighted about money matters [*óforsjál um fjárhagi*], and her goods began to waste away [*eyðask*], so that she possessed nothing except some land and personal articles" (ch. 18, p. 52). This is strong language.

5. "One day, when men were going to the Law Rock, Mǫrðr named his witnesses and announced a suit against Hrútr for his daughter's dowry which he reckoned at ninety hundreds ..." (ch. 8, p. 27).

6. The proverb occurs in *Njáls saga* in ch. 42, p. 109; ch. 99, p. 253; and ch. 134, p. 349.

7. For discussions and reviews of terminology, see *Nature of Narrative*, p. 25; and Michael Curschmann, "Oral Poetry in Mediaeval English, French, and German Literature: Some Notes on Present Research," *Speculum*, 42 (January 1967), esp. pp. 40–41.

8. The relationship between courtship and travel also appears in *Gunnlaugs saga*, and *Bjarnar saga hítdælakappa*, where the betrothal is consummated; in *Hallfreðar saga*, *Kormáks saga*, *Víga-Glúms saga*, *Laxdæla saga*, and *Þorsteins saga hvíta*, where an engagement or love affair is frustrated one way or another; and in *Ljósvetninga saga* in which Brandr seduces Friðgerðr, then travels to Norway where news of pregnancy leads only to feuding and Brandr's eventual death in exile.

9. "Pattern," p. 25.

10. Lee M. Hollander in review article, *Speculum*, 38 (April 1963), 328. For a similar view see Maarten van den Toorn, "Zur Struktur der Saga," *ANF*, 73 (1958), p. 149.

11. "Patterned sequences." The phrase belongs to Scholes and Kellogg, *Nature of Narrative*, p. 27, but the concept is Albert B. Lord's in *The Singer of Tales* (Cambridge, Mass., 1960), pp. 96–97.

12. In "Pattern," Ian R. Maxwell has shown how the first chapter of *Njáls saga* presupposes these first two episodes.

13. Einar Ól. Sveinsson describes this process in his poetic style. "In the conflict of the saga is a regular cadence. This at once becomes apparent in the fixed pattern of the episode, which begins as a rising wave, increasing in might until the main events pass over. Then the turbulence becomes still, and many episodes end with a dead calm and cloudless evening sky. Next morning foreboding clouds can be discerned out against the horizon, which grow and draw near until a new storm is overhead" (*Fornrit*, XII, cxxvii).

14. See M. I. Steblin-Kamensky, "On the Nature of Fiction in the Sagas of Icelanders," *Scan*, 6 (November 1967), 77–84. Kamensky emphasizes the limited selection of similar events, out of the total range

of possible reportable experience, with which the sagas content themselves.

15. I use the word *compose* in its neutral sense. It is quite clear that no conception of inspired creation by an individual author was available to medieval Icelanders insofar as prose was concerned. See M. I. Steblin-Kamensky, "An Attempt at a Semantic Approach to the Problems of Authorship in Old Icelandic Literature," *ANF*, 81 (1966), 24–34.

16. For the concept of displacement, see Northrop Frye, *Anatomy of Criticism* (Princeton, 1957), pp. 33–35, and "Myth, Fiction, and Displacement," *Dædalus*, 90 (Summer 1961), 587–605.

17. Cf. Northrop Frye, *A Natural Perspective: The Development of Shakespearean Comedy and Romance* (New York and London, 1965), p. 61: "Yet the bumps and hollows of the story being told follow the contour of the myth beneath, and as literature develops greater variety and independence of expression, these mythical shapes become the conventions that establish the general framework of narratives. Hence the literary convention enables the poet to recapture something of the pure and primitive identity of myth."

18. Chapter twenty-three of *Njáls saga* presents an example of a displaced mythic reference and the problem of its interpretation. Gunnarr's disguise as the rascally peddler, Kaupa-Heðinn, is finally penetrated when the men of Hǫskuldr's household recall various peeps and gleams of rich clothing underneath his coarse overcoat (p. 64). This is a folklore motif, which is frequently associated with Óðinn, who, as Gunnarr has, wanders about in disguise, his face hidden, and whose true identity only dawns upon his hosts after his departure. But what can one say about its function here? Is one supposed to make a connection with Gunnarr as a godlike hero? Is the combination of his fine clothing underneath his shabby camouflage a symbol of Gunnarr's boldness joined with Njáll's cunning? Or is it just a stock motif, a hint of mystery, that is neither explained nor resolved? One may note how responses on this level involve works from all periods. Perhaps the most familiar undisplaced appearance of this motif occurs in the first act of Wagner's *Die Walküre* when Sieglinde describes to Siegmund the uninvited arrival of a mysterious stranger (Wotan) at Hunding's wedding. A twentieth-century experience of a nineteenth-century opera based in turn on a rehashing of Norse and Germanic legend mingles with a reading of the thirteenth-century saga. The effect obviously was not intended by the saga-man, but nevertheless it is there.

19. For an attempt to find a single structure underlying the large majority of the family sagas, see Andersson, *Family Saga*.

20. Archetypes, in Jung's terminology, are, first of all, forms; they are unfilled, abstract patterns of mental energy (libido) which animate and shape the human psyche and which exist in a region not easily penetrated by the ego of the conscious mind. This energy may be tapped, organized, utilized, brought to the conscious, incorporated, and expended by means of various symbols and ritual acts which serve to manifest and delineate a given archetype. A great many diverse concrete images and acts may belong to a given archetype. See C. G. Jung, *The Archetypes and the Collective Unconscious*, tr. R. F. C. Hull (New York and London, 1959), pp. 79-80.

21. See Robert P. Creed, "On the Possibility of Criticizing Old English Poetry," *TSLL*, 3 (Spring 1961), 97-106, and Lord, *Singer of Tales*, p. 148, who says:

> Each theme, small or large—one might even say, each formula—has around it an aura of meaning which has been put there by all the contexts in which it has occurred in the past. It is the meaning that has been given it by the tradition in its creativeness. To any given poet at any given time, this meaning involves all the occasions on which he has used the theme, especially those contexts in which he uses it most frequently; it involves also all the occasions on which he has heard it used by others.... To the audience the meaning of the theme involves its own experience of it as well. The communication of this supra-meaning is possible because of the community of experience of poet and audience. At our distance of time and space we can approach an understanding of the supra-meaning only by steeping ourselves in as much material in traditional poetry or in a given tradition as is available.

22. The idea was suggested by Whitman's remark in *Homer*, p. 100, that "if [in Homer's style] the sentences are simple, and strung together, the motifs in the large show a strong subordinating syntax, not, indeed, in their direct relations with each other, but in relation to the design of the whole."

23. As an example of such allusiveness, in chapter twelve, Hrútr, as an extra tender of good will, gives Ósvífr a cloak (*skikkja*, p. 40) in addition to the compensation Hǫskuldr is offering. In chapter 123, Njáll, as a final touch, adds a long silk cloak (*silkislæðr*) to the compensation that has been heaped up for Flosi. This is the gesture Flosi chooses to interpret as an insult and hence as an excuse to break off the arbitration and settle for nothing but blood revenge. When the saga is first read, the gesture of Hrútr passes almost unnoticed. On the second reading, it does summon to mind Njáll's fatal gesture 111 chapters further on, acting almost as a Wagnerian *leit-motiv*, calling up in one

brief phrase the memory and knowledge of much trouble to come. I doubt if the association is a deliberate effect of the saga-man's, but, again, it is fitting.

24. Conversely, Njáll's burning is foreshadowed at Gunnarr's last stand, when Mǫrðr Valgarðsson twice suggests that his attackers burn Gunnarr within and is twice strongly rebuked for it by Gizurr (ch. 77, p. 188).

25. Barði Guðmundsson discusses the close parallels between the Burning of Njáll and the Burning at Flugumýr in "Nu taka öll husin að loga," *Höfundur Njálu* (Reykjavík, 1958), pp. 225–34. W. P. Ker translates some of the Flugumýr episode in *Sturlunga* in *Epic and Romance* (New York, 1957), pp. 260–64.

26. *Njal's Saga*, p. 26.

27. "Pattern," p. 22.

28. The saga is named in the last sentence, "And there I conclude the saga of the Burning of Njáll" (ch. 159, p. 464).

29. *Hvat íslenzkra manna væri á skipi*...(ch. 3, p. 12). Sveinsson points out (*Fornrit*, XII, cxxxiv) that skillful placing of primary stress on the most important word of a phrase is one of the marks of *Njáls saga*'s style.

30. For a list of Queen Gunnhildr's appearances in saga literature see under her name in *Nafnaskrá, Islendinga Sögur*, XIII. Most sources suggest she had Lappish parentage, and that was always a sign of trouble ahead for honest vikings. Various writings describe her rule as the worst her country ever had. In Icelandic folklore she was credited with power to assume the shape of different animals in order to enjoy intercourse with the male of the species (see Jónas Jónasson, *Íslenzkir Þjóðhættir* [Reykjavík, 1961], p. 165, n. 4). I am indebted to Richard M. Perkins for showing me work in progress concerning Queen Gunnhildr and for discussions with him about her.

31. For the contribution to the unity of *Njáls saga* of such large patterns as they repeat themselves in the course of the narrative, see Anne Martha Saxon (now Mrs. F. Slater), "Unity and Narrative Technique in the *Brennu-Njáls Saga*" (Ph.D. diss., University of California, Berkeley, 1964).

32. A similar point is made by Andersson about symbolic acts of revenge in *Fóstbrœðra saga* where "the danger becomes more imminent with each act since each act represents an artificial repression, a substitute for direct action" (*Family Saga*, p. 44).

33. I will have more to say on this scene in my concluding chapter. One thing to note here is the undertone of feeling that a settlement by appeal to legal recourse was "the least honorable alternative" (*Family*

Saga, p. 19) and that forbearance and in particular Christian forbearance and mercy were somehow sissy, unmanly, and contemptible (see Albert Morey Sturtevant, "The Contemptuous Sense of the Old Norse Adjective Hvítr 'White, Fair,' " *SS*, 24 [August 1952], 119-21). The issue is squarely faced in *Njáls saga* in the assembly scene in chapter 123 when Flosi rakes up an old taunt of Hallgerðr's that Njáll's beardlessness is a sign of effeminacy and Skarpheðinn retorts: "You can know this, that he is a man because he has gotten sons with his wife. Few of our kinsmen have so lain unatoned for beside our house that we have not avenged them" (p. 314). Skarpheðinn pushes things too far the other way, but the point here is that it is Njáll, a wise, gentle, and by now a Christian man, who is being defended.

34. *Homer*, p. 117.

35. *Serða* is a strong and vulgar word and can imply unnatural as well as normal forms of intercourse. Its use by the young boy helps account for Hǫskuldr's sudden anger.

36. "The 'Children's Judgement' in the 'Njála' and 'Gunnalaugssaga [sic] Ormstungu,' " *Studies in Language and Literature in Honour of Margaret Schlauch* (Warsaw, 1966), pp. 327-33.

37. Cf. Wilhelm Grönbech, *The Culture of the Teutons*, tr. W. Worster (London and Copenhagen, 1931), I, 72-73, where he refers to Hallr's speech of reconciliation as a "great thing, all but superhuman."

38. "Pattern."

39. *Family Saga*, p. 33.

40. Andersson makes this same qualification by allowing for a "coordinate arrangement" of episodes that are not in causal relationship to one another (*Family Saga*, p. 35).

41. "The 'Children's Judgement,' " p. 330.

CHAPTER 4

1. Paul Schach in "Some Forms of Writer Intrusion in the *Islendingasögur*," *SS*, 42 (May 1970), 128-56, surveys and discusses scribal or authorial first person references in the family sagas. His research tends to reverse my feeling that the particular wording at the end of *Njáls saga*, which in its use of the personal "I" differs from other manuscripts of *Njáls saga*, should be assigned to the scribe of the *Möðruvallabók*. This great codex contains ten other sagas in addition to *Njáls saga*, all written out in the same hand, a long labor of love indeed. (There is a facsimile edition, CCIMÆ, 5 [Copenhagen, 1933].) Comparison of the conclusions of the other sagas in the codex to that

of *Njáls saga* shows that most of the other sagas use an impersonal form of conclusion (e.g., *Kormáks saga*, "*Ok lykr þar sǫgu þessi*"), but *Finnboga saga*, the third in order, uses the same phrasing that concludes *Njáls saga*. The point remains that for my purposes it does not matter who wrote down these words. The concept of individual authorship (as we understand the word today) did not exist in thirteenth-century Iceland (see M. I. Steblin-Kamensky, "An Attempt"). I wish here to thank Prof. Ole Widding for his great kindness in allowing me to inspect the *Möðruvallabók* at the Arnamagnæan Institute in Copenhagen and for his time in discussing this passage with me.

2. *Family Saga:* Since I disagree at times with Professor Andersson in this chapter, I should like to acknowledge the many times I have silently agreed with his commentary and the many fruitful lines of thought that commentary has opened.

3. M. I. Steblin-Kamensky in "On the Nature of Fiction in the Sagas of Icelanders," *Scan*, 6 (November 1967), 77–84, contends that no generic distinction may be made between *Sturlunga saga* and the family sagas. Both avail themselves of the same style and the same narrative techniques and forms. But as the matter related moves further back in time, these narrative devices are seen more clearly for the artistic means they are. Denton Fox in "*Njáls Saga* and Western Literary Tradition" observes that *Njáls saga*, *Beowulf*, the Homeric epics, the *Chanson de Roland*, and other epic works seem distanced from their events by two to four hundred years, giving a perspective where significant events stand out or have already been made to stand out by tradition (p. 290, n. 3). Liestøl in *Origin*, pp. 71–73, has remarks and figures contrasting the family sagas with *Sturlunga*.

4. Lars Lönnroth, *European Sources of Icelandic Saga-Writing* (Stockholm, 1965).

5. *Family Saga*, p. 64.

6. Lee M. Hollander argues (in "Verbal Periphrasis and Litotes in Old Norse," *Monatshefte*, 30 [March-April 1938], 182–89) that even verbs such as *þykkja* ("to think to be"; impers., "to seem to one," "one thinks") and *hyggja* ("to think," "to believe") which appear to offer glimpses into the inner thoughts of saga characters often are used in a neutral objective sense; *þykkja* as "to know," "to see"; *hyggja* almost as "to be." W. P. Ker's chapter, "The Art of Narrative," in *Epic and Romance* (New York, 1957), pp. 235–45, contains durable and incisive commentary on the conventions of saga-telling; see also Scholes and Kellogg, *Nature of Narrative*, pp. 171–75. M. C. van den Toorn discusses point of view in "Erzählsituation und Perspektive in der Saga," *ANF*, 77 (1962), 68–83, and in "Zeit und Tempus in der Saga,"

ANF, 76 (1961), 134–52, he interestingly relates the alternation of past and present verb tenses in saga style to the self-effacement of the narrator.

7. I have in mind the passage in Andersson's *Family Saga*, p. 32, where, after describing the conventions of saga-telling, he goes on to say that

> there is no guiding principle laid down by the author in order to give his material a specific import. He draws no general conclusions and invites his reader to draw none. In this sense the saga is not interpretable. The critic, whose congenital belief it has been, from the Homeric commentators on, that a moral or meaning is inherent in literature, has nevertheless refrained from exercising his wiles on the saga. . . .
> In short, the saga comes very close to pure narrative without ulterior aims of any kind, much closer, for example, than the modern practitioners of objectivity whose work is, after all, socially or philosophically loaded.

The statement is representative of prevailing past opinion on the objectivity of saga style. Andersson has stated, however, in a private communication that he will modify this position in an article forthcoming in *Speculum*; in the meantime Lars Lönnroth has published his "Rhetorical Persuasion in the Sagas," *SS*, 42 (May 1970), 157–89. His arguments are similar to mine in that both are indebted to Wayne Booth, *The Rhetoric of Fiction* (Chicago and London, 1961) and both use extensive examples from *Njáls saga*. In development of concepts, however, and in choice of examples our efforts seem to complement rather than duplicate one another.

8. Northrop Frye, *Anatomy of Criticism* (Princeton, 1957), pp. 52–53.

9. In these comments and in what follows my debt to the concepts and terminology of Wayne Booth, *The Rhetoric of Fiction*, will be obvious.

10. Fox, in "*Njáls Saga* and Western Literary Tradition," Maxwell, in "Pattern," and Anne Saxon, in "Unity and Narrative Technique in the *Brennu-Njáls Saga*" (Ph.D. diss., University of California, Berkeley, 1964), discuss issues relevant to this statement; for Gunnarr as representative of the best of the old order see Lars Lönnroth, "The Noble Heathen: A Theme in the Sagas," *SS*, 41 (February 1969), 1–29.

11. "Textual Evidence," esp. pp. 13–14.

12. Njáll forsees the manner of his own death (ch. 55, p. 139) but only tells Gunnarr that it will be caused by "that, which all will least expect." Ian R. Maxwell in "Pattern," pp. 28–29, says very much the same thing about this seating arrangement. I had noted it and had been

led to reflect on it by the apparently functionless disclaimer of further information before I read Maxwell's article. A similar tableau may be discerned in *Beowulf*, ll. 1159b–68a, where attention is drawn to it by the poet's use of extra-length lines. There Hroðgar, his nephew Hroþulf, and his counsellor, Unferð, sit peacefully together, but the poet hints at what he and the audience already know, that those peaceful bonds will be shattered in future years when Hroþulf will seize the throne and have Hroðgar's son Hreðric put to death. See James L. Rosier, "Design for Treachery: The Unferth Intrigue," *PMLA*, 77 (March 1962), 1–7.

13. Skarpheðinn thoughtfully saves one of the teeth and uses it to dash out the eye of Þráinn's nephew, Gunnarr Lambason, at the Burning (ch. 130, p. 333), another reminder that the Sigfússon-Njálsson feud is the central conflict of the saga.

14. Mǫrðr agrees to help Þorgeirr Starkaðarsson only when a large payment is offered (ch. 65, p. 162); stays in his bed rather than intervene in a flight between his friend Otkell and Gunnarr (ch. 54, p. 138); agrees to support Kári only when Þorkatla, his wife, threatens to leave his bed (ch. 135, p. 356).

15. "*It mesta illmenni*" (p. 92). As might be expected Kolr and Svartr appear nowhere else in saga tradition (p. 92, n. 2).

16. That is, Ketill of Mǫrk (ch. 112, p. 283), Runólfr of Dale (ch. 115, p. 289), Hallr of Síða (ch. 119, p. 297), and Gizurr the White who says (ch. 132, p. 345) that throughout the whole affair Mǫrðr has behaved the worst.

17. See M. C. van den Toorn, "Zeit und Tempus," for further effects of the narrator's stance behind the participants (I have used his description of this process). The absence of a directly commenting narrator will also encourage a presentation of events in chronological order as W. P. Ker has noted: "Naturally, where the author does not make use of analysis and where he trusts to the reader's intellect to interpret things aright, the 'facts' must be fairly given; in a lucid order, with a progressive clearness, from the point of view of those who are engaged in the action" (*Epic and Romance*, p. 240).

18. Striking manipulations of point of view occur in chapter 9 of *Gísla saga* (*Fornrit*, VI, 30–31) where Þorkell overhears the women talking about the men they are fond of and in chapter 28 where the identity of the two boys, through whose eyes events are shown, is withheld until the end of the chapter. W. P. Ker comments on two other noted manipulations of point of view (*Epic and Romance*, pp. 240–42 and 254–56); see *Laxdœla saga* (*Fornrit*, V, 151–52) and *Sturlunga saga*, I, 142–50.

19. Mǫrðr's plot against the Njálssons begins when his father

Valgarðr, still a pagan, returns to Iceland and upbraids Mǫrðr for losing followers to the new chieftaincy of Hǫskuldr Hvitaness-Priest (ch. 107). Valgarðr counsels Mǫrðr to slander Hǫskuldr and the Njálssons each to to the other until the Njálssons are driven to killing Hǫskuldr. In the actions that will follow, Valgarðr foresees the Njálsson's death. He points out that in this way Mǫrðr can get revenge for the money Skarpheðinn got out of him in settlement for his share in Gunnarr's death. The last is a causal link between Gunnarr's death and the Burning. Rather touchingly Mǫrðr tries to persuade his aging father to embrace the new faith, but he dies fast in the old ways. Thus the scheme he has entrusted to his son is associated with a pagan malice.

20. An implication of the last remark is that the men are relieved of their fear that Skarpheðinn might become an *aptrgangr*, a revenant.

21. Ketill is in a difficult situation. As the uncle of Hǫskuldr Hvitaness-Priest, he has been bound to an oath to avenge him, but the Njálssons are his brothers-in-law.

22. The establishment of the Fifth Court in *Njáls saga* departs from historical chronology since Ari Þorgilsson's *Íslendingabók* makes it quite certain that the Fifth Court was instituted (c. A.D. 1005) after the conversion of Iceland to Christianity (A.D. 1000). If one insists on reading the saga as history, then the narrative progress of the saga is disturbingly out of order. But this rearrangement reveals certain aims and methods of the saga-man. He wants to get on with the story and yet he has two large historical episodes to digest. He preferred to establish at the outset the conditions necessary for the context of his narrative and not have his story distracted by the maneuvers for establishing the Fifth Court after the conversion. That is, he sacrifices chronology for a thematically climactic structure, for certainly no listener could unravel the chronology here. By this order he also established Njáll as a preeminent figure, wise and respected by all the chieftains, before Njáll is shown accepting Christianity. His choice then becomes all the more influential and significant. Both the shifting in time of the Fifth Court's establishment and the motives offered in explanation of this establishment are remarkably similar to liberties historical novelists allow themselves. The saga-man has availed himself of artistic license in order to build a more effective story, since the order of events is more disturbing to the history-oriented scholar than to the pleasure-seeking reader.

23. Cf. Fox, "*Njáls Saga* and the Western Literary Tradition": "Hermann Pálsson has pointed out to me that the variety of different ways in which the saga can be mechanically divided is an added indication of its essential unity" (pp. 293–94, n. 11).

24. "Pattern."

25. Ch. 78, pp. 192–94. One thinks of Gunnarr (perhaps one is meant to), the prince of the Burgundians, who in *Atlakviða* is thrown into the snake-filled pit: "But Gunnarr alone and fierce struck the harp with his hand; the strings resounded; so shall a bold ring-giver protect his gold against his foes."

26. When one reads *Njáls saga* without reference to other contemporary documents, one cannot help remarking upon the ironic contrast between Þangbrandr's head-thumping methods of conversion and the tenets of the Prince of Peace which he is advocating. Fox calls him a "thug" ("*Njáls Saga* and Western Literary Tradition," p. 302), and Snorri Sturlusson says Þangbrandr "was greatly overbearing and a manslayer, but a good priest and a valiant man" (*Óláfs saga Tryggvasonar, Fornrit,* XXVI, 319). It is hard to tell how apparent this irony was to the saga-man; his later straight-faced remark that Flosi received absolution from the Pope himself and paid a lot of money for it (ch. 158, p. 462) is not out of keeping with his sense of humor. *Kristni saga* (which tells of the conversion but which does not seem to have been a direct source for the same matter in *Njáls saga*—see *Fornrit,* XII, xlii–xlv) represents Þangbrandr as an even more turbulent priest and it may be equally likely that the silence of *Njáls saga* on various unpleasant facts in Þangbrandr's earlier record is a generous one, one meant to represent his activities in the best possible light without departing far from the sources and traditions available.

27. Andersson, *Problem,* p. 114: "How well does the miracle of Njáll's saintly glow and unsinged state jibe with the rest of the saga? Phrased another way, is *Njáls saga* the work of an Icelander steeped in hagiography? The question is of course rhetorical. Christian sentiment cannot be the core but only a small excrescence, external to the substance of the saga. ... Where the Christian bias becomes apparent, we are dealing with a superimposition, or at least with two layers. In other words, the author betrays a personality independent from the saga matter, or stated in reverse, the matter proves its autonomy and priority in relation to the author." Andersson's admittedly rhetorical question is misleading because it obscures the possibility that events in *Njáls saga* suggest the existence of a Christian frame of values without imposing this frame on the characters and audience of the saga. Since we know next to nothing about what traditions concerning Njáll the composer of *Njáls saga* had available to him and nothing about their transmission, it is not even safe to assume that the saintly glow and unsinged state are late additions to the tale. Njáll was burned after the conversion; his reputation might have been a saintly one even then.

28. "*Njáls Saga* and Western Literary Tradition," p. 304.

29. *Fornrit*, XII, cxxiv.

30. *Family Saga*, p. 46, p. 293, and pp. 298–99.

31. "Pattern." Fox in "*Njáls Saga* and Western Literary Tradition," pp. 293–94, has still another division, placing it between ch. 27 and 28.

32. Andersson's analysis of what happens to Gunnarr is a good one: "Gunnarr is at first in perfect control of the situation but becomes entangled in a conflict, from which he initially emerges victorious but in the course of which his own success gradually strengthens the will of the opposition and weakens his own chances for permanent success. What is actually escalated in this series of episodes is the tenuousness of Gunnarr's position" (*Family Saga*, p. 39).

33. "*Njáls Saga* and Western Literary Tradition," p. 300.

34. The root of the idiom is *draga til* which "is used absol. or ellipt. denoting the course of fate" (Richard Cleasby and Gudbrand Vigfusson, *An Icelandic-English Dictionary*, 2nd ed. [Oxford, 1957], s.v. *draga*). Valgarðr uses it when he tells Mǫrðr, "I wish now that you will repay them [the Njálssons] in such a manner that will drag them all to death" (ch. 107, p. 275).

35. Before the main events leading to the Burning get under way, there are two references, one to the retributions that follow the Burning—"Kolr, whom Kári kills in Wales" (ch. 96, p. 239)—and one to the Burning itself—"Glúmr, who went to the Burning with Flosi" (ch. 101, p. 258). As Finnur Jónsson notes, such direct allusions to future events are rare (*Njálssaga*, p. 217, n. 10). Einar Ól. Sveinsson thinks they are remnants from the sources the author was following at those points and have stayed in through an oversight. Speaking of the references to Glúmr, he says, "It is impossible to imagine how much could be learned from a few such sentences. It is apparent that the author of *Njála* had to strike them from his saga at the same time he was fixing the matter of such sentences in his memory, and it is doubtless through inadvertency that here he has deviated from this course" (*Um Njálu* [Reykjavík, 1933], p. 75). But it seems to me that their presence also suggests and emphasizes that the events now getting under way are not to be avoided and there is no use hiding what is to come.

36. See, for example, *Njal's Saga*, tr. Magnus Magnusson and Hermann Pálsson (Baltimore, 1960), pp. 13–14.

37. *Family Saga*, pp. 31–64.

38. There are inconsistencies and irreconcilable differences between historical time in *Njáls saga* such as can be determined from other sources, historical time as the saga itself refers to it (mainly through references to Norwegian kings and other rulers), and saga

time as can be determined by the passing of seasons and the assembling at the Althing (*Fornrit*, XII, lxi–lxviii). The figures I have used are thus rough ones. When the saga is read for its own sake, these inconsistencies do not seem troublesome and they are less than many others encountered elsewhere in medieval literature.

39. "*Njáls Saga* and Western Literary Tradition," p. 304.

40. Various brief mentionings of Gunnarr's deeds and Njáll's Burning are found in *Landnámabók*, the Icelandic annals, and other sagas. Excavations carried out at Bergþórshváll indicate that outlying buildings there were burned in the eleventh century although the main ruins of Njáll's farmstead, if they do exist, have not been found. (See Sveinsson's summary of this evidence in *Fornrit*, XII, v–ix.)

41. Fox notes ("*Njáls Saga* and Western Literary Tradition," p. 293) that *Njáls saga* in its double structure resembles other epic works, such as *Beowulf*, the *Nibelungenlied*, and the *Chanson de Roland*: "One may observe that the apparently broken but actually unified structure corresponds to the apparently double but actually single subject: the hero as an individual (Roland, or the young Beowulf, for instance), and the hero as a member of society (Charlemagne, the old Beowulf)." What is defeated in the first half of *Njáls saga* is one man's attempt to conduct his life among his fellow men without bloodshed; what fails in the Burning, or is shown to be unworkable, is the constitution of a whole society. The image of the spiral also occurs in Anne Saxon's similar description in "Unity and Narrative Technique," pp. 17–18: "The narrator presents a seemingly inexhaustible number of episodes, but their relationship to each other may be compared to a spiral. The motifs of incentive to strife, actual combat, revenge, and reconciliation occur again and again, but with each successive recurrence their seriousness and consequences broaden until most of Iceland and many other parts of Europe are involved."

42. *Family Saga*, p. 46.

43. "Pattern." Maxwell makes it clear that the composer of *Njáls saga* carefully ties together the various parts of this feud and reminds the audience of the binding.

44. For Bjǫrn of Mǫrk, see W. P. Ker's remarks in *Epic and Romance*, pp. 228–29, and Sigurður Nordal's imaginative reconstruction of his character and background in "Björn úr Mörk," *Skírnir*, 93 (1919), 141–52.

45. Perhaps in Bjǫrn's request to Kári there is a faint echo of Hallgerðr's question to Gunnarr when he needs her hair for a bowstring—"Does anything depend on it?"—and his reply, "my life depends on it." Now the stakes are much less.

CHAPTER 5

1. For the steps by which the action of the sagas is brought to a dramatic high point, see *Family Saga*, pp. 31–64.

2. See *Beowulf and the Fight at Finnsburg*, ed. Fr. Klaeber, 3rd ed. (Boston, 1950), ll. 81–85 and ll. 2024–69 for the fate of Heorot and the Ingeld feud which led to its burning and Klaeber's remarks, pp. xxiv–xxxv. Axel Olrik, *The Heroic Legends of Denmark*, tr. Lee M. Hollander (New York, 1919), pp. 16–21, reviews the destruction of Heorot and is concerned throughout with the *Bjarkamál* and *Hrólfs saga Kraka*.

3. Useful accounts of sources, development, and relationships of the matter found in the *Nibelungenlied* and the *Vǫlsunga saga* are the introduction to *The Saga of the Volsungs*, ed. and tr. R. G. Finch (London and Edinburgh, 1965) and the discussion and glossaries at the end of *The Nibelungenlied*, tr. A. T. Hatto (Baltimore, 1965).

4. *Das Nibelungenlied*, ed. and tr. into modern German by Helmet de Boor (Bremen, n.d.), stanza 2371. The epithet is Hagen's but one is nevertheless inclined to agree with his description. A. T. Hatto's translation of it (*The Nibelungenlied*, p. 290) departs not at all from the implications of the word. *Vâlandinne* is glossed as *Teufelin, ein dem Teufel ähnliches weib*; see Georg Friedrich Benecke, *Mittelhochdeutsches Wörterbuch*, 3 vols. (Leipzig, 1854), s.v. *vâlandinne*.

5. In *The Last 100 Days* (New York, 1966), p. 74, John Toland reproduces a remarkable letter written in February 1945 by Frau Martin Bormann in an effort to cheer up her husband in his vigil at the *Führerbunker*. Now in these times, she says, the people of the German nation are reliving the days of *ragnarǫk* as the old Eddic poems describe it. The wolf Fenrir, the great serpent, the giants, and the fiery foes from Hell, all the forces of evil are already at their gates, to the east and to the west, but the gods, and their chosen warriors, and attendant valkyries will fight on. Germany will be swallowed up in flames but one day National Socialism will rise again to greater glory and Balder himself will be reborn.

6. Bertha S. Phillpotts, *Edda and Saga* (New York and London, 1931), p. 72.

7. Gudbrand Vigfusson remarks that *Njáls saga* is "The Saga of Law, *par excellence* ..." (in *Sturlunga Saga*, 2 vols. [Oxford, 1878], I, xlii), a remark which is expanded upon in Karl Lehmann and Hans Schnorr von Carolsfeld, *Die Njálssage Insbesondere in Ihren Juristischen Bestandtheilen* (Berlin, 1883), pp. 6–10.

8. *Vǫluspá*, especially in its vision at the end where one mighty lord comes to rule over all, seems to have been influenced by Christian

teachings, a fact which reinforces the parallel I am drawing between it and *Njáls saga*. Time, place, and manner of composition of the Eddic poems remain unsettled, but *Vǫluspá* is usually considered to have been cast in its present form in the tenth century when Christian currents were reaching into the north. See Frederick T. Wood, "The Age of the *Vǫluspá*," *GR*, 36 (May 1961), 94–98, and "The Transmission of the *Vǫluspá*," *GR*, 34 (December 1959), 247–61; Lee M. Hollander, "Were the Mythological Poems of the Edda Composed in the Pre-Christian Era?" *JEGP*, 26, no. 1 (1927), 96–105, and "Recent Work and Views on the Poetic Edda," *SS*, 35 (May 1963), 101–09; A. Le Roy Andrews, "The Criteria for Dating the Eddic Poems," *PMLA*, 42 December 1927), 1044–54; Bjarne Ulvestad, "How Old Are the Mythological Eddic Poems?" *SS*, 26 (May 1954), 49–69.

9. For the pattern of the night journey as it reveals itself in heroic tales see Joseph Campbell, *The Hero with a Thousand Faces* (New York, 1949) and Herbert Weisinger who puts it to critical use in *The Agony and Triumph* (Lansing, Mich., 1964). The development of creation myths and quest myths and their descent into epic literature are investigated by G. R. Levy, *The Sword from the Rock* (London, 1953). Joseph Campbell, *The Masks of God: Occidental Mythology* (Toronto, 1964), is also relevant. Further descriptions and discussions of their psychological significance are found in C. G. Jung, *Symbols of Transformation*, tr. R. F. C. Hull (New York and London, 1956), and *Two Essays on Analytical Psychology*, tr. R. F. C. Hull (New York and London, 1953). Most of Jung's writings are relevant to these matters but *Symbols* especially was an early and important work. His views are modified, reviewed, and stated succinctly in Erich Neumann's *The Origins and History of Consciousness*, tr. R. F. C. Hull (New York and London, 1954).

10. The primary purpose of archetypal criticism is not to provide a close analysis of the structure of a given work—indeed a small number of patterns underlie all narrative—but to suggest relationships between works, relationships not necessarily dependent on historical influence, and to offer reasons why works written in times and places far removed from the present can still elicit a strong response. There comes a time when one must cope with the fact that past literature, even ancient literature out of its cultural context and translated from its original idiom (e.g., *The Gilgamesh Epic*), can call forth strong emotions in readers *now*. *Njáls saga* is a work of great power, one that profits by as wide a knowledge as possible of its Icelandic context, but one whose effect by no means depends on such knowledge. The argument here is that its general form incorporates a pattern (and uses

images—that is, events, figures, and phrases—reflecting that pattern) which exerts a universal appeal because it belongs to a universal human experience. That form itself, even as it is delineated by purely stock characters and motifs, can call forth a strong response, is evident in the appeal of folktale, soap opera, and other highly stereotyped genres. Great art reinforces on other levels the response called forth by archetypal forms. The relationship between narrative form and the patterns of the mind which have to be behind such forms, the function and the meaning of these patterns, are matters of legitimate critical concern. I think this is the point missed by C. S. Lewis in his otherwise valuable warnings about this phase of literary criticism in "The Anthropological Approach," *English and Medieval Studies Presented to J. R. R. Tolkien*, ed. Norman Davis and C. L. Wrenn (London, 1962), pp. 219–30. The failure of some folklorists to recognize this claim is more disappointing; see, for example, the strictures against certain of "our starry-eyed colleagues of some campus departments of English" by Melville Jacobs, "A Look Ahead in Oral Literature Research," *JAF*, 79 (July–September 1966), 413–27. *JAF*, 68 (October–December 1955), is devoted to articles concerned with myth, folklore, and literature; among the useful and suggestive ones are Stanley Edgar Hyman, "The Ritual View of Myth and the Mythic," 462–72, and Claude Levi-Strauss, "The Structural Study of Myth," 428–44 (also reprinted in Claude Levi-Strauss, *Structural Anthropology* [Garden City, N.Y., 1967], pp. 202–28). Stith Thompson in "Myths and Folktales," 482–88, draws an ominous picture of the critic, shuttled between lunar, solar, and Jungian interpretations of myth until "he is prepared to pass into a *selva oscura* even more revolting and unlikely, a world filled with phallic symbols and fertility rites" (p. 483). But it is misleading, I think, to use the numerous fashions of myth interpretation got up in the prepsychoanalytic era to mock and disparage attempts made afterwards. Finally, the discussions and demonstrations of archetypal criticism in Maud Bodkin's *Archetypal Patterns in Poetry* (1934; reprint ed., London, 1963) and Northrop Frye's *Anatomy of Criticism* have helped shape and guide my ideas.

11. Speaking of her newly born daughter, Hallgerðr says, "She shall be named after my father's mother and shall be called Þorgerðr, because Þorgerðr came from Sigurðr Fafnir's Bane in line of descent from her father" (ch. 14, p. 46). This sort of genealogy is not infrequent.

12. *The Sword from the Rock*, p. 218.

13. See Theodore M. Andersson, "Some Ambiguities in *Gísla Saga*," *BONIS* (1968), 7–42, esp. pp. 41–42, for reflections on how this saga expresses a changed attitude towards the old heroic values.

14. Knut Liestøl asks, "May we not say that, in part, the family sagas derived their soul from the heroic poetry?" (*Origin*, p. 179), and goes on to develop the idea. The continuity between the poetry and saga is the subject of Bertha Phillpott's *Edda and Saga* and of much of W. P. Ker's *Epic and Romance*. Theodore M. Andersson in *Family Saga* (pp. 65-93) reviews earlier discussions of this continuity and suggests in addition that certain formal features of saga narrative are an inheritance from the structure of Eddic poetry.

15. "Escalation" is Andersson's term for the technique by which "each succeeding adventure" is made to be "more provocative or perilous than its predecessor" (*Family Saga*, p. 38).

16. A number of the documents relevant to the discovery and settlement of Iceland, Greenland, and America have been gathered together and translated by Gwyn Jones, *The Norse Atlantic Saga* (London, 1964), which is also provided with a useful introduction. Essential source materials for the settlement of Iceland are the *Landnámabók* and Ari Þorgilsson's *Íslendingabók* or *Libellus Islandorum*, both available in various editions and translations. For them and much other material edited and translated in old, not always reliable, but still convenient volumes, see *Origines Islandicae*, ed. and tr. Gudbrand Vigfusson and F. York Powell, 2 vols. (London, 1905).

17. "*Með lǫgum skal land várt byggja, en með ólǫgum eyða*" (ch. 70, p. 172). The verb *byggja* ("to inhabit," "to people," "to build") is thus opposed by *eyða* ("to lay waste," "to desolate") as noted in Richard Cleasby and Gudbrand Vigfusson, *An Icelandic-English Dictionary*, 2nd ed. (Oxford, 1957), s.v. *byggja*. The saying appears in the oldest collections of Norse laws and in the later Norwegian compilation *Járnsíða* which *Njáls saga* apparently made use of (see *Fornrit*, XII, lxxviii-lxxxi).

18. When I speak of the law I mean the law as it is represented in *Njáls saga*. A consistent picture is given there, but one which has many discrepancies both with law procedure in the days of the republic and with the Norwegian law which replaced it, discrepancies which Lehmann and von Carolsfeld thoroughly analyzed in *Die Njálssage*. But these discrepancies, nagging as they may be to historians, do not affect the use made of law within the saga itself.

19. The Icelandic *goðorð* (rendered here as "chieftainship") was held by men given the title of *goði* ("priest"). They were men of wealth, usually descended from aristocratic settlers. They exercised both secular and religious leadership, but their power lay in their popularity and in the strength of their followings. Men were free to leave the allegiance of one *goði* and seek another. The office could be bought,

sold, or temporarily transferred (a strategem Flosi uses (ch. 141). Their number was fixed at thirty-nine at the time when Njáll was seeking a *goðorð* for Hǫskuldr. See Jón Jóhannesson, "Goðar og Goðorð," *Íslendinga Saga. I. Þjóðveldisöld* (Reykjavík, 1956), pp. 72–82. The introduction of Christianity did not change this structure and it was not until 1190 that the Archbishop at Nidaros decreed that a man could not be an ordained priest and hold a chieftainship as well (Sveinsson, *Age of the Sturlungs*, p. 126).

20. From this chapter and in the rest of the saga it is apparent that Njáll is not a chieftain. But his knowledge of the law and skill at interpreting it endow him with considerable power. Power thus derives from a correct knowledge of technicalities, from sharpness of mind and good memory. See James Bryce, "Primitive Iceland," *Studies in History and Jurisprudence*, 2 vols. (Oxford, 1901), I, 312–58, esp. p. 340, and Eric A. Havelock, *Preface to Plato* (Cambridge, Mass., 1963), pp. 126–27.

21. A system of fines (payable in sheep or cattle) by which blood feuds may be settled is described by Tacitus, who remarks on the dangers to the community when no possibility exists of reconciling private feuds (*Germania*, 21, in *Tacitus on Britain and Germany*, tr. H. Mattingly [Baltimore, 1948], p. 118).

22. See translators' note, *Njál's Saga*, p. 63, and the appendix, *Njálssaga* (Jónsson), pp. 422–24.

23. Hakon Melberg, *Origins of the Scandinavian Nations and Languages* (Halden, Norway, 1949), p. 40.

24. *Grágás*, ed. Vilhjálmur Finsen (Copenhagen, 1852), 1a, 209.

25. James Bryce, "Primitive Iceland," p. 334.

26. While the reciprocal relationship between law and aggression in the sagas is self-evident, an understanding of this relationship and of the action and histories narrated in the family sagas as a whole is enhanced and illuminated by Norman O. Brown's rigorous examination in *Life Against Death: The Psychoanalytical Meaning of History* (Middletown, Conn., 1959) of the interlocking of aggression, guilt, money, the mechanisms of sublimation and projection, and the structures of man's civilization itself. The discussion on the following pages is indebted to his views and logic.

27. See ch. 130, p. 313, n. 4; *Njálssaga* (Jónsson), p. 286, n. to ll. 26–27; *Njal's Saga*, p. 255, translators' note.

28. Several nagging questions occur about this all-important scene. Why does not Njáll answer Flosi when Flosi asks, in apparently unbelligerent fashion, who has contributed the gift? Where has Skarpheðinn obtained those blue breaches? This is the sort of detail which is usually anticipated with care. The lack of any such preparation led Finnur

Jónsson to speculate that this incident was a later addition (*Njálssaga* [Jónsson], p. 287, n. to ll. 3–4). And why is there no common talk at the Althing of Hildigunnr's incitement? That was no private affair and far less important matters are carried by rumor in *Njáls saga*. The answer is probably that these are questions which occur to a reader reflecting at leisure. They would be overlooked in a reading-out of this dramatic scene, and in all events the saga-man has to provide some generally plausible explanation for the breakdown of negotiations which leads to the Burning.

29. Christian men (most likely Irish monks) had reached Iceland before the Norse discovery of it and some were there who fled before the Norsemen as Ari relates in the *Íslendingabók*. But they had sought shelter for solitary devotions and cannot be considered colonists who established a community.

30. *Fornrit*, XII, lxxxv–lxxxvi.

31. *Á Njálsbúð* (Reykjavík, 1943), pp. 1–5.

32. Ari C. Bouman, *Patterns in Old English and Old Icelandic Literature* (Leyden, 1962), p. 4. Bouman says the landscape at Thingvellir is a *paysage spirituel*, but does not elaborate.

33. *Njáls saga* speaks of a church at Thingvellir (ch. 145, p. 408); the reference may be an anachronism.

34. I am informed by a geologist I met at Thingvellir that the mountain range to the east and the plateau to the west are still drawing apart from one another at what is geologically a rapid rate. Large scale forces beneath the crust of the earth are responsible for this action. Iceland itself has been flung up across the mid-Atlantic Rift, a great crack in the earth's mantle.

35. Almost all the travel books about Iceland betray a sense of special excitement and interest when they come to speak of Thingvellir. The astonishment and fascination expressed by Lord Dufferin, *Letters from High Latitudes* (London, 1857), pp. 84–103, are not untypical. The same elements I have invoked emerge in his dainty response (p. 103) to the view from the lakeside: "A lovelier scene I have seldom witnessed. In the foreground lay huge masses of rock and lava, tossed about like the ruins of a world, and washed by waters as bright and green as polished malachite. Beyond, a bevy of distant mountains, robed by the transparent atmosphere in tints unknown to Europe, peeped over each other's shoulders into the silver mirror at their feet, while here and there from among their purple ridges columns of white vapor rose like altar smoke toward the tranquil heaven."

36. An inspection of the headings in Inger M. Boberg, *Motif-Index of Early Icelandic Literature*, Bibliotheca Arnamagnæana, 27 (Copenhagen, 1966), gives an idea of the extent of supernatural activity throughout a

wide range of early Icelandic literature. N. Kershaw Chadwick, "Norse Ghosts," *Folklore*, 57 (June and September 1946), 50–65, 106–27, is also informative.

37. Some articles and references to the power of fire and ice in Iceland are Vilhjálmur Bjarnar, "The Laki Eruption and the Famine of the Mist," *Scandinavian Studies: Essays Presented to Dr. Henry Goddard Leach on the Occasion of His Eighty-fifth Birthday*, ed. Carl F. Bayerschmidt and Erik J. Friis (Seattle, 1965), pp. 410–12; "Eruption of the Öræfajökull," reproduced by W. H. Auden and Louis MacNeice, *Letters from Iceland* (1932; paperback reprint, London, 1967), pp. 81–85; Sigurður Þórarinsson, "Fight with the Fire Below," *Icelandic Review*, 5, no. 2 (1967), 27–33 (spectacular pictures), and *The Thousand Years Struggle against Ice and Fire* (Reykjavík, 1956); and *Iceland* (British Naval Intelligence Geographical Handbook Series, 1942), p. 12, 20, and passim.

38. Cf. Sir George MacKenzie, *Travels in the Island of Iceland During the Summer of the Year MDCCCX* (Edinburgh, 1811), who comments on the indifference of latter-day Icelanders to the scene and phenomena about Geysir: "In looking around as we approached the place, nothing was seen but rugged mountains, far extended swamps, and frightful Jokuls [glaciers] rearing their frozen summits to the sky. Nothing in this direction seemed to invite the curiosity or enterprise of people, already accustomed to the horrors of volcanic eruptions, and fully aware that their only sure subsistence was to be derived from the sea.... At the present day, the number of natives who have visited these springs is comparatively very small; and, by those who live near them, their extraordinary operations constantly going on, are regarded with the same eye as the most common and indifferent appearances of nature" (pp. 221–22).

39. *Kristni saga*, *Íslendinga Sögur*, ed. Guðni Jónsson (Reykavík, 1946–49), I, 270.

40. *The Nine Books of the Danish History of Saxo Grammaticus*, tr. Oliver Elton (London, 1905), I, pp. 85–88.

41. *The King's Mirror* (*Konungs Skuggsjá*), tr. L. M. Larson (New York, 1917), p. 127.

42. *King's Mirror*, p. 131.

43. *King's Mirror*, p. 133.

44. It is tempting to try to link the figure of Mǫrðr with both the Christian devil and the pagan Loki. Einar Ól. Sveinsson is approaching the former when he writes of Mǫrðr in *Á Njálsbúð*, p. 84: "Later the saga states that Mǫrðr greatly envied Gunnarr. Envy is ever the common share which each of the children of men knows and understands. It is sometimes as if men are somewhat wary of naming it by its proper

name in print. But wary this author of old was not." A start into Christian commentary upon the true nature of men whose malicious speech leads to evil deeds might begin with the words of Bishop Jón who rebukes a Norwegian who had given a fiery speech urging revenge and death on some troublesome Icelandic retainers of King Magnus: " 'The devil does not go about so boldly now before men's eyes as before, but nevertheless he finds men to follow his beckoning and to carry out his cursed errands ... and I think that it will be such men who do most to set free the devil himself by their troublesome speeches' " (*Jóns Saga Helga, Byskupa Sögur*, ed. Guðni Jónsson [Reykjavík, 1948], II, 14–15). See also *King's Mirror*, p. 82. Loki, an extremely complex figure (see Jan de Vries, *The Problem of Loki* [Helsinki, 1933]), is like the devil associated with fire, envy, and malicious speech and deeds, but de Vries notes (pp. 181–82) that extant Norse descriptions of Loki may have been influenced by Christian conceptions of the devil.

45. *Ólafs saga Tryggvasonar, Fornrit*, XXVI, 271; *Gylfaginning* in *Edda Snorra Sturlusonar*, ed. Guðni Jónsson (Reykjavík, 1935), viii, 25.

46. This statement and the following remarks are developed throughout Neumann, *History of Consciousness*, but see esp. pp. 42, 125, 142–43, 297–300.

47. Boberg, *Motif-Index*, p. 266.

48. Parallel motifs to Gunnarr's riding off and the stumbling of his horse are discussed in Otto Springer, "The 'âne stegreif' Motif in Medieval Literature," *GR*, 25 (October 1950), 163–77, esp. pp. 175–76.

49. Gunnarr would be looking back to Hlíðarendi, situated on a long east-west running ridge of land that rises from the barren alluvial debris and black sand flats stretching southwards to the Atlantic. The ridge is watered by mountain snows and springs, and the meadow grass along it is astonishingly green in the sunlight. Out to sea there is nothing, only the desolate plain and empty circle of the horizon. The prospect before Gunnarr is bleak and formless; the land behind him is green, cared for, fertile, and beckoning. At Hlíðarendi it is not difficult to see why Gunnarr turned back.

50. Einar H. Kvaran uses this scene as the centerpiece for his article, "Landscape in the Sagas: The Beginning of a Background," *TLS* (August 29, 1936), 685–86. Skaldic poetry evinces more delight in and realization of the sea and landscapes of the Scandinavian world.

51. See Sigurður Guðmundsson, "Gunnar á Hlíðarenda," *Skírnir*, 92 (1918), 63–88, 221–51, esp. pp. 231–33.

52. *Fornrit*, XII, cxxvii–cxxviii. Sveinsson discusses the scene in greater detail on pp. xxxiv–xxxvii.

53. Sveinsson in *Fornrit*, XII, xxvi, calls attention to a similarity in

form and phrasing between this scene and one in the *Alexanders saga* where the Greek conqueror is granted a vision of his homeland, but rejects it. If the other work was in the mind of the saga-man, it is an indication of the company Gunnarr was thought worthy of joining.

54. *"Heldr kvazk* [*hann*] *vilja deyja en vægja."* Gunnarr's assertion is here untangled from the word order of the skaldic stanza (ch. 78, p. 193) in which it is set.

55. *Patterns in Old Icelandic Literature*, p. 9: "Gunnarr's irresponsible return to Hlíðarendi, in spite of banishments, warnings, and prophecies, has to be looked upon, in my opinion, as the insuperable desire for Hallgerðr's presence." But there is no overt support in the text itself for this view.

56. Denton Fox, "*Njáls Saga* and Western Literary Tradition:" "He is Gunnarr of Lithend; if he left Iceland he would lose part of his name and part of his identity..." (p. 298).

57. Magic fogs were, of course, too good a weapon to leave to wizards. In *Oddaverja þáttr* Bishop Þórlakr twice benefits from miraculous fogs that opportunely blind his wicked foes (*Byskupa Sögur*, I, 151–53, 156).

58. Cf. Fox, "*Njáls Saga* and Western Literary Tradition," p. 296, where he states it is by no coincidence that the striking figure of the pagan Svanr appears early in this saga.

59. Mǫrðr is also an early convert to Christianity, but the scene shows Valgarðr, Mǫrðr's father, rejecting his son's plea that he embrace the new faith (ch. 107, p. 275). Thus Valgarðr's plot against the Njálssons comes from a man firmly set in the pagan ways.

60. See Beryl Rowland, "The Horse and Rider Figure in Chaucer's Works," *UTQ*, 35 (April 1966), 246–59, for commentary and references.

61. *Hungrvaka* in *Byskupa Sögur*, I, 24, tells how the bodies of Bishop Magnús and one of his companions remained unburned after he and eighty-two men had lost their lives in the fire at Hítardalr on Michaelmas day (September 30, 1148).

62. The model is the dream of Anastasius (Migne, *Patrologia Latina*, LXXVII, 185); see Á *Njálsbúð*, pp. 8–13 and 171, and G. Turville-Petre, *Origins of Icelandic Literature*, pp. 136–37.

63. See Cleasby and Vigfusson, *An Icelandic-English Dictionary*, s.v. *ryðja*.

64. The quotation is from p. 49 of John Ryan, "The Battle of Clontarf," *JRSAI*, 68 (1938), 1–50. Some other discussions of this battle are Eric Linklater, "The Battle of Clontarf," *Viking*, 15 (1951), 1–14, and A. J. Goedheer, *Irish and Norse Traditions about the Battle of Clontarf* (Haarlem, 1938).

65. *Fornrit*, XII, xlv–xlix.

66. A similar interpretation of the battle's place in the saga occurred to me when I first read *Njáls saga*. I then found that Denton Fox had already developed this idea and by now my expression of it is influenced by his. "What we have in this historical interlude, then, is a full-scale, concrete representation of the fight between good and evil that rages throughout the saga, made explicitly cosmological by the supernatural references, and carried out in terms familiar in the rest of the saga: good is represented by Christianity, mercy (Brian is accustomed to pardon a man three times for the same offense), and loyalty, bad by bloodthirstiness, ravenous self-aggrandizement, and disloyalty" ("*Njáls Saga* in Western Literary Tradition," p. 308).

67. So it is stated in the Frostathings law, a Norwegian compilation, but this section would certainly pertain in Iceland: "*þat er hit iiij níðings verk ef maðr leggr elld í bæ manns oc brennir upp*" (*Norges gamle love indtil 1387*, I, ed. Rudolph Keyser, and P. A. Munch, [Oslo, 1846], p. 148).

68. For the parts of the loom I have used the terminology employed in the Penguin translation, p. 349. Neumann includes weaving webs of fate among a number of sinister activities indulged in by creatures associated with the "devouring chasm" (*History of Consciousness*, p. 87). In *Laxdæla saga* Guðrún is spinning yarn when Bolli rides home to greet her with news of the slaying of Kjartan and her reply virtually equates the two activities (*Fornrit*, V, 154).

69. The sorrow of the Irish that will never grow old is for the fall of their king.

70. Anne Holtsmark, "Vefr Darraðar," *MM*, 31 (1939–40), 74–96.

71. "Of course the weaving of the spear-web is a magic function producing the action which is going on on the stricken field of Clontarf" (*Darraðaljóð* [*sic*], ed. and tr. Eiríkr Magnússon [Coventry, 1910], p. 17). For a suggestion that in *Vǫluspá* a similar activity controls men's fates and for parallels of magic games which shape destinies see A. G. van Hamel, "The Game of the Gods," *ANF*, 50 (1934), 218–42. For the Celtic and Norse motifs that are fused in the poem, see A. H. Krappe, "The Valkyrie Episode in the *Njáls Saga*," *MLN*, 43 (November 1928), 471–74.

72. *Archetypal Patterns in Poetry*, p. 210. Her quotations are from F. M. Cornford, *Thucydides Mythistoricus* (London, 1907), pp. 144–45. She adds, pp. 210–11: "Cornford reproduces in his book the design of a Greek vase of the fourth century B.C., of a class known to have been influenced by tragedy, in which this double effect, a 'supernatural action developed in a parallel series with the human action on the stage,'

is illustrated in spatial form." In the lower tier pictured on the vase
Darius appears on his throne with his men about him; in the upper tier
are figures of the Olympians, who indicate victory in store for Greece,
disaster for the Persians.

73. *Germania*, 8, in *Tacitus on Britain and Germany*, p. 107.

74. Phillpotts, *Edda and Saga*, p. 52.

75. *Harðar saga ok Hólmverja, Íslendinga Sögur*, XII, 290–91.

76. See R. George Thomas, "Some Exceptional Women in the Sagas,"
Saga-Book, 13 (pt. V, 1952–53), 307–27, who uses the phrase. He sees
in the latter type of woman an enhanced sense of individuality.

77. Thomas in "Some Exceptional Women," esp. pp. 307–09, perceives that the sagas reenact a national myth which serves somewhat
the same function (any may contain about the same degree of reality) as
the Western movie does for its audience. Rolf Heller, *Die Literarische
Darstellung der Frau in den Isländersagas*, Saga, 2 (Halle, 1958), p. 154,
notes forty-two examples of women who incite vengeance (*Hetzerinnen*)
in twenty-nine family sagas, with *Laxdœla saga* and *Njáls saga* leading
the list, nine in *Njáls saga* and four in *Laxdœla*. Thus the two sagas
account for a little less than a third of all the examples. Heller expresses doubts (p. 98) that all of these can be considered historical.

78. *Archetypal Patterns in Poetry*, p. 172. She fortifies her statement with a quotation from Euripides to the effect that men blame women
for troubles better blamed on men. The force of the quotation is di-
minished when one finds it is what the chorus of women says to Medea
just before she poisons Jason's mistress and slays her own children
by him.

79. *The Greeks and the Irrational* (Berkeley and Los Angeles, 1951),
p. 17.

80. Neumann, *History of Consciousness*, pp. 272–73. This process
has begun in Gunnarr's speech when he looks up to the hills; never
have they seemed so fair to him. He is reporting a flare-up of inward
feeling, but he is aware of it only as it is reflected back to him in the
enhanced brightness of the hillside.

81. This scene is fully analyzed, from a perspective that takes in
its relationship to similar ritualistic incitements in Germanic heroic
poetry, by Alois Wolf, *Gestaltungskerne und Gestaltungsweisen in der
altgermanischen Heldendichtung* (Munich, 1965), pp. 111–18.

82. *Fornrit*, XII, 290, n. 7.

83. Paul Schach, "The Use of the Simile in the Old Icelandic Family
Sagas," *SS*, 24 (November 1952), 149–65.

84. *Gylfaginning*, xxxiv, 52. I have followed Arthur G. Brodeur's
translation in *The Prose Edda* (New York, 1929), p. 42.

85. S.v. *forað* in Alexander Jóhannesson, *Isländisches Etymologisches Wörterbuch* (Bern, 1956), and Cleasby and Vigfusson, *An Icelandic-English Dictionary*. They point out that *forað* is used to render the "great gulf" of Luke 16:26 separating the rich man in hell from Abraham and Lazarus in heaven. Snorri refers to the hell-hound, Garmr, as *it mesta forað* (*Gylfaginning*, li, 97).

86. The proverb occurs again in *Gísla saga*, *Fornrit*, VI, 61, where it is spoken by Bǫrkr after Þórdís repeats the verse Gísli had spoken, revealing that Gísli had slain Þorgrímr. The scene is similar to the one in *Njáls saga*—a woman sees to it that men are committed to a formidable vengeance. Gísli, when he hears what Þórdís has done, compares her to Guðrún Gjúki's daughter, of whom we have already heard. The proverb occurs once more in *Vǫlundarkviða* slightly altered when King Níðuðr laments his wife's counsel which has led to the death of his sons and the dishonoring of his daughter. Jan de Vries cites a homily on John the Baptist in which a lively exchange between Salome and her mother culminates in the same expression, *kǫld eru kvenna rǫð*; see "Die isländische Saga und die mündliche Überlieferung," in *Märchen, Mythos, Dichtung*, ed. Hugo Kuhn and Kurt Schier (Munich, 1963), p. 173.

87. See *Origines Islandicae*, I, pp. 314–18.

88. Njáll stipulates (ch. 97, p. 245) that the prosecution and the defense each have the right to challenge 6 of the 48 judges appointed to the Fifth Court; if the defense does not exercise its challenge, then the prosecution must challenge the other 6 because only 36 judges may give a verdict. Mǫrðr (ch. 144, p. 401) forgets the last point and calls for a verdict with 42 judges remaining, thus enabling Flosi's lawyer to declare the verdict null and void.

89. See *Íslendingabók, Islendinga Sögur*, I, 4; *Fornrit*, XII, 406, n. 1; and *Njál's Saga*, n. to p. 318. The interpretation offered here may have been intended by the saga-man; on the other hand, the scribes of *Reykjabók* and some other principal manuscripts of *Njáls saga* did not recognize the allusion because they add words saying that Kolr and Þorvaldr were dead and had been among the worst of Flosi's band. Einar Ól. Sveinsson in *Um Njálu* (Reykjavík, 1933), pp. 200–01 thinks this may be a good example of an allusion preserved in earlier sources of the saga which the saga-man did not understand himself but nevertheless passed on. Kolr's death had been a murder, an unproclaimed killing and hence a serious crime, one to be distinguished from a slaying, which was announced to witnesses and dealt with by customary measures.

90. Stanley Greenfield, "*Beowulf* and Epic Tragedy," *Studies in*

Old English Literature in Honor of Arthur G. Brodeur (Eugene, Oregon, 1963), pp. 129–35, distinguishes the hero of epic tragedy, who embodies the best qualities of his culture, who falls because of fate, and whose fall is the end of his people, from the hero of dramatic tragedy, who becomes estranged from his community, falls because of pride and wilfulness, and whose end is not necessarily the end of the society about him. The heroes of the saga would seem to be halfway between these poles. Their pride and willfulness are qualities admired by their own people; nevertheless these qualities play into the hand of a fate that leads them to their lonely deaths. But these deaths are not the ruin of a people.

91. See *Family Saga*, pp. 3–30.
92. *Epic and Romance*, pp. 193–94; *Edda and Saga*, pp. 201–02.
93. *Laxdæla saga, Fornrit*, V, 228.
94. See *Anatomy of Criticism*, pp. 163–66.
95. *Epic and Romance*, p. 232.
96. *Beowulf*, ll. 50b–52b.

Bibliography

Anderson, Sven Axel. "The Attitudes of the Historians toward the Old Norse Sagas." *SS*, 15 (November 1939), 266–74.

Andersson, Theodore M. "The Doctrine of Oral Tradition in the Chanson de Geste and Saga." *SS*, 24 (November 1962), 219–36.

————. *The Icelandic Family Saga: An Analytic Reading.* Harvard Studies in Comparative Literature, vol. 28. Cambridge, Mass., 1967.

————. *The Problem of Icelandic Saga Origins: A Historical Survey.* Yale Germanic Studies, vol. 1. New Haven and London, 1964.

————. "Some Ambiguities in *Gísla Saga*." *BONIS* (1968), pp. 7–42.

————. "The Textual Evidence for an Oral Family Saga." *ANF*, 81 (1966), 1–23.

Andrews, A. Le Roy. "The Criteria for Dating the Eddic Poems." *PMLA*, 42 (December 1927), 1044–54.

Auden, W. H., and MacNeice, Louis. *Letters from Iceland.* 1937; paperback reprint London, 1967.

Auerbach, Erich. *Literary Language and Its Public in Late Latin Antiquity and in the Middle Ages.* Translated by Ralph Mannheim. London, 1965.

————. *Mimesis: The Representation of Reality in Western Literature.* Translated by Willard Trask. 1953; paperback reprint Princeton, 1968.

Baetke, Walter. "Die Kuntsform der Saga." In *Vom Geist und Erbe Thules*, pp. 155–63. Gottingen, 1944.

————. *Über die Entstehung der Isländersagas.* Berichte über die Verhandlungen der Sächsischen Akademie der Wissenschaften zu Leipzig, Philologisch-Historische Klasse, vol. 102, no. 5, 1–108. Berlin, 1956.

Bayerschmidt, Carl F. "The Element of the Supernatural in the Sagas of Icelanders." In *Scandinavian Studies: Essays Presented to Dr. Henry Goddard Leach on the Occasion of His Eighty-Fifth Birthday*, edited by Carl F. Bayerschmidt and Erik J. Friis, pp. 39–53. Seattle, 1965.

Benecke, Georg Friedrich. *Mittelhochdeutsches Wörterbuch*. 3 vols. Leipzig, 1872.

Benediktsson, Hrein. *Early Icelandic Script as Illustrated in Vernacular Texts from the Twelfth and Thirteenth Centuries*. Reykjavík, 1965.

Benson, Larry D. "The Literary Character of Anglo-Saxon Formulaic Poetry." *PMLA*, 81 (October 1966), 334–41.

Beowulf and the Fight at Finnsburg. Edited by Fr. Klaeber. 3rd ed. Boston, 1950.

Beyschlag, Siegfried. "Erzählform der Isländersaga." *Wirkendes Wort*, 1, no. 4 (1950–51), 223–29.

Bjarnar, Vilhjálmur. "The Laki Eruption and the Famine of the Mist." In *Scandinavian Studies: Essays Presented to Dr. Henry Goddard Leach on the Occasion of His Eighty-Fifth Birthday*, edited by Carl F. Bayerschmidt and Erik J. Friis, pp. 410–12. Seattle, 1965.

Boberg, Inger M. *Motif-Index of Early Icelandic Literature*. Bibliotheca Arnamagnæana, 27. Copenhagen, 1966.

Bodkin, Maud. *Archetypal Patterns in Poetry*. London, 1963.

Book of the Icelanders (The Islendingabók). Edited and translated by Halldór Hermannsson. Islandica, 20. Ithaca, 1930.

Booth, Wayne. *The Rhetoric of Fiction*. Chicago and London, 1961.

Bouman, Ari C. "An Aspect of Style in Icelandic Sagas." *Neophil*, 42(1958), 50–67.

————. *Observations on Syntax and Style of Some Icelandic Sagas*. Studia Islandica, 15 (Reykjavík, 1956), 1–72.

————. *Patterns in Old English and Old Icelandic Literature*. Leyden, 1962.

Bowra, C. M. *Heroic Poetry*. London and New York, 1964.

Brennu-Njálssaga. Edited by Finnur Jónsson. Altnordische Saga-Bibliothek, 13. Halle, 1908.

Brennu-Njáls saga. Edited by Einar Ól. Sveinsson. Íslenzk Fornrit, 12. Reykjavik, 1954.

Brown, Norman O. *Life Against Death: The Psychoanalytical Meaning of History*. Middletown, Conn., 1959.

Bryce, James. "Primitive Iceland." In *Studies in History and Jurisprudence*, 1, 312–58. 2 vols. Oxford, 1901.

Bugge, A. "Entstehung und Glaubwürdigkeit der isländischen Saga." *ZDA*, 51 (1909), 23–39.

Byskupa Sögur. Edited by Guðni Jónsson. 3 vols. Reykjavík, 1948.

Campbell, Joseph. *The Hero with a Thousand Faces.* New York, 1949.

————. *The Masks of God: Occidental Mythology.* Toronto, 1964.

Carpenter, Rhys. *Folk Tale, Fiction, and Saga in the Homeric Epics.* Berkeley and Los Angeles, 1958.

Chadwick, H. M., and Chadwick, N. K. *The Growth of Literature.* 3 vols. Cambridge, England, 1932.

Chadwick, Nora Kershaw. "Literary Tradition in the Old Norse and Celtic World." *Saga-Book,* 14 (pt. 3, 1955–56), 164–99.

————. "Norse Ghosts." *Folklore,* 57 (June and September 1946), 50–65, 106–27.

Chambers, R. W. *Beowulf: An Introduction to the Study of the Poem.* 3rd ed. With a supplement by C. L. Wrenn. Cambridge, England, 1959.

Chaytor, H. J. *From Script to Print: An Introduction to Medieval Vernacular Literature.* 1945; paperback reprint London, 1966.

Cleasby, Richard, and Vigfusson, Gudbrand. *An Icelandic-English Dictionary.* 2nd ed. Oxford, 1957.

Codex Regius of Grágás, The. Introduction by Pall Eggert Ólason. Corpus Codicum Islandicorum Medii Ævi, 3. Copenhagen, 1923.

Collingwood, William Gersham, and Steffánsson, Jón. *A Pilgrimage to the Saga-Steads of Iceland.* Ulverston, 1899.

Creed, Robert P. "On the Possibility of Criticizing Old English Poetry." *TSLL,* 3 (Spring 1961), 97–106.

Crosby, Ruth. "Oral Delivery in the Middle Ages." *Speculum,* 11 (January 1936), 88–110.

Curschmann, Michael. "Oral Poetry in Mediaeval English, French, and German Literature: Some Notes on Present Research." *Speculum,* 42 (January 1967), 36–52.

Darraðaljóð [*sic*]. Edited and translated by Eiríkr Magnússon. Coventry, 1910.

Delargey, J. H. "The Gaelic Story-Teller." *PBA,* 31 (1945), 177–221.

de Vries, Jan. *Altnordische Literaturgeschichte.* Revised ed. 2 vols. Berlin, 1964–67.

————. "Die isländische Saga und die mündliche Überlieferung." In *Märchen, Mythos, Dichtung,* edited by Hugo Kuhn and Kurt Schier. Munich, 1963.

————. "Germanic and Celtic Heroic Traditions." *Saga-Book,* 16 (pt. 1, 1962), 22–40.

————. *Heroic Song and Heroic Legend.* New York and Oxford, 1963.

————. *The Problem of Loki.* Helsinki, 1933.

Dodds, E. R. *The Greeks and the Irrational.* Berkeley and Los Angeles, 1951.

Dorson, Richard M. "Oral Styles of American Folk Narrators." In *Style in Language*, edited by Thomas A. Sebeok, pp. 27–51. New York and London, 1960.

Dufferin, Lord. *Letters from High Latitudes*. London, 1857.

Dunstanus Saga in *Hakonar Saga*. Edited by Gudbrand Vigfusson. London, 1887.

Earliest Norwegian Laws, The: *Being the Gulathing Law and the Frostathing Law*. Translated by Laurence M. Larson. Records of Civilization: Sources and Studies, 20. New York, 1935.

Einarsson, Stéfan. *A History of Icelandic Literature*. New York, 1957.

————. "Eiríkr Magnússon and His Saga-Translations." *SS*, 13 (May 1934), 17–32.

Finlayson, John. "Formulaic Technique in *Morte Arthure*." *Anglia*, 81 (1963), 372–93.

Foote, Peter G. "On the Fragmentary Text Concerning St. Thomas Becket in Stock. Perg. Fol. Nr. 2." *Saga-Book*, 15 (pt. 4, 1961), 403–50.

————. "Sagnaskemtan: Reykjahólar 1119." *Saga-Book*, 14 (pt. 3, 1955–56), 226–39.

————. "Some Account of the Present State of Saga-Research." *Scan*, 4 (November 1965), 115–26.

————. "Sturlusaga and Its Background." *Saga-Book*, 13 (pt. 4, 1950–51), 207–37.

Fox, Denton. "*Njáls Saga* and the Western Literary Tradition." *CL*, 15 (Fall 1963), 289–310.

Frank, Tenney. "Classical Scholarship in Medieval Iceland." *American Journal of Philology*, 30, no. 2 (1909), 139–52.

Frings, Theodor, and Braun, Max. *Brautwerbung*. Berichte über die Verhandlungen der Sächsischen Akademie der Wissenschaften zu Leipzig, Philologisch-Historische Klasse, vol. 96 (1944–48), no. 2. Leipzig, 1947.

Fritzner, Johan. *Ordbog over det gamle norske sprog*. 3 vols. Chicago, Leipzig, London, Paris, Petersburg, 1886.

Frye, Northrop. *A Natural Perspective*: *The Development of Shakespearean Comedy and Romance*. New York and London, 1965.

————. *Anatomy of Criticism*. Princeton, 1957.

————. "Myth, Fiction, and Displacement." *Dædalus*, 90 (Summer 1961), 587–605.

Gjerset, Knut. *History of Iceland*. New York, 1925.

Glendenning, R. J. "Saints, Sinners, and the Age of the Sturlungs." *SS*, 38 (May 1938), 83–97.

Goedecke, August. *Die Darstellung der Gemütsbewegungen in der isländischen Familiensaga*. Hamburg, 1933.

Goedheer, A. J. *Irish and Norse Traditions about the Battle of Clontarf.* Haarlem, 1938.

Goody, Jack and Watt, Ian. "The Consequences of Literacy." *Comparative Studies in Society and History*, 5 (1963), 304–45.

Gordon, E. V. "On *Hrafnkels Saga Freysgoða*," *MÆ*, 8 (February 1939), 1–32.

Grágás. Edited by Vilhjálmur Finsen. 2 vols. Copenhagen, 1852.

Greenfield, Stanley B. "Beowulf and Epic Tragedy," In *Studies in Old English Literature in Honor of Arthur G. Brodeur*, pp. 129–35. Eugene, Oregon, 1963.

Gregory of Tours. *History of the Franks.* Edited and translated by O. M. Dalton. 2 vols. Oxford, 1927.

Grönbech, Vilhelm. *The Culture of the Teutons.* Translated by W. Worster. 2 vols. London and Copenhagen, 1931.

Guðmundsson, Barði. "Nú taka öll húsin að loga." *Höfundur Njálu*, pp. 225–34. Reykjavík, 1958.

Guðmundsson, Sigurður. "Gunnar á Hliðarenda," *Skírnir*, 92 (1918), 63– 88, 221–51.

Hallberg, Peter. "Íslendinga Saga och *Egla, Laxdæla, Eyrbygga, Njála, Grettla.* Ett Språktest." *MM*, no. iii–iv (1966 for 1965), 89–105.

———. "Medeltidslatin och sagaprosa. Några kommentarer till Lars Lönnroths studier i den isländska sagalitteraturen." *ANF*, 81 (1966), 258–76.

———. "Några Anteckningar om Replik och Dialog i Njáls Saga." In *Festschrift Walter Baetke*, edited by Kurt Rudolph, Rolf Heller, and Ernst Walter, pp. 130–50. Weimar, 1966.

———. *Snorri Sturluson och Egils saga Skallagrímssonar.* Studia Islandica, 20. Reykjavík, 1962.

———. *The Icelandic Saga.* Translated by Paul Schach. Lincoln, Nebraska, 1962.

Hauch, Carsten. "Indledning til Forelæsninger over Njalssaga og Flere med den Beslægtede Sagaer." In *Afhandlinger og Æsthetiske Betragtninger*, pp. 411–67. Copenhagen, 1855.

Havelock, Eric A. *Preface to Plato.* Cambridge, Mass., 1963.

Hearn, Lafcadio. "The Art of Simple Power: The Norse Writers." In *Talks to Writers*, edited by John Erskine, pp. 72–86. New York, 1920.

Heller, Rolf. *Die Literarische Darstellung der Frau in den Isländersagas.* Saga, 2. Halle, 1958.

Heusler, Andreas. *Die Altgermanische Dichtung.* 2nd ed. Potsdam, 1945.

————. *Die Anfänge der Isländischen Saga.* Abhandlungen der Königlichen Preussischen Akademie der Wissenschaften, Philosophisch-Historische Klasse, no. 9, 1–87. Berlin, 1913.

Hollander, Lee M. "Litotes in Old Norse." *PMLA*, 58 (March 1938), 1–33.

————. "Recent Work and Views on the Poetic Edda." *SS*, 35 (May 1963), 101–09.

————. Review article of *The Saga of the Jomsvikings. Speculum*, 38 (April 1963), 327–28.

————. "The Didactic Purpose of Some Eddic Lays." *GR*, 1, no. 1 (1926), 72–92.

————. "Verbal Periphrasis and Litotes in Old Norse." *Monatshefte*, 30 (March–April 1938), 182–89.

————. "Were the Mythological Poems of the Edda Composed in the Pre-Christian Era?" *JEGP*, 26, no. 1 (1927), 96–105.

Holtsmark, Anne. "Vefr Darraðar." *MM*, 31 (1939–40), 74–96.

Hrólfs saga kraka ok kappa hans in *Fornaldarsögur.* Edited by Valdimar Ásmundarson. Vol. 1. Reykjavík, 1885.

Hyman, Stanley Edgar. "The Ritual View of Myth and the Mythic." *JAF*, 68 (October–December 1955), 462–72.

Iceland. British Naval Intelligence Geographical Handbook Series. 1942.

Ingstad, Helge. *Land Under the Pole Star.* Translated by Naomi Walford. London, 1966.

Íslendinga Sögur. Edited by Guðni Jónsson. 13 vols. Reykjavík, 1946–49.

Íslenzk Fornrit. 16 vols. Reykjavík, 1933–.

Jacobs, Melville. "A Look Ahead in Oral Literature Research." *JAF*, 79 (July–September 1966), 413–27.

Jeffrey, Margaret. *The Discourse in Seven Icelandic Sagas.* Menasha, Wisconsin, 1934.

Jelinek, Franz. *Mittelhochdeutsches Wörterbuch.* Heidelberg, 1911.

Jóhannesson, Alexander. *Isländisches Etymologisches Wörterbuch.* Bern, 1956.

Jóhannesson, Jón. *Íslendinga Saga. I. Þjóðveldisöld.* Reykjavík, 1956.

Johnstone, George. "On Translation—II. A Comment." *Saga-Book*, 15 (pt. 4, 1961), 394–402.

Jónasson, Jónas. *Íslenzkir Þjóðhættir.* Reykjavík, 1961.

Jones, Gwyn. "History and Fiction in the Sagas of the Icelanders." *Saga-Book*, 13 (pt. V, 1952–53), 285–306.

————. *The Norse Atlantic Saga.* London, 1964.

Jónsson, Finnur. *Den Oldnorske og Oldislandske Litteraturs Historie.* 2nd ed. 3 vols. Copenhagen, 1920–24.

Jung, Carl G. *The Archetypes and the Collective Unconscious.* Translated by R. F. C. Hull. New York and London, 1959.

————. "Flying Saucers: A Modern Myth of Things Seen in the Sky." In *Civilization in Transition.* Translated by R. F. C. Hull, pp. 309–443. New York and London, 1964.

————. *Symbols of Transformation.* Translated by R. F. C. Hull. New York and London, 1956.

————. *Two Essays on Analytical Psychology.* Translated by R. F. C. Hull. New York and London, 1953.

Ker, W. P. *Collected Essays of W. P. Ker.* Edited by Charles Whibley. 2 vols. London, 1925.

————. *Epic and Romance.* 1896; paperback reprint New York, 1957.

Kersbergen, A. C. *Litteraire motieven in de Njála.* Rotterdam, 1927.

King's Mirror, The (Konungs Skuggsjá). Translated by L. M. Larson. New York, 1917.

Konunga Sögur. Edited by Guðni Jónsson. 3 vols. Reykjavík, 1947.

Krappe, A. H. "The Valkyrie Episode in the *Njáls Saga*." *MLN*, 43 (November 1928), 471–74.

Kulturhistorisk leksikon for nordisk middelalder fra vikingetid til reformationstid. 13 vols. Mälmo, 1956–.

Kvaran, Einar H. "Landscape in the Sagas: The Beginning of a Background." *TLS*, August 29, 1936, pp. 685–86.

Landnámabók Íslands. Edited by Finnur Jónsson. Copenhagen, 1925.

Lange, Wolfgang. "Einige Bemerkungen zur altnordischen Novelle." *ZDA*, 88 (1957), 150–59.

Lárusson, Ólafur. *Ætt Egils Halldórssonar og Egils saga.* Studia Islandica, 2. Reykjavík, 1937.

Lehmann, Karl, and von Carolsfeld, Hans Schnorr. *Die Njálssage Insbesondere in Ihren Juristischen Bestandtheilen.* Berlin, 1883.

Levi-Strauss, Claude. "The Structural Study of Myth." *JAF*, 68 (October–December 1955), 428–44.

Levy, G. R. *The Sword from the Rock.* London, 1953.

Lewis, C. S. "The Anthropological Approach." In *English and Medieval Studies Presented to J. R. R. Tolkien,* edited by Norman Davis and C. L. Wrenn, pp. 219–30. London, 1962.

Liestøl, Knut. *The Origin of the Icelandic Family Sagas.* Translated by A. G. Jayne. Oslo, 1930.

Linklater, Eric. "The Battle of Clontarf." *Viking*, 15 (1951), 1–14.

Lönnroth, Lars. *European Sources of Icelandic Saga-Writing.* Stockholm, 1965.

————. "The Noble Heathen: A Theme in the Sagas." *SS*, 41 (February 1969), 1–29.

————. "Rhetorical Persuasion in the Sagas." *SS*, 42 (May 1970), 157–89.

Lord, Albert B. "Composition by Theme in Homer and South Slavic Epos." *TAPA*, 82 (1951), 71–80.

————. *The Singer of Tales*. Cambridge, Mass., 1960.

MacKenzie, Sir George. *Travels in the Island of Iceland During the Summer of the Year MDCCCX*. Edinburgh, 1811.

McGrew, Julia. "Faulkner and the Icelanders." *SS*, 31 (February 1959), 1–14.

McLuhan, Marshall. *The Gutenberg Galaxy*. Toronto, 1962.

Magnússon, Sigurður. "The Icelanders." *Icelandic Review*, 5, no. 2 (1967), 21–26.

Malone, Kemp. "J. M. C. Kroesen, 'Over de compositie der Fóstbrœðra saga.'" *Speculum*, 38 (April 1963), 366–68.

Maxwell, Ian R. "On Translation—I. A Review." *Saga-Book*, 15 (pt. 4, 1961), 383–93.

————. "Pattern in 'Njáls Saga'." *Saga-Book*, 15 (pts. 1–2, 1957–59), 17–47.

Melberg, Hakon. *Origins of the Scandinavian Nations and Languages*. Halden, Norway, 1949.

Möðruvallabók. Edited by Einar Ól. Sveinsson. Corpus Codicum Islandicorum Medii Ævi, 5. Copenhagen, 1933.

Morkinskinna. Edited by Finnur Jónsson. Copenhagen, 1932.

Neumann, Erich. *The Origins and History of Consciousness*. Translated by R. F. C. Hull. New York and London, 1954.

Nibelungenlied, Das. Edited and translated by Helmet de Boor. Sammlung Dieterich Band 250. Bremen, n.d.

Nibelungenlied, The. Translated by A. T. Hatto. Baltimore, 1965.

Njal's Saga. Translated by Magnus Magnusson and Hermann Pálsson. Baltimore, 1960.

Njáls saga: The Arna-magnæan Manuscript 468, 4to (Reykjabók). Edited by Jón Helgason. Manuscripta Islandica, 6. Copenhagen, 1962.

Nordal, Sigurður. "Björn úr Mörk." *Skírnir*, 93 (1919), 141–52.

————. "Gunnhildur konungamóðir." *Samtíð og Saga*, 1 (Reykjavík, 1941), 135–55.

————. *The Historical Element in the Icelandic Family Sagas*. Glasgow, 1957.

————. *Hrafnkatla*. Studia Islandica, 7. Reykjavík, 1940.

————. *Hrafnkels Saga Freysgoði*. Translated by R. George Thomas. Cardiff, 1958.

————. "Sagalitteraturen." *Nordisk Kultur*, 8 B (1953), 180–273.
————. "Time and Vellum." *Annual Bulletin of the M.H.R.A.*, no. 24 (November 1952), 15–26.
Norges gamle love indtil 1387. Edited by Rudolph Keyser and P. A. Munch. Vol. I. Oslo, 1846.
Notopoulos, James A. "Continuity and Interconnection in Homeric Oral Composition." *TAPA*, 82 (1951), 81–101.
————. "Parataxis in Homer: A New Approach to Homeric Literary Criticism." *TAPA*, 80 (1949), 1–23.
Óláfs saga Tryggvasonar in *Konunga Sögur*. Vol. I. Reykjavík, 1947.
Olrik, Axel. "Epische Gesetze der Volksdichtung." *ZDA*, 51 (1909), 1–12.
————. *The Heroic Legends of Denmark*. Translated by Lee M. Hollander. New York, 1919.
————. *Nordisches Geistesleben in Heidnischer und Frühchristlicher Zeit*. Heidelberg, 1908.
Origines Islandicae. Edited and Translated by Gudbrand Vigfusson and F. York Powell. 2 vols. Oxford, 1905.
Page, Denys. *History and the Homeric Iliad*. Berkeley and Los Angeles, 1966.
Pálsson, Hermann. *Sagnaskemmtun Íslendinga*. Reykjavík, 1962.
Parry, Milman. "Studies in the Epic Technique of Oral Verse-Making. I: Homer and Homeric Style." *Harvard Studies in Classical Philology*, 41 (1930), 73–147.
Petersen, Niels M. *Historiske Fortællinger om Islændernes Færd*. Copenhagen, 1839.
Phillpotts, Bertha S. *Edda and Saga*. New York and London, 1931.
————. *Kindred and Clan*. Cambridge, England, 1913.
Printz-Påhlson, Göran. "Concepts of Criticism in Scandinavia 1960–1966: I." *Scan*, 6 (May 1967), 1–15.
Quirk, Randolph. "Dasent, Morris, and Problems of Translation." *Saga-Book*, 14 (pts. 1–2, 1953–55), 64–77.
Raglan, Lord. *The Hero*. London, 1936.
Reuschel, Helga. "The 'Children's Judgement' in the 'Njala' and 'Gunnalaugssaga [*sic*] Ormstungu.'" In *Studies in Language and Literature in Honour of Margaret Schlauch*, edited by Irena Dobrzycka, Alfred Reszkiewicz, and Grzegorz Sinko, pp. 327–33. Warsaw, 1966.
Rogers, R. L. "The Crypto-Psychological Character of the Oral Formula." *ES*, 47 (1966), 89–102.
Rosier, James L. "Design for Treachery: The Unferth Intrigue." *PMLA*, 77 (March 1962), 1–7.

Rowland, Beryl. "The Horse and Rider Figure in Chaucer's Works." *UTQ*, 35 (April 1966), 246–59.

Rubow, Paul V. *Two Essays*. Copenhagen, 1949.

Ryan, John. "The Battle of Clontarf." *JSRAI*, 67 (1938), 1–50.

The Saga of the Volsungs. Edited and translated by R. G. Finch. London and Edinburgh, 1965.

Saxo Grammaticus. *The Nine Books of the Danish History of Saxo Grammaticus*. Translated by Oliver Elton. 2 vols. London, 1905.

Saxon, Anne M. "Unity and Narrative Technique in the *Brennu-Njáls Saga*." Ph.D dissertation, University of California, Berkeley, 1964.

Schach, Paul. "The Anticipatory Literary Setting in the Old Icelandic Sagas." *SS*, 27 (February 1955), 1–13.

―――. "Some Forms of Writer Intrusion in the *Islendingasögur*." *SS*, 42 (May 1970), 128–56.

―――. "The Use of the Simile in the Old Icelandic Family Sagas." *SS*, 24 (November 1952), 149–65.

Schlauch, Margaret. *Romance in Iceland*. Princeton, 1934.

Scholes, Robert, and Kellogg, Robert. *The Nature of Narrative*. New York, 1966.

Simpson, Jacqueline. "Advocacy and Art in 'Guðmundar Saga Dýra.'" *Saga-Book*, 15 (pt. 4, 1961), 327–45.

Springer, Otto. "The 'âne stegreif' Motif in Medieval Literature." *GR*, 25 (October 1950), 163–77.

―――. "The Style of the Icelandic Family Sagas." *JEGP*, 38, no. I (1939), 107–28.

Steblin-Kamensky, M. I. "An Attempt at a Semantic Approach to the Problem of Authorship in Old Icelandic Literature." *ANF*, 81 (1966), 24–34.

―――. "On the Nature of Fiction in the Sagas of Icelanders." *Scan*, 6 (November 1967), 77–84.

Sturlunga Saga. Edited by Gudbrand Vigfusson. 2 vols. Oxford, 1878.

Sturlunga Saga. Edited by Guðni Jónsson. 3 vols. Reykjavík, 1948.

Sturluson, Snorri. *Edda Snorra Sturlusonar*. Edited by Guðni Jónsson. Reykjavík, 1935.

―――. *Heimskringla*. Edited by Bjarni Aðalbjarnarson. *Íslenzk Fornrit*, XXVI-XXVIII. Reykjavík, 1945–51.

―――. *The Prose Edda*. Translated by Arthur G. Brodeur. New York, 1929.

Sturtevant, Albert Morey. "The Contemptuous Sense of the Old Norse Adjective Hvítr, 'White, Fair.'" *SS*, 24 (August 1952), 119–21.

Sveinsson, Einar Ól. *The Age of the Sturlungs*. Translated by Jóhann S. Hannesson. Islandica, 36. Ithaca, N.Y., 1953.

————. *Á Njálsbúð*. Reykjavík, 1943.

————. *Dating the Icelandic Sagas*. London, 1958.

————. "The Icelandic Sagas and the Period in Which Their Authors Lived." *APS*, 12 (November 1937), 71–90.

————. "Lestrarkunnátta Íslendinga í förnold." *Við Uppspretturnar*, pp. 166–92. Reykjavík, 1956.

————. *Studies in the Manuscript Tradition of Njálssaga*. Studia Islandica, 13. Reykjavík, 1953.

————. "The Value of the Icelandic Sagas." *Saga-Book*, 15 (pts. 1–2, 1957–59), 1–16.

————. *Um Njálu*. Reykjavík, 1933.

Swannell, J. N. "William Morris as an Interpreter of Old Norse." *Saga-Book*, 15 (pt. 4, 1961), 365–82.

Tacitus, Publius Cornelius. *Tacitus on Britain and Germany*. Translated by H. Mattingly. Baltimore, 1948.

Thomas, R. George. "Some Exceptional Women in the Sagas." *Saga-Book*, 13 (pt. 5, 1952–53), 307–27.

————. "Studia Islandica." *MLQ*, 11 (September and December 1950), 281–97, 391–403.

————. "The Sturlung Age as an Age of Saga Writing." *GR*, 25 (February 1950), 50–66.

Thompson, Stith. "Myths and Folktales." *JAF*, 67 (October–December 1955), 482–88.

Toland, John. *The Last 100 Days*. New York, 1966.

Turville-Petre, G. "Dreams in Icelandic Tradition." *Folklore*, 49 (June 1958), 93–111.

————. "Dream Symbols in Old Icelandic Literature." In *Festschrift Walter Baetke*, edited by Kurt Rudolph, Rolf Heller, and Ernst Walter, pp. 343–54. Weimar, 1966.

————. *The Heroic Age of Scandinavia*. London, 1951.

————. *Myth and Religion of the North*. London, 1964.

————. "Notes on the Intellectual History of the Icelanders." *History*, 27 (September 1942), 111–23.

————. *Origins of Icelandic Literature*. Oxford, 1953.

Ulvestad, Bjarne. "How Old are the Mythological Eddic Poems?" *SS*, 26 (May 1954), 49–69.

van den Toorn, Maarten, C. "Erzahlsituation und Perspektive ·in der Saga." *ANF*, 77 (1962), 68–83.

————. *Ethics and Moral in Icelandic Saga Literature*. Assen, 1955.

————. "Das Publikum der isländischen Saga." *Wirkendes Wort*, 10, no. 3 (1960), 143–49.

————. "Die Saga als literarische Form." *APS*, 24 (1961), 125–39.

————. "Zeit und Tempus in der Saga." *ANF*, 76 (1961), 134–52.

―――. "Zur Struktur der Saga." *ANF*, 73 (1958), 140–68.

van Hamel, A. G. "The Game of the Gods." *ANF*, 50 (1934), 218–42.

Watt, Ian. *The Rise of the Novel*. Berkeley and Los Angeles, 1960.

Watts, Anne Chalmers. *The Lyre and the Harp*. New Haven and London, 1969.

Weisinger, Herbert. *The Agony and Triumph*. Lansing, Mich., 1964.

Whallon, William. "Old Testament Poetry and Homeric Epic." *CL*, 18 (Spring 1966), 113–31.

Whitman, Cedric H. *Homer and the Heroic Tradition*. Cambridge, Mass., and London, 1958.

Wolf, Alois. *Gestaltungskerne und Gestaltungsweisen in der altgermanischen Heldendichtung*. Munich, 1965.

―――. "Zur Rolle der vísur in der altnordischen Prosa." In *Innsbrucker Beiträge zur Kulturwissenschaft, vol. XI: Festschrift Leonhard C. Franz*, pp. 459–84. Innsbruck, 1965.

Wolff, Edward J. "Chaucer's Normalized Diction." Ph.D. dissertation, Michigan State University, 1966.

Wood, Cecil. "Concerning the Oral Tradition." *SS*, 34 (1962), 47–53.

Wood, Frederick T. "The Age of the *Vǫluspá*." *GR*, 36 (May 1961), 94–98.

―――. "The Transmission of the *Vǫluspá*." *GR*, 34 (December 1959), 247–61.

Þiðreks saga af Bern. Edited by Guðni Jónsson. 2 vols. Reykjavík, 1951.

Þórarinsson, Sigurður. "Fight with the Fire Below." *Icelandic Review*, 5, no. 2 (1967), 27–33.

―――. *The Thousand Years Struggle against Ice and Fire*. Reykjavík, 1956.

Þorgils saga ok Hafliða in *Sturlunga saga*. Edited by Guðni Jónsson. Vol. 1. Reykjavík, 1948.

Index

Althing, Battle of, 91, 174–75; mentioned, 63

Althing, the: assemblies shape narrative, 67; as representative assembly, 101; and symbolic landscape, 143–44. *See also* Thingvellir

Andersson, Theodore M.: on saga origins, 13; on bookprose and freeprose, 17, 18–19; analysis of saga climaxes of, 47–48; on saga structure, 96; on saga rhetoric, 98; evidence for oral saga of, 102; on Hallgenðr-Bergþóra feud, 124–25; on objectivity of saga style, 216n7

Archetypal criticism: purpose of, 223–24n10

Archetypes: usage defined, 68, 212n20

Ari Þorgilsson, 45

Atlakviða: cited, 118; vengeance of Guðrún in, 129–30.

Atli (servant of Bergþóra), 107

Auerbach, Erich (author of *Mimesis*): on Gregory of Tours, 36–37, 43; on foreground and background styles, 37–38; on Christianity and literary language, 40–41; observations of, applicable to sagas, 46; mentioned, xii

Baetke, Walter: on bookprose and freeprose theories, 17–18; on thirteenth-century provenance of sagas, 18, 186n2, 196n46

Bandamanna saga, 177

Beowulf, 43, 129, 179

Beowulf: three fights of, 133; mentioned, 8, 118

Bergþóra: introduction of, 33–34; and feud with Hallgerðr, 124–25, 134–35; unburnt after death, 156–57

Bergþórshváll: present impact of, 34–35

Bible: affects of, on saga prose, 45

Bjarkamál, 129

Bjǫrn of Mǫrk: aids Kári, 125–27

Bookprose theory: principal tenets of, 14–17; contrasted to freeprose, 16–17; mentioned, 13

Brian Boruma (Irish High-King): at Battle of Clontarf, 158, 159–60

Burners, the: die at Clontarf, 160

Burning, the: contemporary force of, 76; Gunnarr's death at, 76, 110; Flosi's decision to burn

48–49; chronological order of events in, 50; and characteristics related to social functions, 50–55 *passim*; foreshadowing and backreference in, 68–69, 74–75 (*see also* Foreshadowing); attitudes towards vengeance, 163–66 *passim*; rising curve at end of, 176–78; definition of, 185n1, 215n3; authors of, 200–01n69; representation of battle scenes in, 209–10n3; and attitude towards forbearance, 214–15n33. *See also* Andersson, Theodore M.; Family sagas; *Njáls saga*

Saga style: characteristic features of, 9, 11–12, 38; relationship of, to oral narration, 11–15, 19, 20, 25–26, 37–39 (*see also* Foreground style; *Sagnaskemtan*); objectivity of, 99–100, 101–09 *passim*, 216n7. *See also* Saga narrative

Sagnaskemtan: described, 21–24 *passim*; social function of, 22–23, 46–47; effect of, on saga style, 24–26, 52; existence verified, 194n34

Saxo Grammaticus: on wonders of Iceland, 145

Scholes, Robert. *See Nature of Narrative, The*

Sigurðr Hog-Head: shot through eye, 103–04

Skamkell (farmer at Hof): lies to Otkell, 103

Skapti Þóroddsson: mentioned, 6

Skarpheðinn Njálsson: at Burning, 76, 113–14; and dealings with Flosi, 86, 139–42; slays Þráinn Sigfússon, 104; likes Atli, 107; slays Hǫskuldr Þráinnson Hvitaness-Priest, 111–12

Snorri Sturluson: composer of *Egils saga*, 16; on Icelandic spirits, 146; describes Þangbrandr, 219n26

Snorri the Priest: arbitrates between Flosi and Njálssons, 139–40; acknowledges vulcanism, 145; gives counsel before Althing Battle, 171; alludes to Þorvaldr Crop-Beard, 175

Sturla Þórðarson: recites *Huldar saga*, 26, 201n70

Sturlung Age: sagas composed in, 4, 15–16; undignified practice in, 44; and burnings, 76. *See also* Baetke, Walter; Icelanders; Sagas: relation of, to history

Sturlunga saga: blood feud episodes of, 96; burdened with details, 97–98; mentioned, 26, 45, 49, 60, 209–10n3

Supernatural, the. *See* Wondrous, the

Svanr (uncle to Hallgerðr): initial description of, 8–9; shelters Þjóstólfr, 152–53; engulfed by mountain, 153

Svartr (servant of Bergþóra): killed by Kolr, 107

Sveinn Hákonarson (Norwegian prince): restrains father, 107

Sveinsson, Einar Ol.: on oral sagas, 14; as bookprosaist, 15; on *Njáls saga*, 27, 210n13; mentioned, 120, 143

Thingvellir: as symbolic landscape, 142–44; described, 227n34 and n35. *See also* Althing, the

Tómass saga Erkibyskups: as example of clerical style, 24

Topoi: defined by Scholes and Kellogg, 69–70; analyzed, 70

Translations: author's own, xiv–xv

Þangbrandr (Christian missionary): proselytizes Hallr of Síða, 118; and feats as missionary, 145, 154; as turbulent priest, 219n26

Þjóstólfr (foster father to Hallgerðr): slays Hallgerðr's husbands, 63; sheltered by Svanr,